THE DAY CHRIST DIED

THE DAY CHRIST DIED

Jim Bishop

HarperSanFrancisco
A Division of HarperCollins*Publishers*

Library of Congress Cataloging-in-Publication Data

Bishop, Jim.
    The day Christ died / Jim Bishop.
        p.   cm.
    Reprint. Originally published: New York : Harper, 1957.
    Includes bibliographical references.
    ISBN 0–06–060816–1
    1. Jesus Christ—Crucifixion. I. Title.
BT450.B54 1991
232.96—dc20   90–42233
                                            CIP

91 92 93 94 95 MART 10 9 8 7 6 5 4 3 2 1

This book is dedicated to
<small>JENNY TIER BISHOP</small>
my mother, who taught us to love Him

*History is an approximate account of the past,
just as prophecy is an approximation of the future.*
—PÈRE M. J. LAGRANGE

CONTENTS

INTRODUCTION

It is not irreverent to wish that Jim Bishop had lived two thousand years ago instead, so that the New Testament might have contained five Gospels: Matthew, Mark, Luke, John, and Bishop. His fifth evangel would have been vastly different from the other four in that he would have taken care of all the little details missing in the standard Gospels, which unfold their great story by focusing only on the major events.

The Day Christ Died comes close to what Jim Bishop might have written under those circumstances. Ever the meticulous journalist with panoramic vision, Bishop searches where even scholars sometimes forget to look, and supplies us with all the colorful data from everyday life in first-century Palestine to make "the greatest story ever told" more credible and alive than would seem possible on the printed page. His scrupulous attention to the fine points weaves a rich tapestry for the entire Passion story, which does not close without a careful description of how the body of Jesus was prepared for burial.

Some critics may object that Jim Bishop was not trained as a New Testament scholar and therefore has no business offering us his own research on the culmination of Jesus' ministry. Likely, such critics (whose monographs never achieved best-seller status) cannot handle the English language as gracefully as Bishop, and the Notes and Bibliography in this book demonstrate that the author has done his homework. In this connection, Mr. Bishop's own "For the Record" introduction is must reading to understand his new approach to the old story.

In this he confesses to taking a few modest liberties with the biblical record, not from the point of view of contradicting it, but only to supply the mortar of what most likely *did* happen in order to hold the narrative blocks of scriptural fact together. Is this enough to drop the book from a fact to fiction category? Certainly not. The author faithfully reports his own constructed material, which is brief enough against the whole.

This reconstruction of the last day in Jesus' life also demonstrates that the New Testament is *not* our only font of information on the life of Christ, as most people—believers and unbelievers alike—usually assume. Other ancient sources—archeology, linguistics, and related disciplines—have supplied crucial additional nuggets of information which have been carefully mined by nineteen centuries of scholars. Jim Bishop not only incorporates these treasures, he exhibits them in their natural setting.

"The Day" format is very nearly a Bishop patent, but it has not bound him in these pages. If the browser assumes that we have here merely a record of Jesus' last twenty-four hours from Maundy Thursday through Good Friday, he or she will be mistaken. By means of flashback and three very important "background" chapters on the Jewish and Roman worlds, and the earlier life of Christ, the twenty-four-hour time frame is successfully surmounted.

Now, a score of years since *The Day Christ Died* was first published, I have been asked to update some findings in the book on the basis of scholarship on the life of Jesus since that time and to pen this introduction. Both author and publisher cherish accuracy in recounting the close of so extraordinary a life. Minor items have already been incorporated in the text but the following have not—a surprisingly brief listing in view of the twenty years that have elapsed and the strides being made in New Testament scholarship.

1. The jury is still out on several crucial aspects of the Good Friday trial, including something so basic as its exact time and place. There is as much evidence to suggest a date of April 3, A.D. 33 for Good Friday as there is for Mr. Bishop's preference of April 7, A.D. 30, but the technical arguments need hardly be detailed here. There is now probably more evidence to conclude that Jesus stood before Pilate at the Palace of Herod on the west side of Jerusalem rather than at the Tower Antonia adjacent to the Temple, but this account suffers not one ounce in opting for the latter.

2. The official title of Pontius Pilate is specified as "Procurator of Judea" throughout this book, which was universally assumed prior to 1961. That year, however, an Italian archeological group unearthed the now-famous "Pilate stone" at a theater in Caesarea, an inscription which defines Pilate as *"Praefectus Iudaeae,"* the "Prefect of Judea." Before Claudius became Roman emperor in A.D. 41, governors of Palestine were called prefects. It was Claudius who changed their title to procurators.

My own research on Pilate and the politics behind the Crucifixion differs considerably from Mr. Bishop's views, as readers of my *Pontius Pilate* and *First Easter* will readily note. A strong case can be made that Pilate was *not* so cruel a judge as traditionally portrayed. I will, however, cheerfully confess that Mr. Bishop's opinion of the man remains the majority view to this day! And the brevity of these exceptions are a tribute to the journalist's care in dealing with the facts.

More than anything else, it is refreshing to republish a book like this amid the welter of offerings that have appeared since then. Some recent lives of Christ, by serious scholars, have faulted the Gospels for anti-Semitism and have tried to recast and retell the Passion story, one tome even arguing that Annas and Caiphas, the high priest, were really Jesus' dear friends, trying to keep him out of trouble! But such wrenching of the evidence is futile and dishonest. The priestly establishment of Jerusalem did indeed prosecute Jesus, even while he remained vastly popular with the majority of pilgrim Jews at that fateful Passover. Anti-Semitism, then, has no logic or place in the Gospels as they are, and they require no rewriting or purging, as some misguided critics have suggested.

Other current biographies are nothing less than "put-downs" on the life of Christ—pseudo-scholarly sensationalizings that have tried to recreate Jesus in the author's image depending on the fad in vogue the year of publication. All of these caricatures of Christ have been drawn: Jesus the Radical Revolutionary, the Passover Plotter, the Mushroom Cultist, the Happy Husband, the Superstar, the Rock Redeemer, the Master Magician.

The Day Christ Died is to these as history is to myth, a reverent work throughout, which does not try to distill the supernatural out of the life of Jesus. Miracles remain miracles; signs remain signs. But the wonders, as well as the lavish detail, are consistently related to the larger story of God's dealings with mankind in Christ as Savior, the majestic dimension that lends final meaning to it all.

This book, then, is eminently worth this literary resurrection in Harper's Jubilee series, as the classic it has become.

Western Michigan University   PAUL L. MAIER
April 1977

FOR THE RECORD

This is a book about the most dramatic day in the history of the world, the day on which Jesus of Nazareth died. It opens at 6 P.M.—the beginning of the Hebrew day—with Jesus and ten of the apostles coming through the pass between the Mount of Olives and the Mount of Offense en route to Jerusalem and the Last Supper. It closes at 4 P.M. of the following afternoon, when Jesus was taken down from the cross.

This book, more than any other with which I have been associated, is the product of the intelligence of others. The fundamental research was done a long time ago by four fine journalists: Matthew, Mark, Luke and John. The rest has been added, in bits and pieces and slivers of knowledge from many men whose names span the centuries in the indelible challenge of the written word: Cyril of Jerusalem, Flavius Josephus, Edersheim, Gamaliel, Danby, William, Ricciotti, Lagrange, Kugelman, Hoenig, Benoit, Barbet, Goodier, Prat. These and more added to the sum of knowledge between these covers.

It is, I hope, a practical approach to the events of that day; a journalistic historian's approach rather than that of a theologian. Most of all, I wanted to see Jesus, the man, during this time when he chose to suffer as a man. And I wanted to see him[1] move among his people, among the many who loved him as the Son of God, and among the few in the temple who despised him as a faker. Along the way, I wanted to see, as close up as possible, the twelve whom Jesus selected to carry his word to the world; the thousands of disciples who followed him up and down the hill country; I wanted to understand why Annas, the old man, and Caiphas, the younger one, were desperate to kill the Galilean; if possible, I wanted to probe the self-imposed limitations of Jesus when he came here as man, and I wanted to understand his relationship with God the Father and God the Holy Ghost.

Each chapter of the book is an hour, and there are three background chapters: one is entitled "The Jewish World"; one is called "Jesus" and traces his background and that of his family; and one is called "The Roman World." Of these, the most important is "The Jewish World" because, unless the reader understands the land of Palestine two thousand years ago and gets to see the people, he will not understand this particular day. And it was precisely because so many of the Jewish people believed in Jesus

[1]A section of notes follows page 267.

that the elders of the temple felt impelled to plot against his life—or else, as the high priests said: "He will lead the people astray."

This day bred love and bred rancor and both are still with us. It changed the course of history. In time, it brought nations to the surface, and then submerged them into everlasting limbo. It affected races of people for weal or woe and it affected the lives of billions of individuals. And yet, when friends took Jesus down from the cross, it was not considered by the world—even the world of Palestine—to be an event of importance.

Many of the people of Jerusalem and of Galilee and in the small villages around the land who believed that Jesus was the Messiah were disappointed. To their way of thinking, Jesus should have called legions of angels and struck down the Romans and the high priests who executed his death. He should have sat on a cloud flanked by his apostles and proclaimed a new rule of the world. The fact that he did not—that he chose to die to redeem the sins of man—was, to their minds, a token of failure. Crucifixion was considered to be such a shameful way to die that, for some time afterward, even his apostles did not want to discuss it.

Of paramount concern to me was to try to orient the facts of this day. My sole armament in this was, first, a lifelong belief that Jesus is God and the second person of the Trinity; second, an unquenchable curiosity to which I have become enslaved; and third, a feeling that Jesus truly loved everyone, and proved it.

In the research, I found split trails all along the road. At these points, I felt free to take the one to the left, or the one to the right. For example, was the Roman Procurator, Pontius Pilate, at the Fortress Antonia on this particular day or across town in Herod's palace? A small point, perhaps, but there is evidence favoring both conclusions. In all cases, I examined the evidence and selected what, to me, seemed to be the logical trail.

Nothing in this book controverts the teachings of the Bible. One who believes in the truth of the Gospels (as I have—and do) must confess to a certain lack of objectivity. But I also claim to be a journalist; I felt that my job was, first of all, to proceed independently. While researching material for this book, I made a trip to Jerusalem accompanied by my twelve-year-old daughter, Gayle, to whom I am indebted for endless conversation, innocent questions, and the rich warmth of her feeling that all along the way she was taking care of me.

In Jerusalem—the ancient walled city, not the beautiful new one to the west—one can still walk the way of the cross, kneel in Gethsemane, stand on top of the Mount of Olives and visualize the Holy City as it was, touch the spot where the cross stood, and 120 feet northwest walk into the holy sepulcher. The writer can also meet archeologists of the several faiths, and this one did. These dedicated men—Catholics, Jews, Episcopalians, Baptists, Methodists, Lutherans—are all eager to help, and each one adds a brush stroke to a portrait.

In the white warm sun of Jerusalem, the bearded Father Simon Bonaventure, O.F.M., guided me along the narrow blue-shadowed streets, saying: "Here is where he stood when Pilate said, 'Behold the man!' . . . At this turn is where he fell. . . . Up here is where the women of Jerusalem wept." In the Jerusalem Museum the courtesy of Joseph Saad, its Moslem curator, manifested itself over Turkish coffee and the first-century exhibits of Jewish life; a spoon, an ossuary, some objects of city life in the time of Jesus. One of the finest of the scholars who helped me is the Rev. Pierre Benoit of the Ecole Biblique in Jerusalem. He is a man who can recreate the final day in the life of Jesus in infinite detail, so that it unreels like a motion picture.

And there was a Mother Superior of the Sisters of Notre Dame de Sion who showed to me the Lithostrotos where Jesus was scourged, and the deep cachements where Pontius Pilate stored water for his Fortress Antonia.

It is, I think, a tribute to the enlightened times in which we live that, while I was away, two great men of separate faiths were working on lists of books to be read when I returned. One was Father Ralph Gorman, C.P., editor of *The Sign*, without whose encouragement and assistance this book could not have been written; the other was Dr. Sidney B. Hoenig, a Professor at Yeshiva University, a Jewish scholar who cannot agree with all I have written in these pages. Between them, they saved me incalculable time by advising me against redundance in my research and by helping me to secure those works which would be necessary to the understanding of Jesus and his times.

Father Richard Kugelman, C.P., a master of the times of which I write, was gravely ill throughout this assignment, but he was strong enough to provide much tart criticism ranging from "No!" "Pure guesswork!" to "Not Roman legionaries—just Syrian soldiers!"

In Rome, His Holiness Pius XII said that he had heard of the book in progress and, when I told him that it was not to be a scholarly work but rather a simple book written for the many, he smiled broadly and said: "That is good. That is very good." Such words are of enormous help, especially when the morale of the writer sags and he begins to ask himself if he is qualified to inquire into the life of the Saviour. At another time, when I had interrupted my work on the book to interview the President for a magazine piece, I was delighted that Mr. Eisenhower asked: "In the Holy Land, did you feel that everything was telescoped; everything was smaller than you had anticipated?" This had been my feeling, but I had been worried for weeks that my impression had been a mistake; and yet the walled city of Jerusalem and the Mount of Olives and Bethlehem and Gethsemane, and Bethany, where Lazarus was raised from the dead, and Calvary were all within five miles of one another. Mr. Eisenhower, who had seen it all firsthand, had an identical impression.

There were twelve hundred pages of single-spaced notes before I started to write, and all of them were the products of others. Even the copying of them was not mine. This was done by Miriam Lynch of Quincy, Mass.; Jane Gilliland of Teaneck, N.J.; Floranna Walter of Rumson, N.J.; Virginia Lee Frechette of West Englewood, N.J. Every note had a code number beside it, and these indicated the work from which the note came, the volume number (if one was needed) and the page number. Originally, I planned to explain the code system in the bibliography, so that anyone who might be interested in verifying a particular note, or exploring the matter further, would be able to do it.

This system was abandoned in favor of straight narrative. In rough form the manuscript had critical readings by leading clerics of several faiths.

This book is far from what I could wish it to be. And it is not complete because a great deal of what happened on that final day is lost in antiquity. No liberties have been taken with the facts, except in minor cases for the purposes of narrative continuity or the "logic" of the story, and then only when the weight of probability points in that direction. Two examples of this are (1) the first meeting between Judas Iscariot and high priest Caiphas; and (2) the raid of the temple guards and the Romans on the premises where the Last Supper was held. In the first instance, the Gospels of Matthew and Luke recite a few of the facts. In the second, the presence of young Mark at Gethsemane, wearing nightclothes, points almost inarguably to a prior raid at the home of Mark's father, where the Last Supper was held.

If this book helps but one person to understand Jesus a little better, and to appreciate his mission, then it was worth the time.

I am indebeted to the works and advice of many scholars and theologians, but I must say here that I am indebted to the New Testament as translated by James A. Kleist, S.J. and Joseph L. Lilly, C.M. (published by The Bruce Publishing Company, Milwaukee), since I have virtually always followed its modern form of expression when direct quotation from a recognized biblical source was indicated. Of all the recognized versions of the New Testament, this one provided the language which seemed most appropriate to my purpose—a tale of the most dramatic day in history for a nonsectarian, present-day general audience.

My greatest continuing encouragement came from my mother. This is more than a personal acknowledgment because her stories about Jesus—the omnipotence of him, the forgiving qualities in him, the love of him, and, most especially the fear of him—began when each of us reached the age of three. She did not stop until the sacrament of marriage took each of us away. This was the one book through which I might have won her approval. It is a pity that, while it was being written, she lost her sight.

Sea Bright, New Jersey   JIM BISHOP

NARRATIVE

❖❖❖

April 6, A.D. 30

6 P.M.

They came through the pass slowly, like men reluctant to finish a journey. There were eleven of them, robed in white, their sandals powdery from the chalky stones of the road, the hems of their garments dark with dust, their faces molded with concern. These men were part of the final trickle of humans pouring into the walled city of Jerusalem for the Passover observance.

It was 6 P.M. of the 14th Nisan in the year 3790.[2] In the city, the sun had set a few minutes before, although, from up in the pass between the Mount of Olives and the Mount of Offense, the yolk of it could still be seen hanging between the golden spires of the great temple.

At the mouth of the pass, the leader of the little group paused. He was taller than the others and his men grouped around him as though he might say something of consequence. He didn't. He looked across the small valley and his brown eyes caught the beauty of Jerusalem and mirrored it solemnly. It lay like a fair white jewel, glittering in the prongs of its brown walls. Jerusalem perched high, aloof with pride, over the green valleys and the hills now polka-dotted with the tents of 300,000 pilgrims.

Jesus stared at it with love. And longing. He had wooed it with compassion, and Jerusalem had mocked him and had questioned the honesty of his suit and now Jerusalem—at least the small part of it that mattered—feared him and plotted against his life. The evening breeze stirred his garments and the ten apostles looked upon his face, trying to read something other than sorrow. It was not a "pretty" face. Long ago, the ancients had written that such a one as this would be ugly to those who did not believe in him, and beautiful to those who did.[3] Nothing is known of the way he looked but we may take it that he resembled his mother.

He started down the path into the Valley of the Cedron and the ten followed his long slow stride down, down among a multitude of tents, where there were the sound of infants crying, the smell of roasting meat, the growl of men conversing in Aramaic. They walked through the hilly streets of Siloam and some saw him and turned away and others pointed and whispered behind their hands, doing it with eyes averted because the Jews did not think it seemly to stare boldly into the face of a stranger.

Jesus was a religious celebrity. Many said that he healed the sick, raised the dead, gave sight to the blind and preached a kingdom of love. There were three million Jews in Palestine. The majority of these never saw him. And yet these people had been awaiting the Messiah for centuries with a fervor beyond comprehension. To those of them who had seen and heard Jesus, he was prophet, or fraud, or Messiah, or magician, or prince of Satan, or religious crank. Perhaps eight thousand citizens believed that Jesus was God and the Son of God—the Messiah.

He crossed the Brook Cedron on a stone bridge and entered Jerusalem through the Fountain Gate. There the little group bucked a tide of men outbound to the pilgrims' tents, men who had participated in the third sacrifice at the temple. They carried dead lambs across the backs of their necks, like red furry collars. Some carried them slung by the legs.

Near the pool Jesus started up the broad white Roman steps which lead to the summit of the city. He spoke a few words to those nearest to him and his solemnity seemed to deepen. At that moment Jesus was speaking the common Aramaic, although with the soft slur of Galilee. Sometimes he spoke Hebrew, a language which only the scholars used at this time, and he was conversant with Greek, the tongue of educated men.

He led the way up the Roman walk, a tall, slender man whose ringleted hair, parted in the middle as was seemly of men, flowed to his shoulders; for it was a mark of vanity for a Jew to adorn his hair, or cut it so as to expose his ears, or to coif it in any way except to shear it for length.

This was a lovely walk to take in the evening. The cypresses stood tall and straight on the rise of the hill and, in the fading light, clusters of wild flowers tossed little patches of yellow and red against the dusty grape of the hills. Far below, the apostles could see pilgrims crowding in and out of the Fountain Gate like gray ants moving in and out of a hill. Other than the pilgrims, few people were abroad—on the eve of high holy days as well as the Sabbath, the race was always against the setting sun, and Jerusalem had been filled with suppressed excitement all day. Now, inside the walls and outside, almost half a million people were ready to thank Yahweh for their safe deliverance from the slavery of Egypt. Yahweh alone had appointed Moses to lead these, his chosen people, from the bitterness of servitude across the Red Sea to safety in the land which was promised to them, and en route Yahweh had made a covenant with these people through Moses to keep God's laws. Tonight, and for a week hence, they[4] would celebrate the Feast of the Passover.

At the top of the hill, the little party started through the streets of the city in the dusk. They had been walking across Jerusalem's southern section from the east to the west. The wealthy families lived in the southwest part of the city. As Jesus walked the narrow cobbled roads, he could see servants lighting lamps in the courtyards.

There was no real street lighting because the people of Palestine were usually indoors at dark. They feared the roads at night, and roving bands of highwaymen accented the fear. A merchant, within a few miles of home, often put up at an inn rather than continue his journey.

The roads were good. They had been built by the Romans, who used slave labor to build them in all of the provinces, and taxed the occupied country to pay for them. They were made in three layers; the bottom one was called statumen, which was crushed stone mixed with cement; the second layer was called rudera, and was composed of fine gravel, rough stone and pottery chips; the top was of cobblestones, cut square on all sides so that they were simple to fit together with a thin sandwich of sand between. The architecture of all roads was convex, and rain drained off into a curbed ditch. The reason for the good highways was primarily military: to lessen the travel time for Caesar's legions. While they were built to unite the conquered countries with Rome and to expedite the delivery of merchandise, the roads were so engineered that they never united more than two provinces with each other.

Within Jerusalem, there was a small valley running from north to south and shaped like the roots of a molar. The group now traversed this valley and climbed a short hill toward the west wall. Some paused to look back and, from this eminence, they could see the spikes atop the temple, set there to prevent defilement by birds. The last light of day softened the flat earthern roofs of the houses of Jerusalem and, far to the left, they could see the snowy glitter of Herod's palace.

Within the marble beauty of the temple, the high priest had been reading the twelfth chapter of Exodus. It was timed so that, as the final red tongue of sun disappeared, Caiphas uttered the concluding words: "And the whole congregation of Israel shall kill it." As he said "kill," three Levites, standing over three lambs, lifted the jaws of the little animals and, with a single stroke, drew sharp knives across the three throats. By ritual, the killing had to be done in one stroke and the victim must not utter a cry.

The pilgrims watched this in silent joy. Some of the blood of each animal was caught in a golden basin and handed up along a line of priests until the last one, standing at the sacrificial rock, took the basin and dashed the blood against a stone. It ran down brightly over the bulges and cracks, seeking its own level, falling toward the drains at the lower end of the altar. There it disappeared into the darkness below the temple.

Warm water was poured over these final sacrifices of a tumultuously busy day, and they were hung from racks and flayed. The wool was peeled carefully from the lambs because the skin had to be intact for the oven. When this was done, the carcasses were examined by other priests for imperfections. If any were found to have moles or wens or discolorations of the skin, they were rejected. Three priests signaled that the sacrifices were acceptable and, in a trice, the slaughtering Levites cut the bellies of the hanging lambs with a single downward stroke. They removed the viscera fat, the kidneys and the "caul above the liver."

These were placed upon a fire altar and the offering remained steaming and burning on log embers until it was consumed. Caiphas, as befitted the presiding officer of the Sanhedrin, stood composed in his priestly robes. He saw the priests rub salt into the flesh of the lambs, and, in silence he saw them remove the right foreleg and a part of the head of each animal as an offering to the priests of the temple—for the law said that this "shall be the priests' due from the people, from them that offer a sacrifice, the shoulder and the two cheeks."

The last daily sacrifice was over and, in the outer courts the night watch of the temple came on duty. When a priest standing in the tallest tower cried down that he could see three stars in the east, a threefold blast from silver trumpets shattered the evening sky. This was the moment when the new day began for Israel, and 240 Levites came to take over the new watch. There were twenty-four gates and watch stations around the temple, and ten men manned each station all night. The captain of the temple guard made a continuous round of these stations, demanding assurance from each that all was well. When the night watch began its duties, the only light from the great temple was the red glow from the altar of burnt offerings.

Hearing the trumpets, the apostles knew that the Pasch had begun. It was a solemn feast but it was also a joyous one, for even though Judea was, at present, in bondage to Rome, the Jews were free to worship Yahweh as they pleased and they were also free to follow their own laws so long as those laws did not conflict with the interests of the Roman Empire.

Whatever impulse any of the apostles[5] felt to share in the universal joy had been subdued by Jesus' silence on the trip from Bethany; he seemed to be thinking as he walked. Earlier in the day he had spoken in Bethany and he had seemed almost lively as he announced to his Mother and to his hosts, the sisters Martha and Mary, and to the others among his followers who had come up with him from Ephrem, that he would journey to Jerusalem with the twelve. This meant to them, as he had intended it to mean, that he wanted all the others to remain behind. He would have the feast with those who would carry his word to the world when he was gone. His Mother understood the importance of his constant communion with the twelve—it sometimes seemed as though he would never finish teaching them the many truths necessary to their apostolate—but she must have felt a pang of sadness that he would not sit with her for the four ritual cups of wine tonight. But the tenderness of his farewell to her compensated, in a measure, for his absence.

In the morning Jesus had told Peter and John to go into Jerusalem to prepare for the feast. He told them to walk into the city by way of the Fountain Gate and, once inside, to look for a man carrying water. They must follow this man and, when they had come to his house, he would show them to a large room upstairs. They were to prepare the room for the feast and they must go to the city markets and buy a lamb and take it to the temple for sacrifice.

The assignment was simple. Peter, a big impetuous man who carried a short Roman broadsword at his side, led young John on the two-and-a-half-mile journey to Jerusalem. Inside the Fountain Gate they identified their man easily because, in Judea, men seldom carried water. It was women's work to go to the pool daily with a tall narrow pitcher on their heads, draw water and bring it home. Jesus had not mentioned the name of the man, but both apostles recognized him at once as the rich father of the young disciple Mark.

He had led them up the big Roman steps, across the town to his home, through the courtyard, and up a flight of outside stairs to a room which occupied all the second floor. A roasting oven was already there, and so was the equipment necessary for a dinner for thirteen men.

The two had gone out and bought a lamb, herbs and spices and bread. Then they had gone to the temple and sacrificed. The city was jammed with Jews from all over the known world, since no Jew should, under law, live more than ninety days' travel from the temple of Jerusalem, for it was desirable that he make the Passover pilgrimage each year to the great temple. All Jews knew that the dwelling place of God was in the Holy of Holies inside the great temple in Jerusalem. The Jew might attend services in a synagogue anywhere—Antioch, Rome, Alexandria—but these were to remind him of what he was missing by not being with God in Jerusalem.

Peter and John came back to the upstairs room from the western gate of the temple, the most direct route. They passed the big Roman gymnasium and, like good Jews, bowed their heads and averted their eyes. The gymnasium had been built 150 years before by Antiochus and here the Romans indulged in their sports and cruel games and held their public baths. Judeans were always scandalized by nakedness and they saw no joy in games or competitive sports.

This week, the city was heavy with Roman soldiers. The Procurator always called additional troops up from the coast during the high holy days. If the Jews plotted revolt, or even a demonstration against their conquerors, it would be likely to occur on a big feast day, and it would start on the temple grounds in the court of the Gentiles.

The Procurator was in Jerusalem. His official residence was in Caesarea, on the Mediterranean, but his presence was always required in Jerusalem at times like this. As Governor, Pontius Pilate's attitude was always formal. He was a man of intellectuality; he was also capable of venom and cruelty in equal parts and he never missed an opportunity to lash his subjects verbally, symbolically or physically.

When he came to Jerusalem, Pilate had his choice of residences. Most often, he chose Herod's palace near the west gate of the city because it was big and lavish and the courts were trimmed with alabaster. This was in the most exclusive section of Jerusalem, near the rich homes of Caiphas, the high priest, and the father-in-law of the high priest, Annas.

It was called Herod's palace and, at one time, it had been the home of Herod the Great. The current Herod, Antipas by name, lived in a princely structure called the Hasmonean Palace, when he came to Jerusalem, and this was down the slope of the westerly hill, near the inner entrance to the temple. There was little intercourse between Pilate and Herod Antipas because the King had a grievance. The Procurator had ordered some Galileans slain and Herod, as king, had resented the usurpation of power by the Roman, and was impotent in the matter except to sulk.

Had he chosen, Pontius Pilate could have requisitioned Herod's home for his short stays in Jerusalem but, by forbearing, seemed to be looking for an opportunity to reestablish cordial relations with the King. Pilate's other choice of residence was the formidable Fortress Antonia, which lay like a big stone against the heart of the temple. There, in an ornate chest, the Procurator held the vestments of the high priest and, under Roman dicta, unlocked them on the morning before high holy days and gave them to Caiphas, who was bound to return them to the chest within eight days.

On this occasion, Pilate and his wife had taken up residence in the fortress.

Peter and John threaded their way through the late-afternoon crowds. The city was jammed to the walls with citizens and travelers: the provincial Jews in rough garments, the Galileans with their soft drawl, the Gentile Greeks who dressed elegantly and vainly and who looked like rich tourists, the tough-looking Syrians who came down from the north to work the caravans or to enlist in Caesar's army, rich Jews from Egypt with their snowy robes and purple hems.

The Jews of Jerusalem were condescending and snobbish, not only to the people of the rest of the world, but to other Jews as well. They referred to Jews who were less observant of the law, or chronically unclean, as Amé-Haaretz, which means the people of the land, but in common usage implies stupidity. To be called Amé-Haaretz was a mean epithet. Their opposites, those who followed the law to the letter, were called Haberim (associates).

The two disciples noted that the city had received its annual scrubbing. The pocked roads had been resurfaced after the winter rains—both Peter and John had seen rare snowfalls in this city—and the stone bridges had been strengthened; all sepulchers had been given a coat of whitewash; animal dung had been removed from in front of houses and sometimes from their front rooms. The temple was gleaming and resplendent, as always; it required no special cleaning because, daily, it was served by seven thousand priests and hundreds of Levites, and dust was not permitted to collect even on the huge solid-gold cluster of grapes on the east wall.

When the two men again reached the upper room, the afternoon sun was already low on the hill behind the house and they hurried to build the fire and roast the lamb. It was forbidden to break any bone in the animal because it symbolized Israel, whole and undivided. Peter and John divided the tasks and, while Peter, because he had more experience, spitted the lamb down the middle and set it in the brick and tile oven so that no part of its skin would touch the sides, the other fashioned the round, thin unleavened bread into little cakes. This was the matzoth, ritually prepared bread, so called because the Jews ate it as they followed Moses and he had made of the tribes a holy nation, beloved by God. It was also called the bread of affliction because the Israelites had left Egypt in such haste that their women had no time to leaven the bread.

They also made a salad from one of five kinds of bitter-tasting plants, to remind the diners that the bondage in Egypt was bitter. The two men filled a bowl with vinegar, in which the bitter leaves would later be dipped. Red wine was made ready—the poor were able to buy it at the temple at cost price—and this would later be mixed by the host in the measure of one part of water to four parts of wine. Finally Peter and John made charoseth, a dish consisting of almonds, figs, dates, wine and cinnamon. When properly mixed, charoseth is the color of common brick.

Their work was not finished when Jesus walked upstairs and into the room. The greetings were subdued. Jesus studied the room carefully. This was, to him, an important room, an important night. He did not discuss his feelings; to the apostles he seemed abnormally introspective. They looked for signs of despair, or even of elation—a sign of sorts would have guided their feelings, much as, when lightning flashes and thunder rolls, the sheep look not at the sky but at the shepherd.

The twelve seemed to be composed, but there was an underlying tension in the room. Their greetings were whispered; a group of bearded men, averaging about thirty years of age, men of assorted sizes and coloring, simple men who were certain, now and then, that they were in the presence of the Son of God, although at other moments they became frightened and their belief wavered. Their faith in Jesus was full so long as it was not overburdened. Though they had, of course, withstood trial in the past, this was a moment of great strain. They had heard Jesus discuss his impending death with obvious sadness. And each feared to ask the question they all wanted to ask: "Can you not call upon your father's angels and destroy the city and the world and then let us sit with you today and judge the souls of men?" No one asked it.

They stood in twos and threes near the pillars supporting the roof and they looked at him and whispered and wondered and worried. Mark's father sent two men servants up to serve the Pasch and the smoke of the roasting lamb hung blue over their heads and undulated as they moved.

The servants set the table in the middle of the room. It was shaped like a U about twelve inches above the floor. The open end of the U was nearest the entrance to the room—in this case, the top of the outside staircase—and the host, Jesus, would recline in the middle of the closed end.

For many centuries, the Jews had taken their meals as they pleased, but the Greeks had pointed out that only free men are permitted to recline while eating, slaves must stand, and so the Jews had adopted the custom after they learned it from their conquerors, the Romans.

The couches from which Jesus and the twelve ate were called triclinia. They came in different sizes, from about seven feet in length to twelve. Among the Jews, the curved part of the U was considered the side of special favor, and three places were set on that side. As host, Jesus would be in the middle. The place of honor was to his left, and Peter would recline there. In the formality of Jewish dining, it was considered to be a higher station to be assigned to the lectus summus at the left hand of the host than to be in exactly the same place on the opposite couch; just as it was considered better to be, like Peter, to the left of the host—behind him, in a sense—than to be before him on the right. The place of second honor was to the right of Jesus, and this normally was the place of Judas, the treasurer, though on this night it would be taken by young John. The three would eat from a single low couch, the edge nearest the table being about the same height as their plates and the back edge much lower and open, so that the diner always approached the couch from the rear, lowered himself into it, propped three loose cushions to best suit his comfort, and then leaned on his left elbow, keeping the right hand free for eating.

The apostles had eaten with Jesus in the homes of the rich and they had eaten with him sitting on hillsides. Some of them were jealous of their assigned places in relation to the master, so that after Jesus, Peter and Judas were seated, the remaining ten would often jostle for position. They would not make spectacles of themselves in this matter—always fearful of the wrath of the Messiah—but they would whisper and shove and try to fall on a couch as close as possible to Jesus.

Tonight, as they waited for the signal to partake of the Passover, they stood in twos and threes. Jesus stood by himself, waiting.

A truly compassionate heart hides all other emotions as a mist covers a landscape. Jesus loved all men and, as he waited for the lamb to be made ready, he must have given some thought to Judas. Before this dinner was over, Jesus would accuse one of his men of betraying him and he already knew which one. He also knew why.

Judas had always been the outsider. All of the others were Galileans, while he had come from Judea. He had a working knowledge of economics, and sometimes became so immersed in the business of finding money for Jesus and dispensing alms that he had little time for the eternal lessons being taught to the other apostles. Judas was condescending to the others because his store of experience was vaster than theirs; sometimes he appealed directly to the lord to stop the others from doing things which he regarded as unwise.

The schism between Judas and the others had widened in recent months when some of the wealthy women who contributed to the cause of Jesus charged the money-keeper with stealing. Nothing had been proven, and it is probable that Jesus stopped the matter without listening to the details, but even though the master shielded him from the others, Judas must have known that it would be impossible ever to regain full esteem.

He continued to collect the moneys, as Jesus wished, and he continued to pay all bills, dispense all alms and keep the purse just as though he had not been called a thief. Judas was never out of favor with his master and, had he believed that Jesus was God, he would have known that the gentle Galilean could read his heart. In that case, the dark little man with the superior attitude would have been impelled to explain his act and to ask forgiveness.

There is no record that Judas ever approached Jesus with a personal problem. Absolution awaited him because Jesus had stressed forgiveness again and again. Once, when Peter had asked in a colloquy between disciples if it were enough to forgive a brother seven times, Jesus had smiled a little and said seventy times seven times, and then forgive him again. The attitude of Jesus in this case seemed to be that the erring one should continue to be forgiven. It follows that Judas did not believe that Jesus was God.

Judas, wily and self-seeking, did not ask forgiveness because he believed that Jesus was a victim of self-delusion. And finding that theft was not punished by wrath, Judas was encouraged to sell his master to the high priest.

On this night Jesus regarded Judas with pity and forgiveness. It had been foretold that someone would betray him. What better way could there be than to have it happen at the hands of a man who had no faith except in money?

It was almost seven o'clock, time for the Passover feast.

7 P.M.

The lamb was ready. As it was taken tenderly from the oven, Jesus and the apostles shouted: "There is no God but one!"

Description and martyrdom

The men in that room with Jesus were called, among themselves, "the twelve." In many ways, they were average—representative of the mankind Jesus had come to save. They were pious men in an age when piety was common. For the most part, they were not men of exceptional intellect or training; some may not have even been able to read or write, but all had studied the oral law at the knees of their mothers and fathers. They were emotional and loving and given to arguments, and in a dispute they would usually answer a question with another.

Like all men of that time in Palestine, they averaged about five feet six inches in height, although some, like Peter, were taller. They wore white garments, and one or two who admired fashion had purple hems. All wore full beards and uncut hair, because the Law of God warned against all forms of vanity. Those who were fishermen were proud of it in Galilee and ashamed of it in Jerusalem because, in the holy city, the cosmopolites said that the garments of fishermen smelled of fish oil and lake water.

Before the feast began they stood in groups, washing their hands in the ceremony of purification, and chatting. When there was nothing of importance to cause them to gather around Jesus, they usually broke up into three or four groups, as they had now. Peter and John were busy with the lamb, and the odor of it sweetened the room. This was especially good to these Jews, who ate meat only on feast days.

Most of the men had two names, the second of which was given to each one by Jesus. This caused some confusion among the followers of Jesus because the new name given to one man was sometimes the same as the original name of another. There were at least two Jameses, two Simons, and two Judases.

Of the twelve, there were three apostles who enjoyed the deepest confidence of Jesus: Peter and the brothers James and John. More about them later.

The apostle Andrew was short and dark and sinewy. He was from Capharnaum. His older brother was Peter, and when Jesus appointed Peter as chief of the apostles, Andrew began to call his brother "Father Peter." This man was never known to lead a conversation; indeed, it was a joke among the disciples that Andrew was never known to speak unless it was to ask a question. Among the fishermen in Galilee he was known to be valorous in storms. He had enormous faith, and was a disciple of St. John the Baptist before he met Jesus. No man knows when Andrew died, but long after this night he would be crucified on an X-shaped cross.

Bartholomew, tall, slender and handsome, was the most fashionably dressed of the apostles. It was said that even his undercloak was bordered with regal purple. He looked distinguished, with black hair hanging in heavy ringlets and a yellow beard. He was born in Cana, and his father called him Nathanael. He had been a vinedresser. He was naïve and found it easy to believe a sad story and easy to weep. His best friend was Philip. In the years ahead, he would preach in Persia and the eastern countries and the time would come when the people would flay him alive.

Philip was the merry one. He was short, dark and, to his way of thinking, the long journey through life toward heaven was a most enjoyable experience. He lived in Bethsaida, in Galilee, and there he had a wife and some said three daughters and a sister Marianne. He was, like most of the others, simple and credulous, but he was witty and gregarious as well.

The little man who was standing close to one of the stone columns with his eyes on Jesus most of the time was called James of Alphaeus (not to be confused with the brother of John), and someday he would be called other things, like James the Lesser and James the Just. This man was shy to the point of pain. When he spoke, it was his custom to whisper. He was the shortest of the group. His father was Alphaeus; his mother was reputed to be a woman named Mary who, in turn, was said to be a sister to the Mother of Jesus. James of Alphaeus was always addressed by Jesus as "my brother." And this James loved him dearly but had difficulty believing that Jesus was the Messiah. He was older than Jesus and had known him from infancy.

All Jews, with the exception of the unschooled Amé-Haaretz, were strict Jews, but James of Alphaeus carried the law beyond strictness to the point of fanaticism. He never touched wine or liquor or meat (except where Scripture enjoined him to); he would not anoint his hair or take a bath. He prayed so often on his knees that they became "horny like those of a camel." He had seen his "cousin" perform many works of wonder in the past two years, but James, a paragon of intellectual honesty, found himself admitting, on occasion, that this man was indeed the Messiah and then, a few days or a few weeks later, found himself wavering in his belief.

There was another cousin to Jesus in the group at the Passover supper, and this was Jude. He was not a prominent figure among the apostles, and little is known of him. He was, it is believed by many, the brother of James of Alphaeus, although others contend that he was the son of James. He was called Jude, Jude-Thaddaeus, and Judas of James—meaning

Judas, the son of James. Like James, he was a quiet man, almost introspective, and yet, in the years ahead, Jude would preach the testament of Jesus with a violent passion in Arabia, Mesopotamia, Persia and Syria, where, in time, he would be murdered.

The blank face among these men belongs to Simon Zelotes. Sometimes he is called Simon the Cananaean. There is no record of what he looked like, or even of his place among the apostles. It is believed that he preached in Persia and Egypt, and it is known that he enjoyed travel. In age, the apostles averaged a few years younger than Jesus, who was about thirty, and, if Simon Zelotes was thirty, then he had a long life ahead because it is recorded that he was killed while preaching in Egypt in A.D. 107.

Thomas was a balding worrier. He was certain that few things happened for the best. He was the least shocked of the apostles when Jesus announced that his kingdom was not of this earth and that these men should not expect to sit with him in judgment of the twelve tribes of Judea; rather, he would die and leave them to carry on his word as best they could. Thomas could become enthusiastic about death. Once, when Jesus said that he was going to Jerusalem where plotters were waiting for him, Thomas said happily: "Let us go also, that we may die with him!"

This man was a twin, and had been called by the Greek name for twin, "Didymus." He had worked in Galilee as a carpenter, and, in the early days of apostleship, sat in the evenings with Jesus and discussed the framing of houses and the building of furniture. His devotion to Jesus was beyond the superlatives of words to portray properly.

Among these men, there was one of engaging personality and this was Matthew. He had been a publican, a tax gatherer, and the people of his race regarded him as a sinner and, because he had worked for Caesar, unclean. Originally, his name had been Levi and he had worked in the customs office on the shore of the Sea of Galilee, outside Capharnaum. Here, he collected legal tribute for anything brought ashore, from ironware bought on the far shores to fish netted out of the sea. Passing by, Jesus looked at Levi and said: "Follow me." The tax agent gave up his career at once, and became an apostle.

The Messiah changed his name to Mattija—"Gift of Yahweh." The new Matthew, beard neatly trimmed, hair perfumed, impeccably attired, a charming and learned companion who could speak Hebrew and write it, one who had attended the finest rabbinical schools, asked Jesus if before they left Capharnaum he might be host at a dinner party for his new master. Jesus agreed and, at the gathering, sat to sup with many "sinners and publicans." The Pharisees in Galilee used this against him and said that Jesus was not particular with whom he dined.

It was difficult for Matthew to give up the trappings of personal vanity, and to give up the ease to which he had been accustomed. But it was done. He could, on call, quote much of the Scripture verbatim, and he had a passion for genealogy and the tracing of names and dates.

The busiest man of the company—even now he told the two servants from downstairs how to serve the feast—was Judas Iscariot. He was short and dark and his hair fell in dark ringlets. His name was not Iscariot; it was Judas ish Kerioth—Judas from Kerioth. His father was Simon ish Kerioth. Under his outer garment of white, Judas wore a leather apron with two huge pockets, and in these he maintained the treasury. He was also known to carry a small box under his arm.

His duties made him harsh and tightfisted; he expected the others to account to him for any moneys donated to them, but he did not feel that he was accountable to anyone for total receipts or expenditures. Even though he came from the hill country of Judea and his family had not subscribed to the law, Judas affected a superior manner to the Galileans.

Among the many women of means who contributed to the ministry of Jesus was Salome of Bethsaida. So firmly did she believe in the Messiah that she gave two of her sons to the apostolate—James and his younger brother, John—and she often joined Jesus in his pilgrimages on foot. Her husband, Zebedee, was a rich Galilean fisherman with a big house and servants, a man who hired others to work his boats. He was known and respected even in Jerusalem. His best-known attribute was explosive anger, but it was seldom aroused by those who knew him. When Jesus originally called to James and John, they were working in a boat with their father and they dropped the nets and followed Jesus at once. This aroused Zebedee to a pitch of screams and imprecations.

Of the two young men, John was the one who was beloved of Jesus. He was treated like a son who could almost always bring about a paternal smile of affection: one who could win concessions denied to others. Of all the apostles, these two brothers, together with Peter, were the closest to Jesus.

John inherited some of the violence of his father and once, when a Samaritan village spurned a visit from Jesus, John was in favor of calling down fire from heaven to consume the people.

James, the elder brother, was another of the quiet ones. He spoke rarely, and then tersely. His outstanding attribute was a finely developed sense of fairness. Of all the apostles, he was destined to die first, and he would be the only one who would die in the city where his Messiah died—Jerusalem. From this night of the joyful feast, James had twelve years in which to execute the will of Jesus before his death.

Peter, chief of all the apostles, was a big, broad fisherman with a deep voice coming from the loving heart. Often he was tactless and, more than once, Jesus was impelled to stop him by asking, "What is that to you?" Peter was given to speaking without first thinking, and too often the words came from his heart and not his head. He was impetuous. Once, when he saw Jesus walking on the water, he jumped out of his boat and also walked on water until he began to ask himself by what supernatural right he was doing it. Then he sank, screaming for help.

He had been called Simon, Simon Peter, Cephas and Symeon. He was probably called Cephas in Aramaic by Jesus and this, in Greek, is rendered Peter—the stone, the rock. Originally, he was Simon bar Jona, the son of Jonas. Peter was married and lived in a substantial house in Capharnaum with his wife, his brother Andrew (who fished with him) and his mother-in-law.

When Jesus recruited Peter at the lakeside in Galilee, he promised to make him "a fisher of men."[6] Later Jesus pointed at Peter and said "Upon this rock I will build my church and the gates of hell shall not prevail against it." These words must have come as a shock to the apostles who, until that time, were not aware that Jesus would build his own church. The twelve had assumed, all along, that the Messiah was planning to reorient the worship of the Hebrew congregation at the pleasure of God the Father.

Jesus also endowed Peter with enormous powers—almost unlimited powers—when he said, "I will give thee the keys of the kingdom of the heavens, and whatsoever thou shalt bind on earth shall be bound in the heavens, and whatsoever thou shalt loose on earth shall be loosed in the heavens." In the years ahead, Peter would be arrested three times; he would preach the testament of Jesus far and wide; he would grow old and feeble and, according to some authorities, he would die crucified, asking that he be turned head down.

His greatest utterance, a marvel of faith and humility, was: "You know all things, Lord. You know that I love you."

The apostles moved toward the tables. The dishes of herbs were in place. The two servants walked in and out of the inverted U table, setting ritually clean dishes in place and standing metal goblets, or chalices, before the places for the thirteen diners.

The chill of early evening could be felt in the room and the servants set about lighting braziers. The whole lamb had been set, brown and sizzling, on snowy cloths on the low table. The spices and wild herbs and the fruits had been set along with the bowls. Now the apostles looked to Jesus and he looked around the room at them and said: "I have greatly desired to eat this Passover with you before I suffer; for I say to you that I will eat of it no more, until it has been fulfilled in the kingdom of God."

They looked at one another, as they so often did, for a greater understanding of his words. They took it to mean that he loved them and wanted ardently to eat this important feast with them, and that he would not eat it again until Judea, which had rejected him, had recognized him as God. His ministry, of perhaps two years and a few months, had as its purpose the winning of Judea to his kingdom, and in this he had failed. Now he was prepared, while maintaining the integrity of the old covenant, to add a new one with a new ritual of worship.

When they were all at table, the man of mercy tipped a flagon and filled a large cup with wine. He held it in his left hand, sitting up on the couch to do so, and held the palm of his right hand over it. "Take this," he said softly, "and share it among you; for I say to you that I will not drink of the fruit of the vine until the kingdom of God comes."

They understood this. He was commemorating the first ritualistic cup of wine of the Passover and he would not do it again until all the people of the world became disciples of his father. They drank and, as the cup was passed, glances of envy were passed among them because each one felt that he should be closer to the host. The glances were followed by whispered words and then the words became louder. Some boasted, as men under tension will at times, of their individual service and piety, and a few began to tick off on fingers the great moments each one had lived with Jesus.

Peter did not take part in this invidious discussion, because of his position at Jesus' left. As we have seen, the place to the right of Jesus was, on this occasion, taken by young John although he did not "belong" in this favored place. Younger than the others and quicker of reflex, John had dropped onto the cushions next to Jesus and, at first, nothing had been said. Some of the disciples had been chronically afraid even to ask a question of Jesus, and they envied the young man who had not only taken the cushions next to the master, but had felt familiar enough to lean the back of his head against the chest of Jesus.

John seemed to be able to strike a chord of fatherly amusement in the leader. Jesus often referred to John and his brother James as "Boanerges"— the sons of thunder. It was not that these two made more noise than the others; but because of their father's explosive wrath when he, Zebedee, watched his two sons walk away from their work on the boats and nets to follow Jesus. Thus, the nickname—sons of thunder.

James, the older brother of John, reclined near one of the open ends of the U. Short, broad and deep of chest, he was a modest man and made a habit of looking at his feet when the master addressed him. He slept often and late, and sometimes irritated the others by dozing through situations which they regarded as exciting or dangerous. James had not taken part in the argument about seating arrangements; in fact, he might not have sat next to Jesus, whom he looled upon with perpetual awe, if he had been invited.

The strange feature about the faithful apostles at the table is that not one of them was remarkable. Most of them, when they first met Jesus, smelled of fish oil, lacked gentility, education and intelligence; otherwise they had little in common, except their love for Jesus.

The twelve lived with Jesus and traveled with him throughout most of his two-year public ministry. As Jesus preached up and down the nation, the group expanded. More and more, people came to believe that Jesus was indeed sent by God to save Israel, that he was indeed the Messiah (though in many cases their understanding of the significance of his coming was quite different from his own truth). Some believed that he heralded the end of the world. At times, some of those who followed Jesus left him; others in greater numbers came to believe him, and, after the first year, the followers became so great in number that Jesus picked seventy-two of the men and sent them off as disciples to preach his word in pairs.

Jesus preached in sun and in rain and in chill; he spoke on mountains, in valleys and on the shores of big lakes, in towns, in great cities like Jerusalem and Jericho, and in the homes of the poor. He spoke in parables and in allegories, in Hebrew symbols and in prayer. Mostly, he spoke of love—man's love for God and man's love for man.

More and more people followed him, and some saw him perform miracles. Rich women forsook their homes and lent their purses to the daily needs of the believers; men turned plows on their sides and left them; the sinful and the saintly walked in the white dust behind him; the apostles, who would someday be enlightened by the Holy Ghost, sometimes seemed more interested in elbowing the crowds aside to regain their positions close to the master than in spreading his word. Indeed, with Jesus near, who would listen to any of the twelve?

The night watch manning the Shushan Gate at the temple was the first to see the moon come up on this night. It sat like a huge orange on the mountains of Moab. The first day of the Passover must always be the night of the full moon and sometimes, when mists or clouds veiled the night sky, there was argument among the priests predicting the date of the Passover.

As they turned to go back to their duties, the men on the Shushan Gate saw the notice, which was posted in the outer courts of the temple on this day, adjuring all male Jews within fifteen miles of Jerusalem to come to the temple. Each must bring with him an unmarred lamb not less than eight days old and not more than a year.

It was said that 200,000 lambs had been sacrificed this day. The guards knew that the origin of the sacrifice had been that, in leaving Egypt hurriedly, while the women had baked unleavened bread, each male family head had slain a lamb and sprinkled the blood on the doorposts and the lintels of his home to identify the place to the Angel of Death. Moses had commanded that this event should be commemorated annually.

And this had been done ever since. But, as the years passed and the purists and the liberals reinterpreted the law, changes had been made and were being made in the sacrificial ceremony. Originally, the lamb had been slain in any sanctuary; at this time it could be sacrificed only in the great temple of Jerusalem.

The argument between the apostles subsided. John remained next to Jesus, and Judas fretted on the couch around the turn of the U. Quite possibly, John took the couch of the money-keeper on this one occasion because he had an excuse: during Passover it is customary for the youngest to stand and to ask the host the ritualistic question: "Why is this night different from all other nights?" If John were closer to Jesus, it would be easier for him to do this. And Jesus would then repeat the ancient story of the deliverance. At the conclusion of the story, Jesus would stand and the others would get to their feet as he invoked the blessing: "Blessed art Thou, O Eternal! who redeemeth Israel. Blessed art Thou, O Eternal, our God! King of the Universe, Creator of the fruit of the vine."

John may have taken license because of his youth, but the apostles soon forgot their sensitivies in something new and more important. Their Messiah was not following the prescribed rites. Furthermore, a servant was to pass among them with cups of wine and, instead, Jesus had filled a single cup with wine and water and had passed it among them. He had not sanctified anything; in truth, all he had said was that he desired ardently to eat this Pasch with them, and would do so no more, and he had told them that he would not again drink wine until the world was saved for God.

After the wine had been touched to the lips of all, including James the Just, who took no solace from it, the second servant would walk around the perimeter of the divans with a large basin and a jug. Each diner, according to ritual, was to hold his hands over the basin and the servant would pour water over them. The hands would be wiped dry and parsley dipped in vinegar would be passed around. After that, if the ritual was to be followed, Jesus would break the first piece of unleavened bread on a plate before him.

The apostles—to most of whom the Passover ritual was completely familiar—felt that for the first time the tall Galilean was not following the law under which all of them had been raised. And yet they said nothing. Jewish etiquette, which had nothing to do with the law, was also strict. A guest should conform in everything to his host, even though he might not find it to his liking to do so. Not to follow the wishes of the host was to make oneself like a guest who brought an unbidden guest, a cardinal offense. And yet, when the host asked a guest to drink, the guest did well to hold back, to hold the cup in his hand for a while. To drink at once, greedily, was the same as scraping together the pieces of bread, as though the host had not fed his guests well enough.

Until this evening, Jesus had followed the letter of the law, although he had shown signs of increasing exasperation with the externalism of Jewish piety. Among the priests and especially among the Scribes, he had remarked a punctilious attitude toward the exact letter of the law, which covered greed, jealousy and a lack of faith in the God who inspired the law. Jesus blamed not the people but their religious leaders for the perversion of his Father's ordinances.

The second servant brought the basin and walked around the outside on the couches and paused behind Jesus. He sat up and, instead of holding his long hands over the basin, pushed himself to his feet and took the basin, the water and the towel from the startled servant. The apostles sat up, mute with astonishment. The first servant was not present, having gone downstairs to present the skin of the lamb to the owner of the house, as custom decreed.

The big man set the utensils on the floor, ungirded his outer garment, and pulled it over his head. Sternly, and with hair in some disarray, he glanced around the room at the surprised faces, and wrapped a towel around his waist and tied it roughly behind. Then he picked up the pitcher and the basin and, as a menial, he walked around the table to the disciple at the lowliest position on the right side, and knelt to wash, not his hands, but his feet. In silence, Jesus removed the sandals, set them carefully on the floor, and laved the feet with warm water. Then, in silence, he removed the towel from his waist, dried the feet of his amazed and protesting follower, and moved on to the next man. When that job was finished, he moved to the next and the next and washed and dried the feet of Judas and John and came to Simon Peter.

By this time, the men had found their voices and, as they had argued for precedence a half hour ago, now they argued that it was unseemly of their lord and master to kneel before them and wash their feet. Peter, who loved Jesus deeply and would not have him do this thing, tried to tuck his feet under his loins on the couch.

The Messiah looked up at him reproachfully and Peter, glancing around for support for his refusal, said timidly: "Lord, do you wash my feet?'' Jesus, reaching toward the sandals, said: "What I do, you do not understand now, but you will know later."

The chief disciple, a little bit more emboldened, said bravely: "You shall never wash my feet!" This was a mistake. To these men, Jesus was God or Jesus was nothing. As God, he was beyond the commission of error, and if he chose to wash the feet of twelve men there must be a prime reason for it, and the reason was obvious: to teach these men that humility is a virtue to be carefully cultivated and nourished, and the best way to implant it was to show that God himself was not above the washing of the dusty feet of his servants.

"If I do not wash you," Jesus said softly, "you will have no part of me."

This was an ultimatum. If the feet remained tucked under the garment, Peter would no longer be a follower of Jesus. The pale-bearded apostle not only knew how to fight for the things in which he believed, but he also knew how to surrender completely and abjectly.

"Lord," he said loudly, holding his hands out and running them through his thinning hair, "not only my feet, but my hands and my head too!"

Under other circumstances this would have brought a smile to the face of Jesus, but there was so much yet to be taught and the time in which to do it was down to a little more than six hours. This was not a time for smiling. Jesus washed the feet of Peter, ignored the invitation to wash the hands and head, and went on to the others on the left side of the table. These stopped murmuring, having seen that Simon Peter's protest had availed him nothing.

Now they waited eagerly for Jesus to talk and, as he neared the end of the table, he said: "He who has bathed needs only to wash and he is clean all over." They looked at one another and nodded approval. A man who has cleaned all of his skin needs only to bathe his feet after a short journey. "And you are clean," Jesus said as he stood, "but not all."

They were mystified. Clearly the words meant that some of them, or at least one of them, was not clean. The true meaning escaped them, with perhaps one exception. Here, to be unclean was to be in sin. The apostles waited for a further exposition of the words, and the Messiah stood, washed his hands, dried them, and went back to his place at the head of the table and donned his outer garment.

He reclined, and noted that the others were eating the roast meat and looking toward him with mystification. They had all bathed, only this morning in Bethany, and Jesus knew this. Now he had washed their feet and, at the same time, he was insisting that not all of them were clean.

"Do you know what I have done to you?" he asked, and they looked at one another hoping that one would answer, but they all shook their heads and Jesus decided that, to make the lesson explicit, he had best begin by comparing his position with theirs.

"You call me master and lord," he said, leaning on his elbow and gesturing with his right hand, "and you are correct, for I am. If, therefore, I, the lord and master, have washed your feet, you ought also to wash the feet of one another." This seemed reasonable—a little alien, perhaps, but reasonable—and the twelve nodded gravely. They understood, and they agreed.

"For I have given you an example," the lord said, emphasizing the word *example,* "that as I have done to you, so you too should do." To emphasize a point, Jesus often preceded a statement with the words, "Amen, amen I say to you," which is to say "Verily, verily, this is the profound truth." He used it now: "Amen, amen I say to you, no servant is greater than his master, nor is one who is sent greater than he who sent him."

This was speech at depth. They understood it to refer to themselves; that they, the servants of the lord, could not be greater than the lord, who was not above washing feet. The part referring to the one who is sent not being greater than the one who sent him could, they understood, refer to Jesus and his relationship to God the Father. In sum, he was not greater than the one who sent him here—his Father.

They hurried to agree with Jesus, and his brooding eyes searched from face to face until he was certain that comprehension was complete. "If you know these things, you will be blessed if you do them." Now they ate happily and without restraint, picking pieces of flesh from the bone and wiping their fingers ard dipping them into the bitter herbs. To understand one's smallness was in itself, insufficient. One had to practice humility, preferably publicly, as he had done.

They began to converse in groups again, Matthew with Jude, Philip with John, Judas with James. The dinner proceeded. The second servant stirred the embers in the braziers and warmth suffused the big room all the way to the fifteen-foot ceiling. Jesus too took a little food, now and then listening to something that John said, tilting his head backward to be heard above the hubbub.

The sky was silvered like a concave mirror and the feast of the Passover was being eaten in every part of the city, although some of the elite Sadducees insisted that the first Seder would not commence until tomorrow evening, which was the beginning of the Sabbath. Jerusalem was quiet under the stars. Small squads of Roman soldiers ranged the city streets, but their conversation was muffled and there was nothing sufficiently important to alert them.

The moon began to brighten a little and, when, later, it rose high enough to lift over the Mount of Olives, it would drench Jerusalem in a white glow. Two city streets away from where Jesus reclined, Caiphas, the high priest, reclined with his father-in-law, the powerful Annas, and with his family. Beyond them a few blocks, Herod Antipas, the king, lounged in the beautiful Palace of the Hasmoneans, ignoring the Jewish practices he pretended to cherish. Further north, and to the east, Pontius Pilate sat with his wife, for he was one of the few procurators permitted to bring his spouse to the provinces. All of these would meet in a few hours. At the moment, none but Caiphas gave any thought to the meeting or to what it would mean.

"I do not speak of you all," Jesus was saying, as though he understood that his men were still puzzled by the remark about uncleanliness. "I know whom I have chosen." This was an endorsement of them. "But, so that the Scriptures may be fulfilled"—and now his voice rose a little as Jesus quoted the old words of the Scripture: "He who eats bread with me has lifted up his heel against me."

All dining stopped at once. Did they understand correctly? Each of these men had been raised in orthodoxy and to each the old words were as familiar as the contours of his mother's face. The words meant that a friend had betrayed Jesus. In the past year, the Messiah had used the Jewish Scripture several times to prove that the events of his life had been foretold a long time ago.

Now he was telling them that one of their company was plotting against the lord. They had, from time to time, been asked to believe things which were not easy to believe, but, because their lord had asked them to believe, they had learned to accept his words and to lock them in their hearts as truths.

But this—who? The apostles felt embarrassed to be caught glancing at one another. Who indeed? They looked at one another and looked away. He could not mean the plot of the high priest against his life; they had been aware of that for a week or more and were terrified at the thought of being in Jerusalem near the home of Caiphas. But Caiphas was not "he who eats bread with me."

BACKGROUND

The Jewish World

Palestine, the land in which Jesus had performed his ministry, was, in fact, the Jewish world, the center of which was the Holy City of Jerusalem. The people of Palestine, the Jews, were men of peace. They were brave, sensitive and articulate. Most important of all, they worshiped the one God, Yahweh. At the time of the Last Supper, Palestine was a part of the Roman Empire, but Jerusalem and the Jewish people were "ruled" in a sense by the leaders of their theocracy, the high priest, Caiphas, and his father-in-law, Annas; then, too, by their king, Herod, and by Pontius Pilate, the Procurator or Governor, responsible to Rome. As Jesus moved into the city, as he presided at the Last Supper, he knew full well that these men, together with Judas, would bear a special share in the responsibility of all mankind for his trials, his suffering and his death.

Palestine was a runt country lying in the Mediterranean sand. The distance between Caesarea Philippi to the north and Bersabee to the south was 150 miles. From Joppa on the coast across the country to Ammon was 75 miles. It was so small that Rome made it subordinate to another province, Syria. Still, within its borders were the remnants of twelve tribes, at least three dialects, a group of provinces such as Judea, Samaria and Galilee, a great number of cities and towns, and roughly three million citizens.

It was a land of loamy farms under a subtropical climate. In the hilly country around Jerusalem and Bethlehem the temperature seldom moved above 88 degrees Fahrenheit. In Jericho, only twenty-five miles away, it often climbed to 120 degrees and remained there for days.

There was a rainy season, and a dry season. Most of the annual fall of twenty-five inches of rain came between late November and early April. After that, the deep green of the hills and valleys paled in the arid sun until, in October, the hills became the color of straw and the wadis were not even damp to the bare foot. When the rains began again they were sudden and heavy, with big thunderheads moving sedately from the hills west of Jerusalem, and the water staggered in freshets down the hillsides, digging jagged gullies and creating rapids in the valleys. The table level was always low and individual farmers could not afford to dig wells. They were dug by the towns, and around them each morning the women pounded soiled clothes on rocks, gossiped, and carried pitchers of water home on their heads.

Mostly the land was hot by day and chill by night, except in the dead of summer when the sirocco curled up out of the desert to the south and stung the land with hot sand. The people were more concerned with heat than with cold. The workday began at the first hour and paused at the sixth (6 A.M. to noon). At that time, everyone rested indoors until the ninth hour (3 P.M.) and worked until the twelfth (6 P.M.). From noon until 3 P.M. only dogs, soldiers and insects plied their trades.

It was not a land of timber. There were some trees—cypress and cedar and olive, mulberry, apricot, plum and pine—but they stood in such small hummocks that they were regarded as ornamental rather than useful. Wood was so rare that an epithet of the Jews was to call a menial "a cutter and the son of a cutter."

Homes, walls and even bridges were built of stone. The most plentiful was limestone, which lay like heavy gray cheese beneath a few feet of topsoil and clay. Shepherds cut their homes into the hills, hacking into the soft limestone and fashioning apartments. A huge stone, rolled to within a few feet of the front door, screened the house from the weather and marked its location to all who passed by.

Cereals were planted on the lowlands and along the hillsides. Fruit seemed to be growing everywhere and it was superlative. The women of Rome were always willing to pay a little more for Palestine grapes, olives, dates, figs and sweet chestnuts. Transients often lived on fallen fruit, and one traveler from Lydda complained that, en route to Jerusalem, he walked instep-deep in the juice of figs.

The domestic animals were donkeys, dogs, sheep and goats. The wild animals—plentiful in the mountains—were bears, lions, hyenas, foxes, jackals and mountain goats. In the matter of dogs, the Jews had no affection for them and would not keep a dog who couldn't be trained to guard sheep or protect the home. In Jerusalem few dogs were seen because the city had a strong ordinance against dogs that bit.

Goats were only slightly less rare because the farmers believed that goats were in perpetual fever, and no one would guarantee the health of a goat. Still the milk of goats was highly regarded and sold at a premium. Cows' milk was reserved for calves. Chickens were new and popular in Palestine. Ducks were becoming known, and so were geese. The Israelites were accustomed to pigeons, and had bred them and crossbred them for centuries. Doves were sold for sacrifice in the temple. Their cost was low, and all but the very poorest could afford them.

Farming practices in Palestine were modern, which is to say that they were as advanced as those of Egypt and Greece. The young Jewish farmer had no writings to guide him; he was taught orally by his father or by a relative to whom he was apprenticed.

Plowing was done by locking a neck yoke on two oxen. Attached to the yoke was a heavy tree branch which dragged between the two animals. The rear of the branch held an upright wooden plow—a piece of timber cut to a V point in front and broad in the back—which furrowed the earth and turned it over. The farmer guided the oxen by means of a long slender pole with which he touched the flanks of the animals.

He scattered grain by hand from bags slung from his shoulders. He reaped—and so did his wife and children—with sickles made of flint or iron. Threshing and winnowing were done on a public floor along the main road. Sometimes winnowing was done on the flat roof of the farmer's house.

Almost all plowing and sowing were done in late October and early November, the early planting season. The December rains changed the hills to fresh green and the valleys became lush with growing food. In early April, around the time of the Feast of the Passover, the crops were ready for reaping. The beans and lentils were ready first, followed by barley and other grains.

At this time, the farmer frowned at the sky every morning. A heavy rain now could cancel most of his crop. From November until spring he feared dry spells, east winds, hail, weeds, fungus and locusts. Then, a one-day rain could wreck his economy, and so a common thought is expressed in the phrase: "Better to reap two days too soon than two too late." In his impotence against the elements he sought Yahweh in the temple, he appealed to God for mercy and he offered to God the first fruits of each of his crops. Sometimes, when his crops were safely in, the farmer resented the temple sacrifice of the first gleanings, and when this happened he spared God his venom and turned it on the priests who, he asserted, demanded too much of a poor man.

Wherever he went, the Jew was clean, conscientious and cloistered. He would do business with the Gentile, but he did not fraternize with him. The Jew, in foreign lands, always counted his separation from Jerusalem as temporary no matter how long it lasted. Whether he prospered or not, he was afflicted with an inner misery when he was away from home. He was clannish, sentimental, had fine family spirit, was easily moved to pity, sensitive to insult, understood and used the skills of the tongue better than any other people, and was quickly moved to joy at the sight of a child. He would not fight in an army which battled on the Sabbath, but he was unafraid to die and sometimes bared his neck to the sword rather than submit to an order which ran counter to his law.

The temple at Jerusalem was the center of all Jewish life and to the temple all Jews paid a basic tax of half a shekel per year. There were at least three types of shekels, but the shekel of Jerusalem was a crudely rounded silver coin made of 220 grains of silver. On one side was proclaimed "Jerusalem the Holy," with a chalice called the pot of manna. On the obverse was a triple lily with the words: "I will be as the dew until Israel; he shall grow as the lily."

The Romans circulated a coin designed to make the Jerusalem shekel obsolete. It was made of 120 grains of gold, but the most religious Jews feared to touch it because on it was the image of Caesar Augustus and the words: "Caesar Augustus, son of the god, father of his country." To the Jews one of the important commandments was to spurn the worship of false gods, and any graven image, however innocuous, was felt to be a violation of that commandment. The Jews, sometime earlier, had rioted because the Twelfth Legion entered Jerusalem carrying their battle banners with the face of Caesar on them.

If close to three million Jews paid the temple tax, which would very roughly approximate today's 25 cents, then about $750,000 dropped into the temple as a basic tax. Add to this the harvest offerings; the pieces of meat from 300,000 lambs sacrificed at the Pasch; the sin offerings which occurred daily; the heavy offerings of wealthy families; the sale of animals and birds for sacrifices (guaranteed unblemished, on the temple grounds) and it seems that the rough equivalent of $1,250,000 found its way into the temple coffers each year.

Palestine was a theocracy and, in effect, the temple was the center of all worship as well as being the royal palace and the supreme court of the land. The people were subject to multitudinous laws, the two primary ones being the rite of circumcision and observance of the Sabbath. Circumcision was a mark of male membership in the faith of Abraham. It was also a symbol of a man's right to share in the covenant which Abraham made with Yahweh, and it was an occasion of joy in Judea when a father circumcised his son on the eighth day.

Being a good Jew was, in itself, difficult. Most of the teachings were oral[7] and this led to disagreements among teachers who, in fairness, would quote a given law and then quote the "interpretations" of that law as given by opposing schools of rabbinical thought. The law seemed to thrive on argument.[8]

For example, at dusk on the Sabbath the head of the family had to say three things: Have ye tithed (one-tenth of produce)? Have ye prepared the erub (set the boundary)? and Light the lamp. However, the law continues: "If it is in doubt whether darkness has already fallen or not, they may not set apart tithes from what is known to be untithed; or immerse utensils or light the lamp. . . ."

There were rules, it seemed, to cover almost anything in the daily family life. On the Sabbath: "A woman may not go out with bands of wool or bands of flax or with her headstraps, nor should she immerse herself with them unless she has loosened them. . . ." She might not go outdoors with a hair net, nor with a necklace or nose rings or a ring which bears no seal or with a needle which has no eye. Yet, if she did any of these things, "She is not liable to a sin offering," to wit a contribution to the temple to expiate a wrong.

A man, on the other hand, might not go out with sandals shod with nails, or with a single sandal if he had no wound in his foot, or with phylacteries[9] or with breastplate or helmet. A woman might not leave the house with a spice box or a perfume flask and if she did, she must make a sin offering. Some schools of rabbinical thought permitted a woman to go to a public place with a false tooth or a gilded tooth, "but the sages forbid it."

"Men may go out with a locust's egg or a jackal's tooth or with the nail of one that was crucified, as a means of healing." But the sages said: even on ordinary days this is forbidden as following in the ways of the Amorite.

"If a gazelle enter into a house and a man shut it in, he is guilty; but if two shut it in they are not culpable." But if one alone was not able to shut it in and two shut it in, they both are guilty.

"If a man's teeth pain him he may not suck vinegar through them [on the Sabbath] but he may take vinegar after his usual fashion, and if he is healed he is healed. If his loins pain him he may not rub thereon wine or vinegar, yet he may anoint them with oil but not with rose oil. King's children may anoint their wounds with rose oil, since it is their custom to do so on ordinary days."

A father may deliver a woman on the Sabbath and summon a midwife for her, "and they may profane the Sabbath for the mother's sake and tie up the navel string."

Should someone die on the Sabbath, the law is again exact. "They may make ready all that is needful for the dead, and anoint him and wash him, provided that they do not move any member of him. They may draw the mattress away from beneath him and let him lie on sand that he may be the longer preserved; they may bind up the chin, not in order to raise it but that it may not sink lower. They may not close a corpse's eyes on the Sabbath, nor may they do so on a weekday at the moment when the soul is departing; and he that closes the eyes at the moment when the soul is departing, such a one is a shedder of blood."

A Jew can walk two thousand cubits from the place where he lives. This is about thirty-five hundred feet. However, if he has the foresight to place two meals at a point of thirty-five hundred feet from his home, the place of the meal is considered part of his abode and he may walk another thirty-five hundred feet. If a man falls asleep on a journey and is overtaken by the Sabbath, he may move two thousand cubits in any direction. But the sages say: "Only four cubits."

It seemed, sometimes, as though the learned rabbis were determined to carry their casuistry to the outermost limits of human endurance, although some schools of teaching used the power of interpretation of the law to lend a little ease to the people.

Children from the age of five were taught the rules of the Sabbath before they were taught to add or subtract. There were admonitions against tying or untying a knot, putting out a lamp, sewing two consecutive stitches, writing two letters of the alphabet, lighting a fire and so forth.

The Pharisees, who interpreted the law, split ecclesiastical hairs and then split them again. Originally, the law of the tithe, for example, was for farmers to make a thanksgiving offering of one-tenth of whatever produce they grew. The Pharisees broadened it to include wine and wood—the first of which is made from another product on which a tithe had already been paid—and the second of which was costly and usually had to be imported and paid for in cash. The law on cleaning dishes and pots and kitchen utensils became so exact that, centuries later, when it was copied in Hebrew, it occupied a whole section in the Mishnah.

The Jew believed in oneness. He wanted one god, one temple, one nation, one people, one tribe, one family. He believed in each of these with fervor. This oneness led to one symbol of his allegiance with God: The Ark of the Covenant.

The Ark contained the two tablets of stone on which had been engraved the Ten Commandments. These had been given to Moses by God, and they had been placed in an oblong cask of acacia wood, overlaid and inlaid with gold. On top of it was the Mercy Seat, supported by golden cherubs, and the whole thing was 52½ inches long by 31½ inches in width and 31½ inches tall. The Jews called it 'aron and, to them, it was the most sacred object in the world for the tablets within had been handed directly from God to man. It also represented a contract with God; on the four faces of these tablets were the ten laws which He had laid down for man. To achieve salvation all man had to do was to obey them.

The Ark was placed in the first great temple, and in the course of many wars and uneasy peaces it disappeared. No one knew the day or hour, but it disappeared. The loss was grievous to the Jews, but they consoled themselves with the knowledge that they still had the place where Yahweh dwelt. With or without the Ark, the temple was God's only earthly abode.

The story of the temple begins with David. He lived ten centuries before Jesus and, at the time, the Jews were still new to the Promised Land. The tribes had been ruled by a series of judges, and there was little unity. The people demanded a king and got Saul. But Saul disobeyed a judicial order and was replaced by David.

David felt that there would not be a nation until the Jews found a seat of government. He liked Jerusalem, but he would have to conquer it first. It was walled, then as now, and a lot of blood would be spilled taking it. The King promised a generalship to anyone who could force the capitulation of the city. Joab learned that a rocky tunnel led from the

Virgin's Fountain outside the wall to the citadel in the heart of the city. Joab won command of an army and David had his new capital. The Ark had a home, David had a palace and won many battles. His kingdom eventually spread from the Egyptian borders to the Euphrates River, and he said that this would be a holy place for the children of Israel forever.

The older he got, the more David turned from blood to God. He wanted to build a great temple, but his were not the hands for the work. One day, lifting his eyes to the hill of Moriah in Jerusalem, David saw an avenging angel with sword turned toward Jerusalem. He begged forgiveness for his sins, bought Ornan's rocky threshing floor on the hill of Moriah, and built an altar on the rock wherewith to offer sacrifices to God.

It was David's son Solomon who built the temple on Ornan's rock. He commissioned Hiram, King of Tyre, to do the engineering, and in seven years a temple 1,600 feet long and 970 feet wide was completed. It was the most lavish structure undertaken by man to that time, and its beauty was beyond the credibility of many of the supplicants who worshiped in it. To the Jew, this was truly God's home on earth, and while Jews elsewhere might build holy places of scriptural learning called synagogues, these would never rival the temple.

David reigned forty years. So did Solomon. David died repenting his sins of blood. Solomon died repenting his sins of the flesh. He had longed for the solace of women, and he built a palace on the little hill east of Jerusalem called the Mount of Offense and placed five hundred concubines in it.

After his death, the land of Israel split into two kingdoms—Juda and Israel. There were wars, and Jews on both sides died. The split weakened the nation, and the Babylonians poured across the land and reduced Jerusalem in the sixth century B.C. The country was destroyed.

The Babylonians brought down the walls of Jerusalem. They wrecked the temple and took with them, as prisoners, all Jews "except the poorest." Israel, born to glory, was now a short paragraph in history. The Chaldeans and Medeans moved into the almost empty land. Later, when the Persians defeated the Babylonians, the Jewish prisoners were given an option on returning to their homeland. About forty-two thousand made the trip.

The flame of freedom was bright in the hearts of the forty-two thousand and "the poorest," who were still tilling the land. But there was resentment when it was learned that the Samaritans had adopted parts of the Jewish faith. The true Jews despised the interlopers, who were called Samaritans, and refused to accept their assistance in building the new temple.

While the temple of Solomon was being rebuilt on a smaller scale, the Samaritans built their own temple on Mount Garizim. The Jews now lacked pride. Their women married Gentiles and their children spoke many dialects. They began to speak the tongue of their neighbors—Aramaic—which substituted for Hebrew.

After the fourth century B.C. the reign of Palestine fell to a succession of high priests, who ruled civically and religiously. Jerusalem, as a city, became the toy of any despot strong enough to take it and hold it. It fell to Alexander the Great, to Ptolemy, the Syrians, the kings of Egypt and finally to the Caesars. Each of these had an appreciation of the temper of his subjects and, in the main, the Jews were permitted to worship as they pleased. Local authority remained in the hands of the high priests, who were assisted by a board of elders called the Sanhedrin.

The Herods began to reign as kings about thirty-five years before the birth of Jesus. Palestine, a small province in the Roman scheme of things, was placed under the sovereignty of Herod the Great in 40 B.C. Rome made the appointment, and setting Herod on the throne required three years of work by Roman legions.

In their opposition to the appointment, the Jewish people were wise. Herod the Great was cruel and ambitious. He built great buildings, glittering palaces, splendid cities, and although he professed to be a Jew and offered lavish sacrifices in the temple, he cheerfully bent his knee to Rome.

He married Mariamne, the daughter of the high priest, and after two sons had been born he had her and the boys killed. In all, Herod the Great married ten times. He murdered several members of his family on whim or suspicion. Caesar Augustus said that it was safer to be Herod's pig than Herod's son.

In his time, Herod rebuilt the temple and he rebuilt the castle called Antonia, but in the temple he left a memorial which no student of history would forget.

Herod began the job by employing ten thousand workmen to begin the masonry. Of these, one thousand were Levites or priests[10] who were taught masonry in special courses so that their holy hands could lay the stone for the more sacred parts of the temple. The work required many years, and long before it was completed the temple occupied almost the entire eastern section of Jerusalem. Its alabaster spires glinted pink in the morning sun and a fifty-foot section of solid gold grapes adorned the eastern façade.

From Antonia in the north the Roman Procurators looked down on the Jews walking across the pale tile of the outer esplanade. The eastern side of the temple was called Solomon's Portico; the southern side, facing the Valley of Hinnom, was called the Royal Portico. The area facing the Mount of Olives over the huge city walls had four rows of fluted columns each twenty-three feet high and crowned with Corinthian capitals.

The outer portico was called the Court of the Gentiles and nonbelievers were permitted this far. On the inside of this court was a marble balustrade on which signs were hung in three languages, Greek, Latin and Hebrew, and the signs warned that, if anyone uncircumcised walked beyond this point, the punishment was death.

Inside the balustrade, on the north, was the Court of Israel. Any Jew was permitted in this area, and the eastern part of it was reserved for women. Further inside was the Court of the Priests. This contained the Altar of Holocausts. Beyond this point was the temple proper, consisting of a roomy vestibule and two chambers, the outer of which was called the Holy, the inner of which was the Holy of Holies. Before the Holy hung a heavy veil embroidered with all of the known flowers of the earth and with a variety of the produce of the earth with the exception of animals.

In the Holy was a seven-branched candlestick, a table for shewbread and an altar for incense. The Holy of Holies had held the Ark, but was now empty. Between the Holy and the Holy of Holies was another huge hanging veil, which protected the Holy of Holies from the eyes of all except the high priest and such lesser priests as might be invited, at the time of the high holy days, to worship. The high priest officiated on but one day—the Day of Atonement. This veil, also rich and beautiful and heavy, was draped between five huge pillars, and hung suspended from an arch by gigantic gold rings. Over each veil was a protecting cloth of linen, which kept dust from settling on them, and which could be moved away by means of pull cords. The splitting of the main veil, outside the Holy of Holies, would be a test for the Almighty himself. It had been said that even a prophet had not the strength to knock one of the big solid gold plates from the outer walls of the Holy of Holies.

Herod rebuilt the main structure in a little more than seven years, but the decorations required forty-six years of labor and it was not finished at the time of Jesus. To the Herods, religion was a social custom engendered by fear. They indulged it to such a degree that, while Herod was building the temple in Jerusalem, he was also building pagan shrines for the Romans at Caesarea by the sea.

Before he died, Herod ordered the execution of another son, Herod Antipater, and as he lay on his deathbed he learned that the sages were proclaiming that the Messiah had been born in Palestine. So Herod ordered the slaughter of all male babies up to the age of two—and then expired. He was succeeded by his son Herod Antipas, who became tetrarch of Galilee and Perea. He was a good politician and a fine sneak.

Tiberius now ruled in Rome, and Herod Antipas became his personal spy. The weakness of the new Emperor was that he was suspicious of his servants, and Herod sent personal notes to Rome which exaggerated the private conduct of the Roman Procurators and legates in the Middle East. This little part-time service kept Herod Antipas in favor. As an extra service, Herod built a new city beside the Sea of Galilee and called it Tiberias.

The current Procurator in Palestine was Pontius Pilate, a man of middle years who had none of the marks of greatness except ambition. There is no record of Pilate in Roman statecraft before A.D. 26, when he arrived in Caesarea to be the new Procurator. He may have been a merchant, or a minor official.

He had a regal bearing and he was jealous of the prerogatives of his office, but it is felt that his appointment was due to the ties of his wife, Claudia Procula, to the Roman throne. She is said to have been the granddaughter of Caesar Augustus, but whether this is true or not is of no consequence because her benevolent power came from Sejanus, a counselor to Tiberius Caesar. Sejanus convinced Tiberius that Pilate should be made Governor of the Jews, and not only did he secure the appointment but he also won for Claudia Procula the rare privilege of accompanying her husband to his post.

Claudia was socially ambitious and she entertained often at the Procurator's palaces in Caesarea, Jerusalem and in Samaria. She was also superstitious in matters religious, and although she worshiped the many gods of the Emperor—including the sacred person of Tiberius himself— she feared to interfere with the practices of any other cult, including that of the Jews.

This was not true of her husband. Pilate was an atheist who bent the knee to Roman gods only because it was as much a part of Roman life as a toga or a perfumed coiffure. His Emperor had given him the *ius gladii,* the power to pronounce the sentence of death, and, with the two or three Roman legions who stayed along the eastern borders of Palestine, he needed nothing else.

Pilate despised Jews. He used the *ius gladii* at his whim, and he traveled around his domain accompanied by no less than a cohort of troops— perhaps five hundred men—who, at his wish, beat and killed protesting crowds of Jews. He was intelligent, cantankerous, ulcerous and sometimes brilliant in conversation.

He succeeded Valerius Gratus, who was recalled to Rome because he had chronic trouble with the high priests. Almost as fast as Valerius Gratus appointed them, the chief priests sabotaged his rule. In turn, Annas Ishmael, Eleazor and Simon had been high priests. The last one appointed before Valerius Gratus left for home was Joseph whom the Jews called Qayapha and the Romans called Caiphas.

Pilate met him, preened himself in the aura of servile respect which Caiphas exuded and decided to keep him in office. The Procurator understood that the high priesthood was actually in the hands of old Annas, who had not only served as high priest himself but whose four sons also had served. Caiphas was the old man's son-in-law and Pontius Pilate knew that in civil and religious matters he was talking to the ears and eyes of Annas when he conferred with Caiphas, but as long as there was no insurrection the Governor was content.

Two of the things which Rome had told Pilate before he left for his new duties were that the policy of Rome toward the emotional little province was paternal appeasement; and that Pilate would be responsible for his acts to the Legate in Syria, his new superior.

Among the other fundamentals which the new Procurator learned when he got to his castle in Caesarea were: all Jews were exempt from military service in Roman legions, which made Palestine the only province where the subjects of Rome could not be impressed into the protection of Rome; a Jew could not be called to court on the Sabbath; Roman soldiers could not carry images of their Emperor on banners; Roman coins in Palestine were especially minted and bore symbols rather than engravings of the Caesars.

He had not been in the new job long when he learned that King Herod Antipas would not try to curry favor with him. As Pilate at every opportunity showed the King and the people that the Procurator was the real ruler, bit by bit an estrangement came about between these two cruel men. Pilate hoped that Herod Antipas would quietly sue for peace between them in time, but Herod, too, was proud, and he made no move to warm the chill. It added nothing to Pilate's peace of mind to find that the King enjoyed committing to writing the peccadilloes and administrative errors of Roman governors, and forwarding them to Caesar Tiberius.

For a time Pilate seemed to be stubbornly determined on courses of action only when those actions were wrong. For example, the citizens of Jerusalem had been nourished for centuries on the water from the Virgin's Fountain and the Pool of Siloe. These ran thin and weak in the summer months but the people were accustomed to dry spells and were in no mood to pay for additional water.

In A.D. 28, when Pilate had been in Palestine less than two years, he decided that additional water was needed, and without consulting the people or the high priests and the Sanhedrin, he ordered his engineers to build a stone aqueduct between Solomon's Pools, outside Bethlehem, and the walled city. The Jews protested, and as always they protested with demonstrations in the outer courts of the temple.

To show his contempt, the Procurator took the money for the new aqueduct from the Corban, the temple treasury. This knowledge raced from tongue to tongue, and at Passover time the Jews prepared for a frenzied demonstration against Pilate, and Pilate prepared to cancel their demonstration.

He ordered a group of Roman soldiers to attire themselves as Jews and mingle with the demonstrators in the courts of the temple. This was done, and when the Jews began their opposition by running toward Fortress Antonia and beating their breasts and wailing, the pseudo-Jews brought out clubs and whips from their garments and beat the Jews and left many dead in the Court of the Gentiles.

Too late Pilate learned that the dead Jews were not from Jerusalem, but were pilgrims from King Herod's Galilee. The soldiers had killed the wrong people and the Procurator was too proud to acknowledge his mistake. The chill between Pilate and Herod deepened into animosity.

To the left of the altar of the priests, among the inner courts of the great temple, was a square bare room called the Council Chamber of the Sanhedrin. In here the elders met and, through the high priest, ruled Judea. They met to consider the deaths of the Galilean pilgrims, and they did nothing about it because, even though murder in the temple courts was a frightful crime which ran along the outer edges of the imagination, the Sanhedrin knew they had no power to punish the Procurator. At the same time, the members felt no sympathy for King Herod, who was all the more sinful since he claimed to be a Jew and built temples to the gods of the pagans: a blasphemer.

The Sanhedrin had come into being a few centuries before the time of Jesus. It was the supreme court of Palestine and the legislative body, too. In the main, it was composed of priests, scribes and elders—the finest minds of Palestine. It was called by the people the Great Sanhedrin, and many Jews worshiped daily in the temple without ever seeing it in deliberation.

There were other Sanhedrins in the cities around the country, but the laws they passed, and their decisions too, were subject to affirmation by the Great Sanhedrin of Jerusalem. Sometimes, although not often, a brilliant member of a provincial Sanhedrin came to the notice of powers in Jerusalem and was invited to become a member of the most august body in the land.

Herod the Great weakened the Great Sanhedrin considerably, and on his deathbed he ordered that some members of the Sanhedrin be killed on the day he died to ensure that tears would be shed at his passing. The Romans, who had mastered the art of ruling subject peoples, enhanced the prestige of the Sanhedrin and gave it greater power. They permitted the Sanhedrin to have supreme authority in religious matters and a fair amount of power in civil affairs.

The Sanhedrin was permitted to make and enforce laws which had to do with Palestine's internal affairs; in external affairs Rome made the rules. The Sanhedrin could, in local jurisprudence, pass sentence of death on Jews, or even on Gentiles who were not citizens of Rome, but such sentence had to be reviewed by the Roman Procurator and confirmed.

Normally, the Great Sanhedrin consisted of seventy-one members, including its chief member, who was always the high priest. Sometimes the number was reduced by deaths, but it was in best balance when the court was full.

The membership fell into three classes. The most important were the priestly families; they were apt to be Sadducees—men who denied the authority of oral tradition. They believed in the *written* law. Usually these men had served in the office of high priest or were members of their families. These were the elite of the land—the rich, the conservative.

The second group of members was the Ancients. These were, as the term implies, the elderly men who had attained success as laymen and who were appointed to the high court as a mark of respect. Many of the Ancients were also Sadducees.

The third group was the Scribes. These were mostly younger men, the doctors of the law, the fervent and sometimes brilliant and dynamic fragment of the court. Some of the Scribes were Sadducees, but for the most part, they were Pharisees, that is to say, men who interpreted and reinterpreted the *oral* law and tried hard to find an inner meaning of the ancient written law.

Long ago the Pharisees had vanquished the priestly Sadducees when they won a concession that the whole of the law was not contained in the written law of Moses, but that the bigger part of the law was in the oral elements and in a lengthy dissertation of precepts, called Halakah and Haggadah. Once the oral side of the law was conceded to supplement the written commandments, it was a matter of time and unremitting pressure until the oral law took precedence over the written.

After that, the Pharisees could make as many laws as they chose and they could devise new ones to fit new situations. This gave them almost unlimited power in the field of interpretation. The Sadducees, in disgust, rejected the Pharisees as unorthodox Hebrews and appointed themselves as the true keepers of the law. This, in time, led to a paradox: the Sadducees, as the elite conservatives, dealt more and more with the Gentile world and became lax in their observations of the law; the Pharisees, as the commoners and radical innovators, became so strict in the law that their followers, figuratively, walked an ecclesiastical tightrope.

At times, the affluent Sadducees seemed to have leisure to sit and coin phrases condemning the Pharisees. For example, one of the "games" of the time was to name the seven kinds of Pharisee, six of whom were bad Jews. The answer was: first, the sichem-Pharisee, who was a Pharisee because of the business he could do with Pharisees; second was the nipqi-Pharisee, or "pussyfooter," who hunched his back and shuffled his gait to show his humility; then there was the bleeding-Pharisee, who walked into walls with his eyes closed so that he might not look upon a fair woman; the pestle-Pharisee was one who deliberately bent himself so far forward that he looked like the pestle in a mortar; then there was the tell-me-my-duty-that-I-may-do-it-Pharisee, who wanted everyone to know that he had done more than his duty to Yahweh and could think of nothing else to do; the Pharisee-for-love, which was intended to be an epithet describing the person of no character who was a Pharisee because his friends were Pharisees; and last, the Pharisee-through-fear, the good man who was afraid of Yahweh's wrath.

A Scribe, as we have seen, could be, as he chose, a Sadducee or a Pharisee. The popular side, of course, was Pharisiac. The multitudes would believe almost anything the Pharisees told them, even though, on occasion, it might be contrary to the words of the Sadducean priests. The women of Palestine had boundless respect for the strict Pharisees and, although women had little weight in family or religious counsels, their support meant much because they never lost an opportunity to support a Pharisee in a public dispute.

The priests, Ancients and Scribes who made up the Great Sanhedrin worked under the high priest, who could call a session at any time. If the current high priest was weak, the Sanhedrin was strong; if the high priest was strong, the Sanhedrin became an instrument in his hands. Caiphas was strong, and had the backing of his father-in-law, Annas; the Sanhedrin of his time followed rather than led him.

Under the Sanhedrin were the seven thousand priests of the great temple, and in addition, the temple guards and the rabbis and civil authorities of Judea. In criminal cases the Sanhedrin was always reminded of an old aphorism: "A Sanhedrin which passes the death sentence more than once every seven years is too hotheaded."

The meetings were irregular, depending upon the amount of business which required the attention of the court. It met in the Chamber of Hewn Stone on the southwest edge of the inner court of the temple, although it could and did meet in the home of Caiphas at his order.

Many of the rules governing the behavior of the Sanhedrin in session were not put in writing until centuries later, but it is probably fair to say that the court sat in a semicircle so that the members could look upon one another. They sat in three graduated rows, with the high priest in the center and the Ancients flanking him according to seniority.

Two clerks sat in front, facing the court. One was stationed at the left; one at the right. In criminal cases, when all of the testimony was in, the clerks called the names of the members, starting with the youngest members so that, if they differed with the elders, they would not be embarrassed. One of the clerks collected all the votes for acquittal; the other tallied all those who favored conviction.

The Sanhedrin could sit in judgment with as few as twenty-three members present. If, in the deliberations, a member wanted to leave, he first stood and counted the members. If—excepting himself—he counted twenty-three or more, he could leave. If not, he must sit until there were twenty-three.

The court sat from the Sacrifice of Perpetual Holocaust of the morning (9 A.M.) until the Perpetual Holocaust of the evening (4 P.M.). Civil suits could be opened by plaintiff or defense; criminal cases could be opened only by the defense. In civil cases a majority of one vote was enough for a verdict either way; in criminal cases a majority of one vote could acquit but a majority of two was required to convict.

In civil suits any judge or all of them in concert could plead for the plaintiff or the defendant. In criminal cases, all of the judges could plead for acquittal, but not all could plead for conviction. In civil cases any judge could, at his discretion, plead for the plaintiff, and in the next breath plead for the defendant, but in criminal cases, though a judge who had argued for conviction was permitted to change and plead for acquittal, the jurist who had argued for acquittal originally could not change and argue for conviction.

Trials seldom extended beyond one day's work. Civil cases were tried by day and settled by night. Criminal cases were tried by day and settled the next day, unless the accused was acquitted, in which case the court freed him on the same day. But if he was convicted he could not be sentenced until the following day, by which time the collective mind of the court had theoretically cooled. For this reason it was against the law to open a criminal procedure on the eve of the Sabbath or on the eve of a holy day, because no one could be sentenced on those days.

The average procedure in criminal cases was to open court in mid-morning and, as soon as the charges were read, to begin the examination of the witnesses. Very little weight was given to the testimony of the accused, and the prisoner seldom testified in his own behalf, although he could volunteer testimony if he was willing to face the probing questions of so many members of the Sanhedrin.

Convictions were obtained on the testimony of witnesses, who were questioned first on the seven points of the law: "In what sabbatical cycle?" "In what year?" "In what month?" "On what day of the week?" "At what hour?" "In what place?" "Who saw it?" When all of the testimony was in, the judges paired off, ate sparingly and drank no wine, and then, after the evening meal, they sat alone in their Chamber of Hewn Stone to argue the merits of the testimony among themselves.

Some cases required a few hours of argument before a decision was reached; some took all night.

When the vote was taken, the judge whose name was called would stand and say: "I was for acquittal and I remain of the same opinion," or "I was for conviction and I remain of the same opinion," or "I was for conviction and I now stand for acquittal." There were no other possibilities.

In the event that neither side could muster enough votes for a decision, the high priest sent for two more members of the Sanhedrin and kept increasing the court by two until a decision was reached. The prisoner's best chance for freedom came under a full court. If thirty-six voted for conviction, and thirty-five for acquittal, the court must remain in session until one of those voting for guilt changed his opinion.

The word *Sanhedrin* comes from the Greek *synedrion*—an assembly, council or conference—and the Jews used the word formally, but in daily conversation the Great Sanhedrin was referred to as a Beth Din (court of judgment). Its chief was called the Nasi (the leader).

Politically the Sanhedrin maintained a balance between the two parties: Sadducees and Pharisees; believers in the written law and believers in the oral law. As the supporters of the oral tradition, the Pharisees were louder and more voluble and their public behavior was more holy than that of the Sadducees. Judaism was doomed, they shouted, unless the Pharisaical oral interpretations of the law of God became the law of all Judea.

In spite of the political balance, the Pharisees were in some respects the strong men of the Sanhedrin when Caiphas was Nasi. He was a Sadducee, and he drew his power from another Sadducee, Annas, but the voices most often heard in the high court were doubtless those of the Pharisees, whose perpetual attitude was one of outraged piety. They had no more votes than the Sadducees—perhaps a few less because a Sadducee was the current high priest—but the Pharisees had the ears of the people with their predictions of doom and perdition.

Another factor was that the Sadducees had been declining in power for centuries. They, who had led the people toward God, were now reduced to following the vociferous Pharisees. In fact, the system of selecting new members of the Sanhedrin leads one to believe that the majority party could, if it chose, maintain itself in power.

When a new member was needed to fill the roster to the required number of seventy-one, the judges sat facing three rows of nominees for the Great Sanhedrin. The nominees were priests, merchants, elders, rabbis (religious teachers) or common people.

To become a nominee, scholarship in the law was required. The candidates were examined and reexamined in the law and in the several schools of interpretation and, on passing, were taken from their congregations and placed in the third row of nominees. Besides knowledge of the law, a candidate had to have an appreciation of justice, mercy and general wisdom.

When the Great Sanhedrin had to replenish its numbers, it summoned all the nominees and selected a man from the front row. Then, after further examination of the candidates in the second row, one of their number was moved to the first row; one from the third row, after questioning, was moved to the second row; and, finally, from among the newest nominees someone was taken from a congregation and moved into the third row.[11]

Membership in the Great Sanhedrin was for life. Some, in old age, withdrew to retirement. The rule was for the members to die in office. So far as is known, only two classes of men were excluded from membership: bastards and converts.

Politically, the power of the Sanhedrin was great at the dawn of Christianity. The people were looking to the high priest for leadership against the Herods and the Romans. At this time the high priest was more than the leader of the Sanhedrin; he was, in effect, the chief of state, and the Sanhedrin was bound to look to him for leadership and was inclined to follow his dictates.

The Sanhedrin had its own laws, and the most important of these, so far as Jesus was concerned, was: "A tribe, a false prophet and a high priest are not judged save by a court of seventy-one." If the Saviour was to be arrested and tried, it would have to be under this law, as a false prophet. And he could not be judged by any less a tribunal than the Great Sanhedrin.

The strength of the court was never shown more clearly than in the trial of a judge who defied a decision of the Sanhedrin. The penalty was strangulation. When he was brought to trial before the Great Sanhedrin, the judge's life was spared on the ground that, while he had orally defied the decision, he adhered to the will of the Sanhedrin in his official acts.

Most trials were a bedlam of sound. The judges sat on their crescent benches and, across the chamber, the nominees sat on their benches. As each piece of evidence was adduced, the Sanhedrin fell on it and argued pro and con across the benches. The nominees were also permitted to argue the merits of each piece of evidence, although they were not permitted to participate in the final deliberations, nor cast a vote.

No case could be moved to trial without witnesses because Jewish law was based on the testimony of others than the defendant. The judges were prosecutor, defense counsel and final court of appeals. There were no lawyers to plead for or against, other than the judges. No member of the Sanhedrin, no matter how prejudiced, could hear one side of a case without insisting on hearing the other.

All sentences in criminal cases were severe. There were no prisons; no asylums. Banishment was a minor sentence. The usual sentence was death in one of four ways: stoning, burning, decapitation or strangulation. Of these, the most common was stoning. This was accomplished by collecting a crowd and pushing the condemned from an eminence. The crowd looked down. If he moved, they threw stones at him until he was dead.

Each sentence of death was passed on, before execution, to the Roman Procurator. He usually affirmed it without question. If he felt so disposed, or if someone had pleaded the case with him privately, the Procurator might summon the accused and accusers and hear the case before his own judicial chair. If he reversed the verdict, the condemned was acquitted and the Sanhedrin was powerless. If he confirmed it, the Governor often forced the prisoner to undergo the Roman form of execution: crucifixion.

In addition to the Sadducees and Pharisees, there were political splinter parties in Palestine. The Zealots out-Phariseed the Pharisees. They were also the jingoists of the nation, the supernationalists of Palestine. They would admit no one's authority except God's and carried out this principle with such rigor that the Zealots often submitted to cruel punishment and death rather than bend the knee to anyone.

The Essenes were a special group who lived in villages throughout Palestine, but were centered on En-Gedi on the near shore of the Dead Sea. They were ascetic religionists numbering perhaps four thousand and they administered their affairs like monks. To be accepted as an Essene a Jew had first to serve a year's novitiate, and then two years of probation before the solemn vows of membership were permitted. They practiced communism; there was no private ownership of goods or tools or produce or money. Marriage was forbidden to Essenes. They worked on farms, and when they were not working the Essenes prayed. Other than prayer, silence was enjoined upon them at all times. They were so ultrastrict in their interpretation of the law of Moses that, on Sabbaths, they refrained from all bodily functions whatsoever.

It is doubtful that the city of Jerusalem ever housed more than 100,000 people. The circumference of the walls was less than three miles, and inside were about 300 acres. The great temple area occupied 1,600 feet by 970 feet. The Fortress of Antonia bit into the northwest corner. The west side of the city was dotted with palaces and the big homes of the rich. The population may have been less than 100,000—the bulk of it concentrated in the southeast corner where the poor lived near the waters of Siloe.

The city was half a mile in the sky, and this brought with it a certain clearness and coolness of air. Most of the homes were made of whitish gray limestone cut from the surrounding hills. The streets were narrow and hilly and full of plodding donkeys laden with the commerce of the metropolis. They walked slowly and independently, unafraid of the long reed in the hand of the owner who shuffled a few paces behind.

The people in their striped cloaks seemed to be always on the move in the narrow alleys, in two opposite streams melting and blending and falling away from each other. They walked through patches of white sunlight into patches of deep blue shadow. Now and then the servants of a rich man would call for clearance for his litter, carried by slaves. In the open places, camels hauled sleds loaded with stone for new buildings.

Sandal makers stared absentmindedly from shops, their lips full of small nails; a Scribe sat at the base of a wall and wrote letters for those who could not write; a rich woman bought brocade for a coat. It would be placed on a scale, and everyone watched as she placed gold coins in the opposite scale; when they hung in balance, the brocade was hers.

The shops along the streets were narrow across the front and open. Some, like the potters, banded together and mass-produced jars and urns and dishes along factory lines. There were butchers and grocers and wine merchants and exporters and jewelers and doctors and carpenters and vendors and hairdressers and basket weavers and morticians, stone quarriers, fishermen, artisans of bronze and iron, blacksmiths, sailors, locksmiths, tailors, cask makers, midwives, chemists, shoemakers, painters, millers, itinerant laborers, couriers and slaves (who wore large identification tags on chains around their necks).

On an average day, there might be 150,000 pilgrims in the city, present to worship Yahweh in the place where He dwelled. Many of these came out of the diaspora, from the far corners of the civilized world, as the law said that Jews must. The bulk of them landed at Joppa, the nearest port, and many of them walked the rest of the way to Jerusalem.

These were always overwhelmed by the size and beauty of the temple, and by the seven famous markets for which the city was renowned. There were complete markets for ironware, cattle, wool, clothing and bolt goods, wood, bread, vegetables and fruit. The big market days were Mondays and Thursdays; then the courts met and there were readings of the Torah.

The prices of all commodities were fixed by the municipal officials of Jerusalem, who were appointed by the high priest with the assent of the Procurator. No Jew could undersell a competitor. Nor could he ask more than the fixed price for superior wares. All prices were constantly being adjusted by the city fathers so that the merchants could realize a set profit on their merchandise—no more, no less. The local eating houses did a flourishing business; what they had to offer was a menu of fresh fish or salt, fried locusts, hot vegetables, soup, pastry, fruitcake, wine and Egyptian beer.

The bankers were licensed by law and were permitted to charge up to 8 percent interest annually on loans. These were called *shulchanim* and they set their tables up every morning in the outer courts of the temple. There they earned more money exchanging coins than lending. The average fee for changing Greek or Roman or Egyptian coinage into temple shekels for offerings was the rough equivalent of four cents per coin. Still, in spite of the riches to be gained in such work, few Jews aspired to it because the law frowned upon moneylenders.

The sons of the wealthy fell more readily into the importing and exporting trade, or into the insurance of caravans. Palestine exported wheat, olive oil, balsam, honey, dried fruits. The country bought wood, metals, apples from Crete, cheese, fish, wine, Medean beer and Egyptian beer, dress goods from India, veils, sandals, dinnerware, baskets, jugs and basins.

The city authorities, backed by the Sanhedrin, devised ordinances to cover daily contingencies. A wholesale dealer had to clean his scales once a month; a retail dealer, twice a week. In fluid measure, all merchants were ordered to add an extra ounce for every gallon and a half sold, to make up for spillage. A bargain was not closed until both parties had taken possession: the merchant of his money, the customer of his goods.

Anyone who could prove that he had been cheated, or that the fixed prices of Jerusalem had been violated, could demand the difference in money, besides demanding punishment of the violator. Wine for sale could not be adulterated. A member of the Sanhedrin condemned tradesmen who gave small gifts to children to attract the trade of their parents.

A woman who borrowed a loaf of bread from a neighbor must, at the time, fix the value in money, because a sudden rise of the price of flour might increase its value. In renting a field, it was incumbent on the lessee to pay at once, and in cash, or else the owner of the field could raise the price if the market for farm goods rose.

Unions were organized and labor guilds were held in esteem. Before a new union was organized, it was necessary to get the permission of the Roman Emperor, who withheld it only if his advisers told him that the union was being organized for seditious purposes. The unions throughout Palestine regulated the working hours for various crafts, regulated the days of work, negotiated for better salaries, and insured members against losses in donkeys and tools.

On the hills around Jerusalem and throughout the country, shepherds seldom drove their flocks of sheep. They led them. Each shepherd had his own whistle, which his sheep could hear from afar, and they would move toward him at once. When shepherds met, their flocks intermingled so that even Solomon, in all his wisdom, would not have been able to separate them with justice. When the shepherds parted, one whistled softly.

His sheep—all his sheep and no others—extricated themselves from the mass and followed him.

At a pool, a shepherd could order his sheep to wait. No matter how thirsty, they would stand. While drinking, if the shepherd saw another flock coming to the pool, he could order his charges to stop drinking and they would obey. A sick lamb was always carried slung across the back of the shoulders, with its belly close to the warmth of the shepherd's neck. Small stone enclosures were set up for night counting of sheep. The entrance would admit only one sheep at a time and the shepherd sat on the little wall and counted as they filed inside.

Jewish friends showed their esteem for one another by always walking hand in hand. No one ever slept in the dark; a lamp was always burning in the family sleeping quarters. Bread was never cut; it was broken in wedge shape so that it could be used as a spoon for dinner, and was dipped into a common dish.

The market of Annas marred the serene beauty of the temple. Sellers shouted and waved to pilgrims all day long, and haggled over prices. The animals bleated and snorted and filled the courts with the ammonia-like fumes of dung. On ordinary days a poor man could buy two pigeons for sacrifice for the equivalent of a few cents. But at Passover time the price was often multiplied by fifty. In bitterness the poor called this place "The bazaar of the Sons of Annas."

Later in the first century, Flavius Josephus summed up the feelings of the Jews for their religio-political government when he wrote:

"What form of government then can be more holy than this? What more worthy kind of worship can be paid to God than we pay, where the entire body of the people are prepared for religion, where an extraordinary degree of care is required in the priests, and where the whole polity is so ordered as if it were a certain religious solemnity? For which things foreigners, when they observe [our] festivals, are able to observe for a few days time, and call them 'mysterious' and 'sacred ceremonies,' we observe with great pleasure and an unshaken resolution during our whole lives.

"What are the things then that we are commanded or forbidden? They are simple, and easily known. The first command is concerning God, and affirms that God contains all things, and is a Being every way perfect and happy, self-sufficient and supplying all other beings; the beginning, the middle and the end of all things.

"He is manifest in His works and benefits, and more conspicuous than any other being whatsoever; but as to His form and magnitude, He is most obscure. All materials, let them be ever so costly, are unworthy to compose an image for Him, and all arts are unartful to express the notion we ought to have of Him. We can neither see nor think of anything like Him, nor is it agreeable to piety to form a resemblance of Him.

"We see His works, the light, the heaven, the earth, the sun and the moon, the waters, the generations of animals, the productions of fruits. These things hath God made, not with hands, not with labour, not as wanting the assistance of any to cooperate with Him, but as His skill resolved they should be made and be good also; they were made and became good immediately. All men ought to follow this Being, and to worship Him in the exercise of virtue: for this way of worship of God is the most holy of all others."

Long before the first century A.D., the Jews reasoned that in time the dead would outnumber the living, and cemetery space would be a problem. The elders resolved it at once. First they decreed that it was unclean to bury the dead anywhere within the limits of a city or town. Next, it was decided to bury the dead by families. Each one had a stone sarcophagus raised six inches above the cemetery ground. After a period of time, the member of the family who rested in the sarcophagus was considered to be not much more than bones. At that point (usually seven years after burial) the body was removed from the full-size sarcophagus and placed in a small stone ossuary. This measured eighteen inches long by eight inches high and was placed beside the original sarcophagus. In time, an entire family was buried in the one sarcophagus and later moved to the little "jewel cases."

Housing for the living was not as much of a problem. The poor built stone or mud huts. The most expensive part of these was the crossbeams needed to hold the flat roof. Wood was rare and costly. But once purchased, it was embedded in mortises at the tops of the walls and, over it, palm leaves and branches were tossed to make a thatched roof.

In the country many farmers lived in limestone caves cut into the hillsides. These were almost always on a slope and seldom faced the strong winds and rains of winter. Like the mud houses in the city, the hillside homes were made of one large room with a three-foot elevation of earth to the left rear for sleeping. Under the sleeping section was the winter oven which kept the family warm on chilly nights. Entire families slept together and usually slept in their underclothing. There were no beds for the poor. They slept on straw mats woven by the housewife. One sheet covered the family.

The rich built houses of stone or baked brick, and these always had front courtyards and oil lamps hanging from the courtyard walls. The mortar used in the brick houses was inferior in quality, and in a heavy tropical storm the cement became "soapy" and slid out from between the bricks. The homes of the very rich were made of squared stone and often lasted five hundred years.

Windows in all homes were few and high from the ground. Sometimes they were hung with bars; mostly they were closed with draperies. The floors of the average homes were of packed earth. Earth was also laid on the thatched roofs and after a storm the mud on the rooftops was rerolled with a cylindrical stone. Outside the house a flight of stone steps usually led up to the roof. The roof had a score of uses; often a man sat up there and plied his trade as tailor, leather worker, weaver or shoemaker. Farm roofs were used for the winnowing of grain; also, for drying unpressed grapes or ripening of fruits—and now and then for sleeping.

The poor who lived in towns often kept animals in their homes. In the rear of the single-room dwellings, to the extreme right, a stone archway was built with room for an ass, a cow and fodder bins. On the outside of the archway were steps leading to the top of it. There the family stored reserve foods—cheeses, breads, wines and the special earthenware for feast days.

The rich man had a couch. It had small legs and sometimes a back and two sides, like a settee. He used a pillow and a mattress, and these were made of broken rushes, which were noisy, or feathers, which weren't. He paid to have his coverlet dyed purple, because this was the color of kings.

At night the poor, who had no windows in their homes, used thick homemade candles made of tallow molded around a rush. People who needed new fire used a piece of flint and a piece of iron. But usually new fire was borrowed from a neighbor on a knot of wood. They obtained heat at night by placing stones in front of the mounded oven. The charred embers inside the oven reflected off the stones and canceled the chill; the rest of the heat seeped up through the mud to the sleeping family on top. The rich man had braziers and could afford wood. These little grates were made of bronze. Servants filled them with faggots, lit them in the courtyard, and, when they were reduced to ruddy char and no smoke, brought them into the house.

Although it is true that most crimes were punishable by death, including stealing, in several types of burglary the thief was punished, according to the book of Exodus, by having to pay to the person he wronged double what he stole. If a man stole cattle, he must pay double. If he killed or sold the cattle he must pay four times their worth, except in the case of an ox, when the payment became fivefold. Should the thief plead that he was too poor to pay, then he had to become the servant of the man from whom he stole.

It was a lawful duty to show the routes and roads to travelers asking for information, "and not to esteem it a sport," as Josephus wrote, "when we hinder others by setting them in the wrong way."

"He that kicks a woman with child so that the woman miscarry, let him pay a fine in money as having diminished the multitude by the destruction of what was in her womb, and let money also be given the woman's husband by him that kicked her; if she die, let him also be put to death, the law judging it equitable that a life should go for a life."

If a man carried poison in his home, and had no just reason for having it on the premises, then he must be put to death with the poison, "the same mischief he would have brought upon others." If a man maimed someone, or caused someone to lose a limb, the court decreed that the one who was injured had a choice of satisfaction: either to accept money from the man who inflicted the injury, or to inflict the same injuries on the wrongdoer.

The law, in its wisdom, even remembered expectant mothers. The pregnant woman must not take hot baths for fear of miscarriage. She must avoid green vegetables, salt food and fat. She must eat fish and mustard. Newborn babies were bathed in warm water, massaged with salt and wrapped in swaddling clothes. Males were to be circumcised on the eighth day. Most babies were breast-fed until they were at least two years of age, sometimes three.

Education in Palestine was compulsory. Every town had a school and each child, at the age of six, had to attend. Earlier than the age of six, it was the duty of the mother to instruct the child in religion, in household tasks not beyond its ability to perform, and in good behavior.

The Pharisees said that it was unlawful to live in a village without a school. Many of the schools were in synagogues. Students always stood while being taught, unless the teacher invited them, in good weather, to sit outside under a tree. Everyone was taught religion and reading, and writing, although it was not considered necessary for girls to study beyond the minimum of reading and writing. Most youngsters studied the Scriptures (essentially what we now call the Old Testament) diligently until the age of ten. After that they were taught oral law, or interpretation of law. At about the age of fifteen, a boy could, if he chose, enter theological discussions in the Bet Midrash at Jerusalem, or in his town synagogue after Sabbath services. The boy would be faced with a circle of twinkling eyes and bantering questions. If he stammered or halted he received more help than he could use or even understand.

At this time many of the learned men of the world—which consisted largely of the Mediterranean basin—understood some of the study of science and were eager to learn more. It was fashionable among the more successful Jews to apply themselves to science. The basic truths of mathematics and the principles of engineering and the laws of stress had been understood and applied fifteen hundred years before this century. The people of Mesopotamia had been studying astronomy and passing their knowledge on to Jews and Romans and Egyptians alike for more than two thousand years. Six hundred years before, they had laid out the phases of the moon and the sun, and most of the stars of the first magnitude.

The Jews of this time were not lax in matters of hygiene. They understood that filth brought disease, and disease brought epidemics. Their sanitation measures in Jerusalem did not match those of Rome, but Jerusalem was considered a provincial city and, as such, it ranked higher than might be expected.

All street and sewage drains were pitched toward the Valley of the Cedron, which lay east of the city and west of the Mount of Olives. All cisterns had, by law, to be covered. No cemetery could be within eighty-seven feet of the city walls; no tannery could operate within the city limits at any time. Bakeries and dyers' shops could not operate on the ground floor of a building if someone lived on the floor above.

Lepers were not permitted in any town under pain of death, and were kept as far from any settlement as possible. Neighbors were not permitted to have windows which looked down on the courtyards of others. All rooftops, however flat, must slope two degrees or more to carry off rainwater. It was against the law to have an open well, an uncovered pit, a rickety staircase or a noisy dog.

There were no trends or fashions in clothing. The oral law detailed the clothing that a male Jew should wear as well as female clothing. The men wore a tight-fitting cotton cap. His cloak was a tallith, a prayer shawl. This had horizontal striping on both ends, which hung below the waist. They wore a loose white dress, usually without sleeves, and this covered the body from neck to ankles. On long trips, or on formal occasions, they wore sandals. Otherwise, they walked barefooted, and the washing of feet was almost as important as the washing of hands.

The women wore the kolbur, made of linen and looking like a petticoat hanging to mid-thigh; over that was a baldinajja, a full-length linen dress; then the istomukhvia, a tie-on robe; a mid-body scarf referred to as the pirzomata; over the outer dress was a colored girdle, striped in the colors of the tribe. The scarf worn on the head was full and protected the modesty of the woman by hiding much of her face. The ends were folded so that they hung down her back like a long, pointed veil.

Indoors the men wore a short tunic with sleeves which was made of one piece and was bought with no hole for the head, to prove that it was not a secondhand garment. After purchase, the Jew cut a V-shaped hole. Sometimes, in addition, his wife would sew a few strong stitches in the bottom of the garment, leaving two large holes for his legs. When the man was ready to labor in the fields he often tucked the loose ends of this garment up into his girdle—"girding his loins."

The tallith, worn by every male Jew as ordered in the law, was a reminder of the separateness of the people of Israel.

This was a good thing internally for the nation, because it bred a homogeneity not found anywhere else. But in Palestine's relations with the rest of the world it bred a certain intolerance. The Jew had a pact with God.

Practically all Jews were believers. If there were heretics or atheists, they were among the Amé-Haaretz. The Jew who believed was forced, by his faith, to a special feeling of dedication.

The Jew's sense of "separateness" was often even stronger when he lived in Gentile cities like Rome and Athens and Alexandria. This feeling contributed to antagonisms in which his religious beliefs and his business acumen were libeled and distorted by alien peoples who had little understanding of them. He was reviled, beaten, cheated and killed. This cruelty, in turn, strengthened his suspicion of others; it made firm his feeling that he was separate and alone. In foreign lands he learned to study his public rights, and fell naturally into studies of law.

The people ate two regular meals: at noon and after sundown. Some drank a brew of herbs or ate bread at dawn, but in the main, Palestine was a two-meal country. The poorer families sometimes boiled a sheep tail in a pot of vegetables. They ate cucumbers, beans, lentils, onions, leeks, vegetable marrow and garlic. The diet, severe as it was, was augmented by dates, figs, olives and watermelon.

The olive was the most important commodity of all. The groves seemed to be everywhere. The poorest home had its olive tree out front, small and lacy-looking, with a twisted trunk festooned with burls. A good tree would yield ten gallons of oil. Olives were picked in October and the harvest was plucked by the women and the children. They beat and shook the trees and what fell they gathered.

It was forbidden by law to go over an olive tree a second time, so that when the harvest was done there would be something left over for the poor. Olives went to the presses to be squeezed for their heavy chartreuse-colored oil. Some olives were preserved in jars of salt water.

When the oil had been compressed from the olive, it was allowed to settle until the sediment went to the bottom. Then it was poured into jars and taken from the gethsemane (olive press) and stored in stone cisterns. Almost ritualistically the very first olives—at least a small amount of them—were placed in horsehair bags at home and trodden by the feet of the women of the family, to whom the honor fell of pressing the first oil of the season.

Grapes, too, were important, and vineyards splashed the low slopes of mountains with dark green. June grapes, unripe and tart, were used as a laxative. The real harvest began in July and this was a happy festival, a time for laughter, a time for romance.

This was anything but a backward country. The people were forward-looking, progressive, and the only item they never hesitated to import from the Gentile world was knowledge. In the field of medicine, for example, all qualified physicians had to have some experience in surgery.

The doctors understood the necessity for amputation in cases of gangrenous members and they knew how to seal off arteries. They used an anesthetic called nepenthe and this was the most common of the deeper sedatives, although others used a drug called mandragora to keep the patient drowsy and apathetic during surgery.

Mesopotamia had a medical code two thousand years old. Greece had already tried state medicine and had failed. Only in Rome was the physician despised as a charlatan, for this fountainhead of new culture preferred home remedies. In Rome, slaves were taught to be doctors; the rich were charged exorbitant fees, the poor were treated free.

In Palestine the doctors used lancets and cutting instruments of unique design; in Egypt the doctors operated on the human brain and did tracheotomies for obstructed larynxes. In all countries around the Mediterranean Sea, the doctors used needles for suturing, had forceps of varying sizes, catheters, surgical scissors for excising diseased parts of the female procreative agencies, and had invented a rachet for dilation.

Long ago, the Sanhedrin had enacted into law a requirement that every town in the land must have a physician-surgeon. A physician was appointed to attend priests at the temple. One of the achievements of the doctors of Palestine was that they were the first to operate on the human eye for cataracts.

False teeth had been in use for five hundred years. They were made from the teeth of dead people and animals. The Jews brushed their teeth daily and used a dentifrice made of powdered bones and oyster shells bound into a paste with honey. For toothache the remedies were vinegar or myrrh, niter and hartshorn.

In the field of mechanics, the Jews learned from others. They used water power extensively and their mill wheels could be adjusted to a delicacy of strength so that, for example, olives could be crushed without breaking the olive pits, which would taint the oil. The people understood the use of the crane and fashioned fitted wheels and gear slots for raising different types of weights. They had borrowed the original models from the Romans, who called the crane a machina tractoria.

The Jews also borrowed from the Romans a meter which, attached to a public vehicle or chariot, would after a certain number of revolutions of the wheels pop a pebble into an empty box. At the end of the ride, the passenger counted the pebbles and paid the driver.

The entire province was old-fashioned in the matter of keeping time. The Jews reckoned each day as beginning at sunset, but of course the moment of sunset varied with each new day and this caused error. They divided the night into three watches: evening, midnight and cock-crowing.

The people were aware of timekeeping devices, but would not use them. They had no means of breaking one hour into smaller components and could not keep an appointment with accuracy. Sunrise was another variable.

The Romans had used a sundial for three hundred years, but finding that it was useless on overcast days and useless at night, they turned to water clocks. The water dripped with greater accuracy than sand, and when the Romans brought the clocks to Palestine it was expected that the people would fall upon them with glad cries. They didn't. God, they felt, was the keeper of time, and any system which evaded the use of his sun, his moon and his stars was a pagan system. The Jewish months were dictated by the phases of the moon. They did not come out evenly, and the first phase of Nisan, the opening month, was different from year to year but always fell in the latter days of March or the month of April.

Above all, the Jews awaited a Messiah.

The Messiah was a sweet national obsession. It was ecstasy beyond happiness, joy beyond comprehension; it was balm to a weary farmer's bones as he lay with his family waiting for sleep; it was the single last hope of the aged, the thing a child looked to a mountain of snowy clouds to see; it was the hope of Judea in chains; the Messiah was always the promise of tomorrow morning.

This solemn surge of singing in the heart of every good Jew was the core of Judea at the time of Jesus. This was the topmost stone in the climb toward eternity.

The Messiah. In Hebrew, the word is Mashiah—the anointed. Every Jew understood that two great events were to precede his resurrection from the grave: the first was the coming of the Messiah; the second was the end of the world. Sometimes the two events were linked as though the Messiah would come and bring with him the destruction of the earth. Sometimes these events were distinct. They were discussed by sages endlessly, who quoted from the words of the prophets and from the books of their people. They discussed them carefully and with concealed joy, and no one ever tired of hearing of them.

No matter how many were born and grew up and grew old and died, each new generation was sure that it would live to see both of these events, and the more they heard that other generations before them had similar aspirations, the more sure each new one was that they were nearer to the fulfillment. The old prophets had promised that the Great Elect would come from God himself, and he would liberate the tribes of Israel; then, if the people were worthy, the enemies of Palestine would be destroyed. Israel would reign over all the pagan nations of the world and bring them to the one true God, Yahweh, and this would be His final triumph.

All of the sages were in agreement that the Messiah would be of the House of David. He would be called the Son of Man, and it was acknowledged that the Messiah had existed before the stars and the sun had been fashioned; he was truly of the hand of God. The people read the Book of Daniel and the Psalms and other parts of the Scripture, and they were sure that the time must be near because so many of the words of the old prophets had been fulfilled.

In the Book of Enoch, probably written less than a hundred years before the time of Christ, the Messiah is called the Elect of God, with whom he abides. He would come as the staff of the just, the light of nations; all the peoples would prostrate themselves before him; "in him dwells the spirit of wisdom and the spirit of enlightenment, the spirit of knowledge and of strength, and the spirit of those who have fallen asleep in justice. He will judge all nations, punishing those who have oppressed the just; at his coming the dead will rise again, heaven and earth will be transformed and the just, become heavenly angels, will abide with him throughout life everlasting." In the Psalms, the Messiah is seen in prophecy coming as a king, crushing Israel's enemies, purging Jerusalem, routing nations. After that the Messiah was to govern Palestine in peace and justice, and the Gentiles would come from the ends of the earth to contemplate the glory of Jerusalem.

There had been many predictions about this, in many ages. Even Isaias had said that the Messiah would come to earth. Most of the prophets rendered accounts which varied to a degree from others, but they seemed to agree—especially those who were specific in their utterances—that his birth would be unknown to many; that he would suddenly appear, do his work toward effecting the salvation of Israel, and disappear—probably for "forty-five days"—then return again and destroy the sinful powers of the world.

It is at this point that Israel and all its people would be brought back from the corners of the world and would again share their own land—the ten tribes living together—but all of this only on condition that the people had repented of their sins.

The dead would be raised; the sinners in Gehenna who had lain under perpetual fire would be restored. Those Jews who had died and been buried elsewhere in the world would, by the miracle of the Messiah, roll underground (not without suffering) until they reached Jerusalem and then they would be returned to life. The general resurrection would be announced by the blowing of a great trumpet.

Some of the ideas concerning the coming of the Messiah were confused. For example, many of the sages would proclaim that when all this had come to pass the city of Jerusalem would glitter in the sun and the Sabbath boundaries for walking would be marked with pearls and precious stones. The city and its walls would be moved upward to a height of about nine miles. The Messiah would decree the new temple which he would build and which, in all its beauty, would have five things restored: the Golden Candlestick, the Ark, the Heaven-lit fire on the sacrificial altar, the divine presence (Shechinah) and the Cherubim.

The prophets spurned something which turned out to be irresistible to the sages: expanding the Messianic doctrine. Once the elders started to rationalize the prophecies into ever greater detail, they began to slide and sink in the ecclesiastical quicksand. One insisted that once the temple had been restored, it would naturally follow that all of the ancient rituals of Moses would be restored, too. This seemed reasonable to many, because one could not imagine a Messiah whose teachings were not compatible with those of Moses.

Someone else said that, in that case, how would the defeated Gentiles worship? Some said that the Mosaic law would be imposed on them, too, while others thought that the Gentiles were unworthy of Moses. A third school of thinking asked if it were not reasonable to expect that the Messiah would arrive with his own ideas of how to worship God. This tossed all the earlier thinking into a conflicting whirl of perplexities, and when the theories had settled, many asked if the new law would apply only to the Gentiles, or to Israel as well? It was finally decided—and not by any majority—that the new law would be binding on Israel and that the Messiah would give to the Gentiles a list of ordinances—perhaps thirty commandments.

The objective scholars (and especially the liberal ones) were sure that, after the Messiah came, the only holy day would be the Day of Atonement, and that the temple sacrifices would be cut down to thank offerings only. Even the laws of pure and impure food would be abolished, they felt.

All were certain that this would be a period of joyful holiness, of forgiveness, of peace. Nowhere would there be oppressors or enemies. Once the Oriental imaginations of the Jews set to work visualizing what life would be like in those times, they outdid one another in extravagance: the angels of God would cut gems forty-five square and set them in the outer gates of Jerusalem; windows and gates would be made of precious stones; the walls would be made of silver and gold encrusted with gems;

jewels would be strewn about the streets for all Jews to take; Jerusalem, the Holy City, would be as large as Palestine, and Palestine would be the size of the world.

The soil would become fertile in the blink of an eye; there would be the finest dresses and the loveliest cakes; wheat would be as palm trees; on the mountaintops the wind would whirl the wheat and convert it into flour and cast it to the bottoms of the valleys; all trees would bear great fruit, even those which were not designed for it; every day the woman of the house would bear a child, so that, in time, each family would number as many as all Israel at the time of the Exodus; sickness and disease and any instrument of hurt to human beings would be extinct; death would be abolished for the faithful by order of the Messiah; Gentiles would die at the age of one hundred and, at that age, would be as children.

The fifth world monarchy would be raised to take the place of the fourth (the Roman). Jerusalem would be the capital of the world and the home of the Messiah. When the ten nations of the Gentiles fell, the final judgment would be at hand. This would occur in the Valley of Jehoshaphat, and Yahweh would preside, surrounded by a heavenly Sanhedrin composed of the elders of Israel. The Gentile nations would plead for mercy and would be denied and sent to punishment.

When this was done, heaven and earth would be renewed in eternal happiness and there would be no darkness in either place, and the yetser hara (impulse toward evil) would be destroyed. There would be no sin. The question of whether there would be any animal functions in the body was never settled.

On the other hand, most of the sages were in agreement with the Prophecy of Baruch that, in the general resurrection, men would come forth from the grave looking exactly as they had in life, so that, when they were recognized by their families and friends, the truth of the resurrection would be manifest to all. After Yahweh had bidden the good to come to Him, and the evil to be punished, the righteous would be transformed into beautiful angels and the guilty would fade away.

It was a satisfying image to all Jews, but more than that, it was a reasonable matter. It fitted nicely with all the current ideas of God and the hereafter and justice and rewards and punishments, and it echoed the words of the long-gone prophets. This was the thing a good man lived for. It might happen in his time; it might happen in the time of his sons or their sons, but that did not matter because, no matter when it came, it would unite all the good people who loved one another.

If there was a weakness in the whole rich promise of a Messiah, it was the question of how to recognize him when he came. The clues were few and thin: he would be of the house of David, his birth would be unknown to his contemporaries; Israel would be assailed from outside.

The house of David was now numbered in many thousands; babies were being born to the Davidites regularly; the people were sorely pressed by the infidel Romans.

The pious were perplexed. They looked but they did not know where to look, or even when. And, to confound matters, false Messiahs entered Jerusalem now and then accompanied by the Amé-Haaretz, who shouted, "Hosanna to the Son of Man!" and strewed the path of the stranger with flowers and palms. The fakers were of two kinds: charlatans and the insane. The latter were, of course, sincere.

And always, it seemed, there was the same denouement. The priests of the temple hooted at the false Messiah and the Pharisees baited him with questions designed to trap him and the people demanded miracles as proof of divinity. In almost all cases the man would soon be exposed, and then Jerusalem would go back to its normal life, determined not to be seduced spiritually again.

The man who might have been of assistance to the people was the high priest. As the interpreter of the law Caiphas had the right to insist that anyone who claimed to be the Messiah be sent to him for examination. And if Caiphas had been sincere in his desire to find the Messiah, he would have been the first man to fall to his knees in the event that he was convinced.

His true attitude was reflected in the actions of the Levites, priests and the Pharisees who lived on his favor; uniformly they strove to prove that there was no Messiah, that anyone who claimed to be he was automatically an "Egyptian magician" who deserved death for blasphemy. This was wrong even when the spurious Messiahs were descending on Jerusalem because it left no room for acceptance and obeisance should the true Messiah come.

Caiphas was interested in only one proposition: the continuance in office of Caiphas as high priest, and the maintenance of the temple in its current status—spiritually and economically. There must be no threat to either of these things. In the old days, as Caiphas knew, the high priest had been chosen for life, but with the coming of the Herods and the iron rule of Rome, high priests were political pawns and they were deposed quickly and mercilessly if they did not please their earthly masters.

Caiphas had been the fifteenth high priest in the past sixty-five years. Let there be a disturbance on the temple steps which irritated Rome, and there would be a new high priest. In the case of Caiphas this was a particularly obnoxious possibility because he would be the last of the family of Annas to hold the office, and if a new man was appointed it would be from another sacerdotal family. Then, in spite of the great political power of Annas, the money-changers and the market salesmen would be responsible to someone else.

No one in all Judea was more keenly aware than Caiphas and his father-in-law that the very vestments of the high priest reposed in a Roman locker deep down in Fortress Antonia.

NARRATIVE

❖❖❖

April 6, A.D. 30

8 P.M.

The apostles sorrowed and worried. Jesus had to die. They knew this because he had told them many times. But, like children gifted with exorbitant faith, they had been secretly certain that, when the time of trial arrived, Jesus would summon legions of avenging angels who would decimate his enemies, wipe out the Roman armies, destroy the world by fire, and he would then sit with his apostles on golden chairs in the clouds over the Valley of the Cedron and there judge the living and the dead. Only a few weeks ago, the mother of the Sons of Thunder had, with material anxiety, hung onto the sleeve of Jesus to ask him for good golden seats beside his throne for her boys.

Jesus was dipping his thumb and index fingers into the bitter herbs. He saw the sorrowing, and his own brown eyes became heavy-lidded. "I tell you now before it comes to pass," he said, almost apologetically, "so that when it has come to pass you may believe that I am he."

He loved them and it grieved him to see their depression, but the statement also took cognizance of their frailty, when they sometimes doubted that he was the Messiah. He knew that, before he died, they would need proof piled on proof to cement their faith. So he resorted to prophecy to prove that "I am he." And, to make them understand that he and they were one in their mission to redeem mankind, he said: "I say to you, he who receives anyone I send, receives me; and he who receives me, receives him who sent me."

Jesus bowed his head and clasped his hands on the cushion at his side. He was a man with an inner worry, a secret and shocking knowledge, and he remained thus for a moment and then blurted the words: "Amen, amen I say to you, one of you will betray me."

The great brown head was again lowered and the fingers wrung against each other as though he felt shame for what one of them was doing. The apostles looked at one another in disbelief. He had led them on, gently but steadily, toward this great announcement. And yet they were not prepared for the news. Mouths hung open; a few glared angrily at one and all; some sat up as though ready to flee. Each apostle began to tap his own bosom and beg: "Is it I, Lord? Is it I?"

Jesus did not answer. The feast, an hour old, was disrupted. The servants stood away from the table, the wine and cups glistening on trays, wondering if they should run downstairs and tell their master that the Passover upstairs had closed in dishonor. Peter, mouth open, stroking his beard absentmindedly, wanted to ask straight out who the traitor was, but he was afraid. He had been in trouble only a half hour ago, and even if he never learned the identity of the traitor, he was not going to risk more displeasure.

So, looking across the back of Jesus, he saw young John lean his head against the chest of Jesus and, catching John's eye, he made mute panto-mime motions: "Who is it of whom he speaks?" John, whose heart was so full of love that he had not learned to be fearful, looked up into the eyes of his master and said bluntly: "Lord, who is it?"

Jesus lifted his head, the eyes full of anguish, and he whispered: "It is he to whom I will give the morsel after dipping it in the bowl."

Judas had stopped eating and was obviously as shocked as any of the rest of the company. He, too, had asked, in pained surprise: "Is it I, Lord?" and, like the others, he received no answer. Inwardly he trembled, and his feeling was that beyond doubt someone in the entourage of the high priest had discussed the plot in the streets, or perhaps told a follower of Jesus that one of the apostles had promised to deliver him to Caiphas in the dead of night. But did Jesus know who? Judas doubted it.

The host took a morsel and dipped it into a bowl of charoseth. He shook the loose wine from it and held it to Judas. The money-keeper, who had not heard John ask the question—nor the whispered reply—looked pleased and held his mouth toward the tidbit and ate it. Judas regarded this as a mark of favor.

Smug, and now certain that he was not under suspicion, Judas asked again—this time not in concert with the others—"Is it I, Master?" Softly, the Nazarene murmured: "Thou hast said it," which was an Aramean colloquialism meaning "yes," but meaning more than yes. It also meant "You have said it, not I." He would use this expression once more before he died.

With the exception of John, and perhap Peter, no one at the table comprehended the tableau. The others were troubled, and they talked in a babble about convincing Jesus to go back to Bethany or all the way to Ephrem, where no plotter would dare to arrest him. These men did not dispute the will of Jesus to die for the sins of all mankind. But they expected at the very least that his death would be a glorious act, worthy of God. They wanted him to raise himself up on a cloud of fire and go straight to his Father in heaven. They expected to witness this, and some of them felt that they might be invited to go with him. The thing they dreaded most was a death of shame, an end as a criminal. And that they knew, was what he risked by being in Jerusalem tonight.

Judas swallowed, and glanced toward the man he had told the multitudes was the Messiah. Jesus stared at him steadily, no rancor in his eyes, and he said: "That which you must do, do quickly." Judas understood. Some of the others heard it, and thought that the master had ordered Judas Iscariot to go out into the night and buy things for the festival, which had a week more to go, or that he had told Judas to go out into the night and give some money from the common purse to the poor.

The Judean pushed himself back on the low couch and stood. For a moment he looked down on the reclining figures of his friends and then, without adieu, he walked around the table, the leather purse swinging from his hand, and down the stairway and out into the night. Only three persons in the room knew that he had betrayed the Prince of Love—John, Peter and Jesus.

Of course Judas could easily have been stopped from leaving the room. Had Jesus asked for the attention of the others and said: "This is the traitor!" the apostles, in their anger, would have restrained him and possibly injured him. The fact that Peter and John knew the identity of the renegade and did not themselves spread the alarm as Judas walked out implies that Jesus must have silenced them. For, in this instance as well as in many others, the divine side of the character of Jesus overruled that of the fearful man. As God, he knew that he must die, sustaining every bit of agonizing pain for the sins of man. As man, his impulse must have been to stop Judas and to flee from Jerusalem with his apostles. He had doomed himself when he said, "The son of man departs, indeed, according to the fixed decree; but condemnation awaits that man who is instrumental in betraying him!"

A man devoid of faith, like Judas, needs something to sustain him, to nourish his emotional life, and most men in this position boast of their practical side. Judas was practical. As one of the original twelve, he had subscribed to Jesus as the Messiah as long as there was a good living in it. And for the money-keeper of this fervent enterprise it was a good living indeed, because hundreds and then thousands came to believe that this man Jesus was indeed he whom it had been predicted Yahweh would send to Israel. This being the case, the rich recruits to the cause not only knelt before him and wept or begged for forgiveness or kissed the hem of his dusty garment, but they would not be satisfied until they had contributed their wealth to the furtherance of the Messiah.

At times, in the presence of miracles such as the recent one of raising Lazarus up after he had been in the tomb four days, Judas must have half believed in Jesus. But then his practical side told him that such things were in the nature of Egyptian magic, as everyone knew, and Judas believed that there was collusion between Jesus and Lazarus and Jesus and the other beneficiaries of miracles. It was a good scheme to be allied with, as long as it flourished. And Judas remained with it exactly that long.

In recent weeks, when he heard Jesus speak more and more poignantly about his impending death, Judas began to suspect that the scheme had been drained of its good. When he learned that Pharisees were taunting the Messiah he knew that the end was near, because they were many and strong and Jesus was one and weak. Then, when some of the followers hurried from Jerusalem to Ephrem to warn Jesus that Caiphas, the high priest, was plotting to arrest and condemn Jesus for blasphemy, Judas knew that this particular venture was at an end.

The question then was a practical one: How could he get out of it with profit? Judas could flee and not be seen in the Jerusalem area until Jesus had been forgotten. He could remain with the group, hoping for a few more shekels, but in this he would risk arrest as one of the apostles. It was not a part of his practical nature to risk anything. The clever thing to do would be to go to Caiphas and offer to deliver Jesus. This would accomplish several things: it would ally him with the high priest, and obviate the risk of arrest. It would enrich him, because Caiphas did not dare to arrest Jesus by day because of his numerous and volatile followers. And a man like Judas could set a price on delivering the Nazarene: it would even make a sort of temple hero of Judas, the man who had worked for Yahweh to deliver the blasphemer. It would also put him in the good graces of the high priest sufficiently to be able to ask for a temple concession—like the selling of doves. Finally, by being righteous in apprehending the blasphemer, he would be in the position of taking funds—but from an official criminal—and so no one would be able to accuse him of stealing.

This was logical thinking and practical. It was the best possible way out of an increasingly deteriorating situation. The only way in which it could prove to be a poor solution would be if Jesus of Nazareth turned out to be the true Messiah, the Son of God. In that case, Judas would be—as he knew—the meanest traitor in the history of the world, and he must have given some thought to this side of the matter, since Jesus had proclaimed himself the Messiah, and Judas had endorsed his proclamation before the crowds in every town.

Judas' practical mind told him that Jesus was a misguided religious fanatic. Judas cannot have thought of Jesus as a fraud: he had seen enough of Jesus to know that the man had given all of himself in love and devotion to all people—Jew and Gentile alike—and that he had asked nothing for himself. Judas, a fraud, understood frauds. To his way of thinking, Jesus must have been a naïve religious who, through mental aberration, believed that he was God. The miracles of Jesus could be set down to what some of the people called magic and others called the works of Beelzebub.

Judas hurried out into the streets and walked north a street or two to the home of Caiphas. The apostles did not say this and would not write of it, but Judas had to earn the thirty pieces of silver which Caiphas had promised, for this was the price of a slave. The high priest had accepted the offer only if Judas could effect the arrest of Jesus when the multitudes of his followers were not about.

This was the time, and what better time than when he was already inside the walls of the city? The courtyards of Caiphas and his father-in-law, Annas, adjoined by a common gate, and a servant studied the glistening face of Judas under a flickering yard light and told him to wait. He waited. He trembled with excitement; he was going to earn money and get the favor of the most powerful man in the Jewish faith at the same time. It did not matter to Judas that a man who would buy the betrayal of another man was unworthy to be high priest of a faith which set high store on the word of God and justice and the equities of free people.

Judas, the practical betrayer, was about to meet Caiphas, the practical religious leader, in one of the most solemn moments of history. Had either been a man of good will, had either been honest, the story would have been different. Judas cannot have thought that Jesus might suffer a penalty less than death, because he knew the severity of the Jewish law. A blasphemer was a creature more vile than a murderer. He understood the penalty in store for Jesus, as Caiphas did.

Judas waited, and it was near the third hour of the night watch when Caiphas came out. The high priest was a dark, balding man of superior garments and manner. Judas would have meant little to him on any occasion. Now he met him only on the chance that this mean little Judean mercenary might be ready to deliver up the Nazarene.

Caiphas had small patience with this man. He asked by what right Judas expected an audience at this hour. The faithless one said that he bore good tidings, that Jesus and the apostles were sitting at the Pasch this moment, only three throws of a stone away from where the high priest stood.

Caiphas was pleased. It would have been difficult to hide it. Jesus had hurt him in many ways, and the ways were increasingly grievous. The Nazarene had come from nowhere proclaiming himself a prophet, or acting like a prophet, and the Amé-Haaretz had flocked to his words as though he really were a prophet. The high priest had had much experience with others who had proclaimed that they were sent by God; in fact, Jerusalem seemed to attract the mad ones.

But these others usually fell of their own weight. They promised to restore the Ark of the Covenant to the temple, or to make God appear on a cloud of fire, or they tried to restore sight or cure lepers, and the people who had first followed them in faith now picked up stones when the great miracles failed to materialize.

Jesus was different. He did not even follow the prescribed law. He dined with publicans and sometimes he did not even undergo the ritual washing of the hands. He performed miracles, and the Levites and Pharisees who went with him to mock came back to the temple shaken and frightened, saying that they had seen him do these things. Furthermore, this Jesus had excoriated the priests, condemned the external worship of many of the Pharisees, and preached love of God and of all men. He had come to the temple and had kicked over the tables of the money-changers, mocked the business of selling animals for sacrifice on the temple grounds, and had caused Annas to ask his son-in-law if he proposed to permit this traitorous conduct to continue—whether he lacked the courage to do something about it before Jesus turned the people away from the great temple, which would provide the Romans with the schism they needed to take over the great house of worship for pagan ends.

Caiphas had plotted the arrest of Jesus with the members of the Sanhedrin early this week, but many had wanted to wait until the Passover was over, so that the people would not become excited at the beginning of the high holy days. But word of the plot had reached Jesus and the apostles and, wonder of all wonders, his second-ranking apostle had come forward and offered to deliver him at the first opportunity.

Now Caiphas was both pleased and worried. He had not expected the opportunity to take this spurious Messiah so quickly. No arrangements had been made. The temple guards could be summoned in ten minutes, but, in a case of this kind, it would be wise to ensure the cooperation of the Romans, and the best way to do it would be to acquaint Pontius Pilate with the case, have him order his soldiers to accompany the temple guards on the raid.

The high priest, finger to lips, paced the courtyard. He, too, had a problem. In all Palestine there was only one man greater than Caiphas, and this was Annas. His father-in-law was a maker and breaker of men, a personage so great that his frown could cause sleepless nights for King Herod Antipas and for Pilate, too.

He was called Annas, although his real name was Hananyah. He was small and delicate, pedantic, precise. When Jesus was eleven years of age, Annas had been appointed high priest by Publius Sulpicius Quirinus, who was then beginning his second term as Roman Legate of all Syria. Annas became rich, influential beyond the boundaries of his country. He was a brilliant schemer, and men in positions of power greater than his feared him.

After ten years Annas was deposed. Valerius Gratus, the Roman Governor of Judea at that time, decided that he could break Annas. The Procurator removed Annas from office, but Annas kept the temple business as a private industry, and no one bought a lamb, a dove, or even an ox as a sacrifice without paying Annas, because it was the men of Annas who sold these things on the temple grounds. It was Annas who placed the money-changers at their tables in the Court of the Gentiles, and no Jew could contribute anything except a temple shekel to Yahweh—and of course there was the fee for changing money.

Annas also kept the high priesthood as a personal instrument. In succession, five of his sons became high priest. Now his son-in-law Caiphas was in office. Caiphas would not initiate any action beyond exercising the ritual prerogatives of the high priesthood. When Jesus first came to the attention of Caiphas as a Galilean rabble-rouser, the high priest at once brought the matter to Annas, who decided to do nothing. In his time, he had seen several Messiahs come, and although they always attracted a small lunatic fringe of believers, they always disappeared in a short time. So the advice of Annas was: let the man be. You have been high priest for almost twelve years and you have seen these Messiahs come into Jerusalem in state, and leave a short time later with donkey dung in their beards. If he appears to attract too many followers, send the Pharisees out to bait him with questions. Make him the butt of ridicule and his own believers will laugh.

Caiphas had done this, and Jesus had replied to the questions with such lustrous brilliance that some of the Pharisees had come back to the temple murmuring, "This one is different. He speaks as a great judge. This one talks with the voice of Moses and Isaias." Could this Jesus be the real Messiah?

And the high priest had begun to worry. He was alarmed when Jesus had the temerity to come to the temple to preach his alien doctrines. And Caiphas was panicked when the Galilean publicly condemned the Pharisees and their works, and then kicked over the tables of Annas' money-changers.

He had gone to his father-in-law with the story, and then Annas realized that he had misjudged Jesus. This one was indeed different. Given a few more years, the cumulative power of Jesus would be sufficient perhaps to crack the walls of the great temple and most assuredly to usurp the power of the Sadducees. Then this happy man Annas nodded to his son-in-law and ordered him to proceed "with caution" to try Jesus on a charge of blasphemy as one who had reviled Yahweh.

Now they had him. Caiphas asked Judas where the criminal was, and the Judean told the high priest the exact house. The high priest nodded with some surprise because he knew the father of Mark as a rich and substantial citizen of Jerusalem with considerable influence in the temple. One never knew where to look for disciples of Jesus.

Caiphas told Judas to wait in the courtyard and, in a moment, he was alone. The high priest had lifted the hem of his costly garment and had hurried across the court to tell Annas the news and to get counsel.

If Judas noted the happiness on the face of the priest, he must have thought at once that he had sold Jesus too cheaply. Had he known how important the tall villager from the north was to the socially superior Sadducees of Jerusalem, he might have asked a hundred times the thirty pieces of silver they had promised. When they told him that it would be legal to offer him the price of a slave,[12] he had agreed.

He stared around the courtyard and noted the lamps hanging from staffs inside the white walls. In some wonder, he studied the large colored tiles underfoot and, though he wasn't worthy to be asked inside, he admired the beautiful home of the high priest and saw the servants standing on the balcony to light the braziers against the chill of this bright night.

In ten minutes, Caiphas was back. He was now curt. The chief of the temple guards had been sent for, and would arrive in a little while with a complement of men. They would wait, with Judas, for additional Roman legionaries. Caiphas himself would be off in a moment to seek personal audience with the Procurator, Pilate, and ask him to assign a centurion to the job of assisting in the raid on the upstairs room.

Judas was shocked. He had assumed that this was a small thing, a matter to be forgotten in the morning. Now this elegant personage had consulted the great Annas and had summoned, not one temple guard, but a group of them, and would now go, at this late hour, to consult with the representative of Caesar, who would assign a centurion, no less, and more soldiers.

Caiphas said that, as a dutiful son of Judea, Judas must be prepared to testify in the morning that Jesus had preached that he was the Messiah, the Son of God come to save the people of the world. Thus the niceties of proving blasphemy would be done through one of Jesus' own men. Judas trembled. Testify? No. No, he would not testify. Never. Jesus had been his benefactor, his friend. Judas had agreed to lead them to him, to point him out for identification, but he would not stand up and accuse this man. Let the high priest get someone else.

Caiphas pointed out that the arrest was one thing; proof of blasphemy under Jewish law was another. A disciple who would stand up in court and point at Jesus and merely tell the truth, "I heard this man say that he is God and the Son of God," would be sufficient. Judas shook his head obdurately. Like a petty thief he knew his limitations, and all he asked was thirty pieces of silver and freedom.

In the dim saffron of the oil lamps Caiphas smiled. Judas was one who would steal coins from a dead man's eyes but would ignore the big jewel on the dead man's finger. The high priest warned him to remain standing where he was. He would be needed later to lead the soldiers to his Lord.

The Pasch proceeded in the upper room. Eleven apostles reclined with Jesus. They dipped and ate. They washed their hands. They drank wine.

When Jesus was silent they conversed animatedly. When he spoke they fell silent. Now and then, as in the case of all men dining, there was a loud assertion, or a shouted question, or laughter.

They became alert when Jesus, his features no longer sagging in sorrow, said to them: "At last the Son of Man is glorified, and in him God is glorified! Since God is glorified in him, God, in turn, will glorify him in himself; and without delay will he glorify him."

He smiled, which was rare for him, and the face broke up into little planes of love. "Dear children," he said softly, "only a little while longer am I with you. You will miss me and, as I told the Jews, so I tell you at present: where I am going you cannot come."

They beamed in the warmth of his smile, although they were certain that this was another allegory of great depth and beyond their understanding. "A new commandment I give you," he said. "Love one another; as I love you, so I want you, too, to love one another. By this token all the world must know that you are my disciples—by cherishing love for one another."

This was hardly a new commandment, except that it was explicit. He had often preached love to the people and the apostles could doubtless remember every date and the place. Love God as God loves you; love your neighbor as he must love you. The only thing new about it was that it now had a note of finality—and a new tone, which said, "As I have loved you."

The others looked to Simon Peter. He bent across the back of his Messiah and, trying to speak quietly, said: "Lord, where are you going?"

Jesus turned his head across his own right shoulder to glance briefly at the face of his chief disciple. "Where I am going," he said slowly, but loudly enough for all to hear, "you cannot at present follow me. But you will follow me later."

For a moment, Simon Peter digested this reply. Not understanding that he could not go now, but would go later, he pressed one more question. "And why, Lord, cannot I follow you right now? I will lay down my life for you."

Jesus did not turn his head as he answered: "You will lay down your life for me?" He shook his head from side to side. "Before cockcrow you will disown me three times."

9 P.M.

Jerusalem was quiet. The metropolis of the monotheistic God seemed to be deserted. The streets were clear of people and animals and reposed in dark velvet, only the roofs and alabaster pinnacles catching the glow of the moon. On the ramparts of Fortress Antonia a Roman guard folded his arms against the chill of an east wind and watched his off-duty comrades roll dice on the huge flagstones below. He was chuckling at the braying arguments after each roll when his attention was diverted by the sentry at the twin west gates, who stepped into the roadway and bared his broadsword.

He watched the sentry, who spoke sharply to someone in the gloom outside the twin gates. In a moment the sentry was waving someone inside the huge courtyard, but whoever it was would come no farther than under the twin gates. In the pale courtyard lights, the soldier on the ramparts could see that it was the high priest, and beside him was the burly chief of the temple guards.

The sentry spat. The Jews would not be here unless they wanted something of Pilate. Always, it seemed to the sentry, they wanted something done or they wanted something stopped. He watched and saw the soldier below sheathe his sword, cup his hands, and roar across the courtyard that Caiphas, the high priest, desired immediate audience with Pontius Pilate, Procurator of Judea and Samaria, at the pleasure of his imperial Majesty, Tiberius Caesar.

The man on the ramparts wondered why the Jews did not come into the fortress. Then he remembered that these strange people felt unclean—sinners—if they entered the establishment of a Gentile. Sometimes, now that he thought of it, the sentry remembered that a few would come into the fortress courtyard and stand waiting; others more strict, like this one, waited outside or under the stones of the twin gate. None that he could recall ever went inside the fortress, even when invited by the Procurator to his private apartments upstairs. The exceptions, of course, were prisoners. They were dragged into the dungeon below, near the stone cachements, and they invariably wailed that they were being defiled. This was amusing to the Syrians who served in the Roman army here, because the culprits were thieves or murderers or tax dodgers before they entered the fortress.

The Syrians did not like Jews for several reasons. One was that Syrians were conscripted into the Roman army; Jews were not, because the Jewish faith forbade fighting on the Sabbath. The Syrians were expected to add the name of Caesar to the gods they worshiped; the Jews escaped this— the only province exempt from the imperial decree to adore Caesar. The Jews despised the soldiers and lent money to them at usurious rates. In the markets, the Jews mocked the Syrian soldiers in a language the legionaries did not understand.

The Jews did not like the Syrians for several reasons. Jews who lived in Syria sent word home that the natives treated them cruelly, cheated in marketing goods, mocked them, stoned their shops, violated their women. In all the known places of the world, only the Syrians regarded it as a sport to go hunting for Jews. The Syrians were crude and uncultured, compared to the Romans and the Greeks and the Egyptians. In Palestine, the Jews regarded it as humiliating enough to be under the heel of Rome, but to suffer at the hands of Syrian mercenaries was almost too much to bear.

The sentry on the rampart was happy to note that Pilate kept Caiphas waiting.

Fortress Antonia was, in essence, a renegade's revenge. It had been built by the father of King Herod Antipas, the current ruler, Herod the Great. He was a half-Jew fond of building elaborate structures and beautiful cities. When the Romans made him king of the Jews, he named the fortress, which kept Jerusalem in subjugation, after his friend Mark Antony.

Antonia was cleverly built. The temple occupied almost half the east wall of the city. The Valley of the Cedron lay immediately outside this wall, giving it an imposing eminence. The south wall was protected by a small valley and the west wall presented similar problems to an invader. So Antonia, like a big stone wedge, was laid partly inside and partly outside the northeast wall, where the ground was fairly level.

It had adits to permit reinforcements from the north to get inside the fortress from outside the wall, in the event that the Jews had sealed all other gates. It also had, on its south side, subterranean exits onto the temple grounds, so that, at a time of insurrection, the Romans could move into the Court of the Gentiles in force and, if necessary, invest the entire temple.

Many of the stones in the wall around the Holy City of Jerusalem were thirty-four feet long and seventeen feet broad, and they had been brought from distant places. The walls, not taking into account the valleys which sheered off below them, averaged about thirty-five feet in height, above which were battlements and turrets of about nine feet.

So the great wall was formidable, but Herod's Antonia, a gift to Rome, canceled the value of the wall. Antonia was 536 feet long, 300 feet wide and 84 feet high. The original building was somewhat smaller and had, in the old days, been called the Tower of Hananeel and was known to the prophet Jeremias. Flavius Josephus, who would be writing about it a generation later, said: "The niceness of the joints and the beauty of the stones were in no way inferior to the holy house itself."

Antonia contained porches, baths, huge courts made of tremendous stones, private apartments, two cisterns, each big enough to hold a platoon of soldiers without crowding, quarters for a full garrison of legionaries (the Twelfth Legion was often quartered inside its walls); a public highway ran through it, leading from Golgotha to the Probatic Gate. The roadway inside the fortress was made of flagstones eight to ten inches thick and serrated with etched stripes so that beasts of burden would not slip on its surface in wet weather.

The entire fortress was well lighted at night with several hundred bronze and iron lamps hung high on the walls and fed with olive oil. On the temple side there was a tower 120 feet high. Inside the fort were shops, and all flooring stones in the courts and on top of the fortress were pitched slightly so that the rain ran into grooved gutters and then fell forty feet below the streets to the cisterns.

To the Jews, the Antonia inside their walls was an exposed nerve in a large molar.

In the upper room, the Passover supper proceeded, punctuated by the ceremonial cups of wine and the breaking of the unleavened cakes. It is not known how closely Jesus followed the rubric. It is plausible to think that after the opening remarks and the dire prophecy that he would eat no more of the Pasch, he followed the ritual closely and dipped the bitter herbs into vinegar, spoke the blessing, and handed herbs to each of the eleven. He broke the matzoth, and put it aside—called the Aphiqomon—which was to be eaten after supper.

As he blessed the first matzoth, he elevated the dish which held them and said: "This is the bread of misery which our fathers ate in the land of Egypt. All you who are hungry, come and eat. All that are needy, come, keep the pascha."

The ceremonial cups of wine were drunk at proper intervals and the apostles borrowed cheer from the wine and forgot—or seemed to forget—that Jesus had announced the imminence of his death, and they no longer pondered the accusation of a traitor in the group. Nine of the eleven did not know that the accused was Judas, and the two who did reposed such complete faith in Jesus that they held their silence.

The guards along the walls of Jerusalem called out the fourth hour of the night watch. In thousands of homes, the first Seder was nearing an end.

10 P.M.

Jesus looked around the table at the eleven who were left to him. They ate with the gusto of the hungry and, as he listened to bits of their conversation and examined the innermost recesses of their hearts, he found what he already knew—that these men were good. And the Messiah was troubled because these were his final hours and there was much—so very much—that he still had to impart to them.

He ate little bits and pieces of food so that their attention would not focus on his lack of enthusiasm for the Passover. Jesus obviously knew that Caiphas would not arrest him in this room. Had he thought that he would be apprehended here, he would not have kept some of his most important words for the walk to the olive press later.

Jesus knew that Caiphas wanted no disturbance in the city. He had multitudes of followers among the Jews in and out of the city and up and down the land: his public arrest would create a stir which might lead to rioting—and rioting always led to bloody ''police'' action by the Romans.

If possible, this arrest must be achieved on tiptoe. Caiphas knew this. Jesus knew this. And now, after the visit of the high priest to Antonia, Pilate knew it too. He would furnish help to the high priest. But not for the sake of peace; it was his intention to add to the troubles of the Jews by precipitating an event which was bound to split these people into two violent groups.

After the arrest was effected, Pilate knew that he could then take this little case out of the realm of secrecy and throw it, like a clod of mud, into the public eye by merely pretending that he was so interested in seeing justice done that it would be necessary to bring the prisoner through the streets to him for a hearing.

Each man had more reasons than were at first apparent for the things he did on this day.

The Son of Man knew these things and many more, as though the drama had been written in the dawn of time—as indeed it had. The words uttered that day were to burn their way into the fabric of the centuries ahead.

He waited until after the third cup of wine and he saw that a few of them were now looking at him, waiting for him to conclude the rites. He pushed himself up off his elbow so that, in half sitting, he could look upon the faces of all including Peter.

"It has been my heart's desire," he said in a deep, clear voice, "to eat this paschal supper with you before I suffer." Their faces sorrowed; something of the agony which lay ahead penetrated their imaginations. "I tell you," he said, slowly raising his right hand, "I shall not eat it again till it is fulfilled in the kingdom of God."

They whispered among themselves. They were mystified as before, but now they wondered about the nature of the events which must precede fulfillment, as they did about the nature of fufillment. What did fulfilled mean? Must the Passover be fulfilled? Where would be this new Passover? From where to where? Maybe he meant the imminence of the parousia—the end of the world. They were still whispering when they saw him take up a loaf of flat, round unleavened bread. The apostles subsided and watched.

Jesus stood. He placed the palm of his hand a few inches over the bread and his dark eyes turned upward. The whispered words of a blessing came from his barely parted lips. In the silence, he gave thanks and broke the bread into fragments and passed among them, giving to each of the eleven a morsel.

"This," he said, "is my body, which is about to be given for your sake. Take you and eat." They began to eat the bread, not understanding except to know that this was an abrupt departure from the Passover ritual. He smiled down on them. "Do this as my memorial," he said. They now understood. He wanted them to do this, again and again and again, after he had gone.

Jesus returned to his couch and picked up a big metal chalice on the table. It was filled with wine mixed with water. The apostles were still chewing and swallowing and looking when he again lifted his eyes upward and murmured a second blessing. Then he gave thanks and passed around behind each of them, handing them the cup in turn and saying: "Drink you all of this. For this is my blood of the new testament, which shall be shed for many for the remission of sins."

They drank. He watched, pleased. "I tell you," he said, "I shall not again drink of the produce of the vine till the kingdom of God is set up."

Although these plain men had yet to acquire the superior knowledge which the Holy Ghost would give to them, they understood at once the meaning of the bread and the wine because he had called the one his body, the other his blood, and he had said that they should do this "as a memorial" to him. The apostles knew that, at this moment, Jesus the Christ had departed from the ritual of ancient Judea and was establishing a new faith, a new pact with God, a means of salvation for all men; the God-man was offering himself, in love, as the newly sacrificed lamb.

A few may have wondered why Jesus had done this enormous thing, this giving of his body and his blood into their own, in the absence of the money-keeper. Conversely, two of them now understood why it had been necessary to wait until Judas had left before introducing the new sacrament. It was the fresh hope of the world undefiled by the presence of a sinner.

The sands were running close to 11 P.M. and Caiphas waited in his courtyard. He was impatient. This thing which had to be done should be done at once and quietly. The Roman guards had not arrived and Caiphas fumed at Pontius Pilate for the delay. The high priest was surrounded by his servants, who waited for his words.

He called Judas to him and watched his deep obeisance with scorn. Caiphas was an intelligent man and he knew that if Judas would live with one who proclaimed himself the Christ and then betray him for a pittance, then Judas, if given the opportunity, would betray the high priest for an even smaller sum.

Caiphas tried to think of all the possibilities. He ordered the apostle to lead the arresting party to the house of the feast, and to make sure that he pointed out the right man to the Roman soldiers. He envisioned a general melee when the raid was in progress, and he did not want Jesus to escape. If he slipped through the net tonight, he might flee to Galilee or the wilderness and not be seen in Jerusalem again until the high holy days of the autumn.

Furthermore, the high priest did not want to arrest the apostles on this night. They were sheep. They would disperse at the first sign of attack on the shepherd. He called the chief of his servants and made it plain that he desired to have the apostles *threatened* with arrest. That would be sufficient. The law must be complied with and he wanted the trial of only one person. It would be better if the apostles were able to tell the followers of Jesus that he had been arrested and tried and convicted of blasphemy. Then this new cult or sect would expire, and the people would return to the field of proper worship, the temple.

Exploring the possibilities, Caiphas had demanded of Judas what would happen if the prey escaped from the cenacle. Judas said that the feast would probably continue for another hour or so, and that it should be simple to surround the house and to send a raiding party up the outside stairs—there was no other exit—and then he would lead the group into the room and would identify Jesus by walking up to him and kissing him. By this they would know the man.

If, by any chance, Jesus and his followers had left the upstairs room, then Judas would suggest that they go to the gethsemane at the foot of the Mount of Olives, because when Jesus was in Jerusalem he often slept there with his men. Should they not be there, the soldiers should go to Bethany to the home of Martha and Mary, because that was the only other place Jesus would repose. And as Bethany was only three miles from where the high priest stood, the arrest could be made long before dawn and the awakening of the city.

Caiphas was pleased. So long as the quarry was surely in one of three neighboring places, there was little cause for anxiety. It would, of course, simplify everything if Jesus could be caught in the cenacle, resist arrest, and receive a Roman spear wound as a consequence. This would take the onus off the high priest, the Sanhedrin—in effect, the temple. The thousands of followers of Jesus in and around the city would then have to expend their venom on the Romans, an ideal situation for Caiphas. Still, resistance was hardly to be expected, unless the Pharisees had read their man incorrectly. The newest of the Messiahs preached love and passivity, nonviolence and forgiveness, and these characteristics did not lend themselves to a midnight brawl with soldiers.

Caiphas had been lax in the matter of Jesus. He knew this. The high priest had been aware of this man for more than a year. It would have been easy to apprehend him earlier. He could have been tried before the Sanhedrin as a blasphemer, and if he had been found to be witless he might have been banished. If he had turned out to be dangerous, he could have been stoned to death before he had had an opportunity to build up this large following. Now, almost too late, he had to take a chance on arrest and trial and death before Jesus, with his ever-growing host of believers, split the authority of the temple.

These were his thoughts as he stood in the night. Caiphas was pleased that Jerusalem was so very quiet. He had noted, en route to Antonia, that few people were abroad. These few carried shaded lamps; most of the populace was indoors concluding the sacred dinner and preparing to go to bed. Now, if only the Romans and their burnished shields would arrive— the arrest, the trial, the condemnation and the stoning could be concluded by dawn. To the priestly mind of that time, there should have been five possibilities concerning this man of mercy: (1) he was the Messiah; (2) he was a faker; (3) he was deluded and thought himself the Messiah; (4) he was a good spirit; (5) he was an evil spirit.

There is nothing to show that Caiphas or, for that matter, the Great Sanhedrin, had ever considered other possibilities than that Jesus was a fraud. Perhaps the trouble lay in the fact that there was such a weight of politics—practical politics—in administering the business of the great temple that the spiritual side of an august priest became callous, and over the years he lost the very thing he aspired to save—his soul. He tended to weigh all matters, spiritual and temporal, in the same soiled scales. In time, such a man will scoff at any manifestation of the supernatural. The decay he saw in all others was in his own heart.

The Jews believed, as part of their faith, in the efficacy of spirits. The world of now and the world of the hereafter, they believed, were filled with innumerable spirits. There were good spirits and evil spirits. The good ones were always sent by God and they guided man into paths of righteousness and the better life; all evil spirits were subject to God's authority but fought His will and hated man. All spirits were composed of an ethereal fluid substance which was either luminous or faintly opaque.

The Hebrew world classified all spirits as "angels." There were angels of the presence—those who stood eternally before God; there were angels of the ministry—these were sent to earth, sometimes in human guise, to perform special duties for God. Others guided the stars and the earth in their orbits. Some were detailed to the duties of the dead. A few were assigned to the nations or the races of people of the earth; many were ordered to help individuals. Some had no other duty than to torment demons.

Among those spirits always in the presence of God, seven were specially elect, and three of these were Michael, Raphael and Gabriel. Michael's work was the vindication of God; Raphael was the angel of bodily cures; Gabriel was in charge of special revelations. The leader of the evil spirits was called the Satan, that is "the accuser," "the adversary." Later, toward the time of Jesus, he acquired other names: Belial, Beelzebub, Asmodeus, Mastema.

The evil spirits always occupied the air closest to the earth and preferred to live in deserted and unclean places: abandoned houses, tombs, ruins and sometimes, if they felt that they might be welcome, in the homes of men. They worked only at night and they engendered all physical and moral ills, all accidents, madness, scandal, discord and war. Their work was to tempt the just, guide the impious to further degrading acts, promote idolatry, teach magic and corrupt the law.

Caiphas knew all these things, just as he knew the slender clues to the identity of the Messiah. The thought that Jesus might be a true Messiah would be, to Caiphas, a frightening thing; it would imply his power over all men and all nations, and might include the summary destruction of Caiphas and his temple. Such a thought would be enough to freeze a man in a state of hesitation forever. The bare possibility would cause an average man—not to consider a learned priest—to disassociate himself from any plot against the life of such a man. It would, in fact, lead him to hope faintly that the great promise of the prophets might at last be at hand. He would have to investigate most diligently, and if his probing proved that the newcomer met all the religious requirements, and in addition healed the diseased, raised the dead, gave sight to eyes that never before had it, could read the hearts of men and do other things, in public and in the presence of strangers, things reserved to the supernatural powers of God himself— he would have to drop to his knees before such a one and beg forgiveness.

Caiphas was blind to the possibility and so was his father-in-law, because they had consulted about this matter and, beyond doubt, had also consulted with certain influential members of the Great Sanhedrin. Jesus, in their eyes, was a faker who was becoming more dangerous to their way of life day by day. As the common Jews of the villages turned more and more toward Jesus, giving up their homes and their worldly goods to follow him, the select few in the temple turned more and more against the Messiah.

In the cenacle, the apostles were in attitudes of rapt attention. The master was speaking and he spoke with a pressing fervor, like a teacher who knows that he has time to say each thing but once. Peter, full of good food and always as boastful as a child in his love for Jesus, was the subject of admonitory remarks:

"Simon, Simon," said Jesus, "mark my words: Satan has demanded the surrender of you all in order to sift you like wheat; but I have prayed for you personally, that your faith might not fail." Then, softly, as though he did not want to refer to his death again, he said: "Later on, therefore, when you have recovered, it is for you to strengthen your brethren."

Peter, always big in body and in spirit, interrupted. "At your side, Lord," he boomed, "I am ready to go to prison and to death." The apostles nodded in agreement.

Jesus shook his head. "I tell you, Peter," he said again, "the cock will not crow today before you three times deny having anything to do with me."

Peter raised his hands to expostulate. Then he looked at his Lord and subsided. He saw the strong, sensitive hand held up to stay his words. Two servants came up to collect dishes and bowls and to bring more wine, if it was needed. When they had left, the tall Galilean seemed to lapse into a moody silence. He fingered the chalice, now empty, and then he looked up, his eyes moving from one face to the other, slowly, reluctant to move on.

"Now," he said, "the Son of Man is glorified and God is glorified in him." He was referring to the new and holy sacrifice which he had instituted. "If God is glorified in him," he said, "God will glorify him in turn, and immediately will he glorify him."

Again the apostles wondered. They could not understand fully because Jesus was now talking about the immediate future; his Father would glorify him in death by redeeming the souls of all mankind, and would glorify His son by an almost immediate resurrection.

One of the apostles lifted a small carrying bag to the couch beside him. He may have wanted to put in it a piece of bread for later. The Messiah watched him and then, turning to all, he said:

"When I sent you on a mission tour without purse or bag or sandals, did you lack anything?" They shook their heads no and some said: "No." He nodded. "It is different now. He that has a purse must take it with him; so, too, he that has a bag; and he that has not either of these must sell his cloak to buy a sword." This was something all of them understood at once. Soon, they would be without their Lord and, when that happened, life was not going to be easy for them. No longer would they be protected against hunger, cold, poverty and the attacks of the enemies of God. They would have to preach the words of Jesus and they would have to do it in hardship.

"Yes," he added, "I tell you, this Scripture text must be fulfilled in me: 'And he was classed with the lawless.'" He shrugged ever so slightly. "Indeed, my career is at an end."

"Look, Lord," they said, pointing happily to the weapons leaning against one of the pillars in the room. "Here are two swords."

He waved the thought away. "It is enough," he said.

11 P.M.

The final cup of wine had been drunk and the feast was over.

They stood and sang the hallel (Praise Ye) and, as the solemn notes died in the big room, so, too, the followers of Jesus had bridged the distance between what would become the *old* and the *new* testaments. Until this night, there had been *a* testament. From now on, there could be an old testament and a new testament and the second would be a continuance of the revelations of God the Father through Jesus, His Son.

Jesus rose from his couch and they all stood. He did not seem disposed to leave at once, so the men fell into conversation and conjecture. They discussed the new holy sacrifice and they seemed, in the gravity of the moment and despite the enormity of its implications in the light of what they had been taught, to understand the import of the act. They saw it as a new high point in their careers, and they understood that they were now priests in a new religious faith.

A few reminded the others that a year ago Jesus had told them in the synagogue at Capharnaum that he would give them his flesh to eat and his blood to drink or else they would not have life. At the time, most of them had been sickened at the thought. Now they understood. Now they knew that, as Jesus blessed the bread and made it his body, and blessed the watered wine and made it his blood, they, partaking of it, were being blessed by having his spirit within them. They also understood that when he said, "Do this as a memorial," they could do it all their lives and they could also communicate the power to do this to others.

Four of the apostles—Peter, Thomas, Philip and Jude—fell from this to a discussion of the imminent departure of Jesus, and it saddened them to such a degree that conversation died. The Messiah was so touched that, for the first time, he addressed them with a diminutive form of affection, repeating in essence what he had said earlier, but this time addressing them as "little children."

"My little children, yet a little while I am with you. You shall seek me, and what I said to the Jews[13] I say again to you: 'Where I go, you cannot come.'"

Now he was more the affectionate father than the teacher, and he again repeated himself almost exactly: "A new commandment I give to you: that you love one another as I have loved you. By this sign shall all know that you are my disciples—that you love one another."

All of the apostles were sorrowful. Their spirits were not now lifted by the tender words of love. They stood with lowered heads, looking at the floor or looking up briefly at him. None had anything to say, but the sadness was as tangible as the cool night air.

Jesus felt the gloom and he wanted to lift them from it. Still, as man, he must have felt the chill of sadness also; he was young and vigorous at thirty-four years; he had had only two years and a few months of public ministry, and, as man, he had an enormous capacity for love which reached all the way from his mother down to the children of strangers. It hurt, and hurt deeply, to know that he was ordained to die as a criminal, to part from all of these who could make his heart glad. The human side of Jesus turned away from the thought of his own death, as one turns away from anything that carries terror.

"Do not let your heart be troubled," he said gently, almost smiling. "You have faith in God: have faith in me also. In my Father's house are many rooms. I should have told you if it were not so. The fact is, I am now about to go for the very purpose of preparing a place for you." Some lifted their heads, and there was hope in their eyes. "And when I am gone and have prepared a place for you, I will come back and take you home with me. I want you to be where I shall be." Now all the heads were up and all were smiling. They had believed, with some human wavering, that this man was the Messiah; they had believed it for two or more years and had given up their normal lives and their goods, and, in some cases, their families. When he said that he would die, they were in despair. But when he said that he would die and come back for them and bring them "home," their joy was solemn and deep.

"The way to where I am going you know, of course," he said to them. Their triumphant faces suddenly clouded. They knew the way? What way?

They looked at Thomas because often, when they were in a delicate situation with the Lord, he alone knew how to ask the necessary question. Thomas coughed, hesitated and said: "Lord, we do not know where you are going; how do we know the way?"

They sometimes risked his displeasure in asking questions—more often than not Peter was the offender—but this time Jesus was not disappointed in the inquiry. He raised his hand to his own chest.

"I," he said, "am the way, and the truth, and the life." They knew the way to eternal life, because the way was through him. "No one comes to the Father," he said, holding out both hands for understanding, "except through me. Since you know me, you will also know my Father." The puzzled expression started to show on their faces again and, almost like a father who is in mock despair because his children cannot seem to comprehend the simplest matters, he said: "In fact, you know him now, and are looking him in his face."

It could hardly have been plainer. He was saying that God the Father and God the Son were one. This, as might be expected, was too much for the minds of the apostles to embrace all at once. Some nodded as though they understood, but they didn't.

"Lord," said Philip, stroking his thick beard, "let us see the Father, and we shall be satisfied." Uppermost in the habits of the time was the justice of a bargain; show us and we shall believe. Ask him to appear here, now, however briefly, and all questions will end; "we shall be satisfied."

"Philip," Jesus said sternly, "so long a time have I been in your midst, and you do not know me?" The Messiah punctuated his words with a finger of one hand tapping the palm of the other. "He . . . who . . . sees . . . me . . . sees . . . the . . . Father." He shook his head, almost in exasperation. "How, then, can you say: 'Let us see the Father?' Do you not believe that I am in the Father and the Father is in me?" He had made it as plain as he could and he was wearied by their lack of comprehension. "Take the words I speak to you: they are not my own invention, are they?" They shook their heads slowly, solemnly. "And as for the things I do, the Father who dwells in me is personally responsible for them. Believe me, all of you, when I say that I am in the Father and the Father is in me; but if not, at least believe on the strength of what I am doing."

He maintained patience with these men because he understood how difficult it was for the human mind to imagine two divine persons in one divine being. He knew that he could make them all believe him—even Caiphas and Annas would fall prostrate before him if he would consent to show his divinity by some tangible thing—but the major point of his teaching was that man must believe without seeing, and sometimes, without understanding. God the Father had already tried to make them see. He had come down to a mountaintop and talked to Moses and had given him the tablets of the law. Perhaps it was as a result of this that man felt himself in a position to bargain with the Creator of all things. He would promise to keep the law if God would first tell him what kind of a reward he would get. He wanted to know specifically where and when and how much and for how long would be God's side of the bargain. What was more, he would like to see some proof.

Jesus, who was love incarnate, never lost patience with his Father's creatures. "I tell you the truth," he said, looking at the eleven, and through them to all mankind of all the ages yet to come, "he who believes in me will himself do the things I am doing; in fact, he will do even greater things than I do, now that I am going home to the Father; and should you ask for anything in my name, I will do it, that the Father may be glorified in the Son. If you ask me for anything in my name, I will do it." His eyes pleaded for faith: if they could not understand, then they must have faith. There was so much, so very much, to say to these simple, good-hearted men. His eyes lowered. "If you love me," he whispered, "you will treasure my commandments."

Jesus was ready to leave. He looked around and made a sign to Peter. It was almost midnight when they left. Jesus led the way down the outer stairs, pausing at the foot to whisper his thanks to the father of the young disciple Mark. Then they walked out into the night, a little band of men murmuring to one another in brilliant moonlight. They turned south, toward the Valley of Hinnom, but they were still inside the wall and no one could be seen on the streets.

A breeze came from the west, and in the darkness they could see white clouds move across the sky toward the moon. They saw the thousands of stars, the gaudy jewelry of the heavens. The moonlight was so bright that night that the huge limestone slabs in the Roman steps showed white, and little trees cast a shadow across them.

Jesus discoursed as they walked slowly. It is not easy for one man to be properly heard by eleven while walking, so when he had something to say he stopped and the eleven clustered around him in the silver light. He would say the things he had to say, and then move on and, in a little while, he would stop again. These discourses continued through the southern part of Jerusalem and then down the long Roman steps to the Fountain Gate.

"And I will ask my Father," he said, "that He will grant you another advocate to be with you for all time to come, the Spirit of Truth. The world is incapable of receiving him, because it neither sees him nor knows him. You will know him because he will make his permanent stay with you and in you." In the half-light he sensed their fears. "I will not leave you orphans; I am coming back to you," he said.

The word "advocate" used by Jesus, in Greek, is *parakletos,* which means a consoler, or counselor. When he said "another advocate," he implied that he, Jesus, had been a paraclete to the apostles; now he would send a spiritual one who would remain with the disciples and with the followers of Jesus for all time. This, then, is the introduction of the Holy Ghost.

"Yet a little while, and the world sees me no longer; but you will see me, because I live, and you, too, shall live. On that day you will come to understand that I am in the Father and you are in me, and I in you. He who accepts my commandments and treasures them, he is the one that loves me. And he that loves me will, in turn, be loved by my Father; and I will love him, and will manifest myself to him."

They started walking again, down the steps broad enough for almost the whole party to walk abreast, and Jude, ordinarily quiet and self-effacing, stopped the group with a question.

"And what is the reason, Lord, why you intend to manifest yourself to us and not to the world?" It was good that Jude, generally so silent, had decided to ask a question, because the answer which came at once explained a great deal.

"*Anyone* who loves me will treasure my message, and my Father will love him, and we shall visit him and make our home with him. He who does not treasure my message does not love me; and, mind you, the message you have heard is not mine but the Father's, whose ambassador I am."

Anyone . . . he stressed the "anyone" as he spoke.

"I have told you all this while I am still lingering in your midst; but the Advocate, the Holy Spirit whom the Father will send in my name, will teach you everything and refresh your memory of everything I have told you. Peace is my legacy to you: my own peace is my gift to you. My giving to you is not like the world's way of giving."

Jerusalem was at its quietest. In a few minutes, at midnight, the watches would change, and the lonesome cry of the soldiers on the ramparts of Antonia would be heard. Soon the great gates of the temple would open and many of the early risers would be there to offer chagigah, and the poor in the outer courts would beg for alms and meat on this holy feast of the Passover.

Now the city was still under the high moon, and only in the northeast could sounds be heard. There, leaving the double archway of Antonia, was a detachment of Roman soldiers, their heavy sandals making a rhythmic scouring sound on the Lithostrotos. Ordinarily, a centurion would command a group such as this, but Caiphas, in his plea for assistance from the Romans, overstated his case and the man who led this detachment was the Tribune himself—the ranking military man in the city.

The Tribune understood the legalities of the situation. He was not to meddle in the arrest because blasphemy against Yahweh was not a crime against Rome, and there was no statute under the rule of the Empire on which Jesus could be tried. This was a Jewish problem; they were dealing with a provincial troublemaker who, somehow or other, had hurt the prestige and practices of the great temple. All the Tribune had to do was to assist the temple guards in executing the orders of the high priest. If there was any resistance, the Romans would be fully authorized to beat many Jews to death.

Lanterns were carried before and behind the column of soldiers, and the Tribune walked along the flanks of his men, making certain that they had the proper bearing. He marched them west along the roads and turned left at the small crossroads gate outside of which was the small hill which the Jews called Golgotha, which is to say, a skull.

They moved south along the hill to the right of the Tyropoeon Valley and on down between the Palace of the Herods and the Palace of the Hasmoneans. The men kept a smart pace, the swinging lanterns causing their bare legs to dance in black on the pavement. Their orders were to report to the high priest. He would lead them to the culprit.

Caiphas had waited so long that, in impatience, he had sent a messenger to Antonia. On the way the man had seen the soldiers and had hurried back to inform the high priest. At the news, Caiphas forgot his irritation with the laggard behavior of the Romans and once more questioned Judas for probable flaws in his story. The high priest knew that if Jesus was not found on this night, the Romans would laugh at him derisively and news of the failure would spread abroad from Antonia in the morning. He had to find Jesus; he had to take him into custody during this night.

Judas, summoned from across the courtyard into Caiphas' presence, said that he doubted that Jesus and his band would go as far as Bethany tonight because the Galilean was most strict in maintaining the erub—he would not travel on the Sabbath farther than the law allowed, which would be a little more than half a mile.

Now that he had had time to consider, Judas said, there were two places Jesus would go if he was not at the cenacle. The first would be to an olive press at the foot of the Mount of Olives, the very place the apostle had told the high priest about earlier. The other was a huge cave one-third of the way to the top of the Mount of Olives. Sometimes, though not often, Jesus and the apostles slept there. One thing was certain: they would go no farther.

The temple guards had been present in the courtyard for some time and had been given their orders. They had only to wait for the Romans, who would lend authority to the proceedings.

They were standing in the huge courtyard which fronted on the lavish homes of both Caiphas and Annas. The daughter of Annas, when she married Caiphas, had suggested that her marriage home be built next to that of her father, and that the two be made as one with a common entrance.

Old Annas never came out on his porch that night to inquire about the multitude of men who stood murmuring and swinging their clubs. It was not necessary. In his wisdom he had probably suggested soliciting the help of Pilate. As the one-time Nasi of the Great Sanhedrin, there was little going on in the city that he did not know about, and even less that a dutiful son-in-law would not bring to his attention.

Annas knew that the cenacle was only about two streets from his home, and that Jesus could have been taken at any time that evening by a few servants of the high priest. The extra precautions, the use of Pilate and his soldiers, were because he wanted no scandal to remain after this night in the gossip of the Pharisees. He had told Caiphas to follow the legalities of the matter down to the last little letter. Let no one say later that they had killed this charlatan out of hand.

Once Jesus was arrested, the next move would be to send the servants out at once to convoke the Sanhedrin for an immediate session in the home of Caiphas. The Sadducees believed it was legal to call the session, but a man could not be tried for a crime in the dark. Perhaps the members of the court could use the time before dawn in questioning this man on the law and the breach thereof. If so—if he posed as the Messiah—he might be brash enough to expose himself.

If not, witnesses would be needed. Caiphas knew this, and he expected that Judas, despite his earlier refusal, might be pressed into compliance. In the event that witnesses could not be found, Caiphas had arranged for the testimony of a few temple guards who had heard Jesus speak.

It would be of interest to know more about the meeting between the high priest and the Procurator. There is no record of it; no record that there was such an interview on this night. But it is known that Roman soldiers were sent to Caiphas to support the raiding party. Pilate had charge of all Romans in Palestine, and he disliked the Jews. And it is reasonable to assume that he would not send soldiers to assist Caiphas in a religious problem unless he could sense an advantage in it.

The Procurator understood Jewish law as well as he understood the laws of the Empire. He must have known that the penalty for blasphemy was death, and he knew that the sentence could not be carried out unless and until he confirmed it. He also knew that Jesus had become a chronic and ever-growing problem to the chief priests and this must have pleased the Governor.

He had no interest in Jesus; no more, let us say, than he would have had in a scorpion lodged in the high priest's couch. He was on the side of the scorpion until it had executed its function; after that, Pontius Pilate would grind it under his sandal. If, for example, the Jews arrested and condemned Jesus, the Governor would be happy, in his judicial capacity, to set the man free if it would confound Annas and his son-in-law.

One thing is certain: he would not have sent his soldiers to assist in the arrest if Caiphas had been foolish enough to send a deputy to ask for them. The tactful thing, the priest knew, was a personal audience. This was distasteful to Caiphas, not only because he understood the Procurator and was conscious of his hatred, but also because it might have meant personally defiling himself by setting foot inside the Gentile fort at the feast of the Pasch. He had to weigh these things against the advantages to be gained if he could enlist Roman aid.

He could gain two advantages: the first was to make the aliens his partners in the arrest and, thus, in the eyes of the followers of Jesus, make it appear to be a Roman matter rather than a plot by the high priests; the second was that, by enlisting Roman aid now, he tended to predispose Pontius Pilate to concur in the death sentence which was sure to follow. Rome could hardly be a party to the arrest and then concede that an innocent man had been apprehended.

The wiliness of the two schemers tended to cancel out evenly. Each understood the strategic treachery of the other. Each understood that Jesus was a pawn in a bigger game. The fight was for power: Caiphas and Annas for the retention of power in Jerusalem; Pilate to bring the Jews to heel.

But Pilate, as a condition of the night audience with Caiphas, insisted that the high priest come to his apartment in Antonia. This explains how the wife of the Procurator, Claudia Procula, became interested in the case later. She may have been a spectator of the conference, but if she wasn't, then Pilate told the story to her before they retired.

Pilate's gesture of sending a large group of soldiers may have been an act of deliberate sarcasm. It was like sending a major general and two brigades to apprehend a cripple.

BACKGROUND

Jesus

Jesus was born about the time of the winter solstice in 6 B.C.[14]

The Messiah was born in a cave in Bethlehem—the only child of Mary. There are two aspects of this birth: the natural and the supernatural. Each is so thoroughly integrated with the other that, like a two-color garment, it is impossible to pull the thread of one for examination without destroying the raiment.

Mary was of the house of David. So was her husband, a bearded young carpenter named Joseph. It is probable that Mary was between twelve and thirteen years of age when she was betrothed. This was the custom of the times. When she was married, she may have been fourteen. It is hardly likely that she was older.

In the absence of any evidence, Biblical or historical, to the contrary, it may be assumed that this marriage followed the Hebrew norm. The parents of Joseph sought the parents of Mary and the preliminary conversations were held. The bridegroom-elect may have been between eighteen and twenty-four years of age; certainly he had finished his apprenticeship as a carpenter, otherwise he could not have supported a wife.

In spite of royal lineage in both families, it is doubtful if a dowry was discussed because these were poor branches in the Davidic line. The probability is that Joseph had seen Mary in company with her parents and felt attracted to her. Then, when Joseph's elders began to talk of marriage to him, no doubt he expressed a preference for Mary. The conversations would result from that.

As soon as both families were in agreement, the qiddushin, the betrothal ceremony, would take place. It was as binding as a wedding and had the same finality. Once the betrothal contract was made, the only way in which the bridegroom could be rid of the bride was through divorce. The qiddushin, in Judea, entitled the couple to sexual relations even though each must live with his parents until the wedding ceremony. In Galilee, where Joseph and Mary lived, and in other parts of Palestine, a state of sexual purity was maintained until after the wedding, which occurred a year after qiddushin. If the bridegroom died in the interim, the betrothed woman was considered to be his legal widow. On the other hand, if the betrothed girl was unfaithful in the same period, she was punished as an adulteress.

The time from engagement to marriage was spent building a small home, or renting one, and furnishing it. The nissu'in, or wedding, consisted of the solemn reception of the bride into the home her betrothed had prepared for her.

Sometime between the betrothal and the marriage, Mary was visited by the angel Gabriel at the home of her parents in Nazareth. He said to her: "Rejoice, child of grace! The Lord is your helper! You are blessed beyond all women!" The young virgin was neither overwhelmed nor pleased by this. She shook with an unknown terror. The angel said: "Do not tremble, Mary! You have found favor in the eyes of God. Behold: you are to be a mother, and to bear a son, and to call him Jesus! He will be great: 'Son of the Most High' will be his title, and the Lord God will give to him the throne of his father David. He will be king over the house of Jacob forever, and to his kingship there will be no end!"

The Jews had been taught that angels are the messengers of God, and in every town up and down the land it was common for the elders to discuss the historic cases of neighbors who had been visited by angels, with either miraculous or disastrous results, depending on whether the spirit was a good one or an evil one. So the visit itself did not frighten the virgin from Galilee. It was the portent of the visit. What was it God wanted?

"How will this be," Mary said, "since I remain a virgin?"

The angel became specific. "The Holy Spirit will come upon you, and the power of the Most High will overshadow you. For this reason the child to be born will be acclaimed 'Holy' and 'Son of God.' Note, moreover: your relative Elizabeth, in her old age, has also conceived a son and is now in her sixth month—she who was called 'the barren'! Nothing indeed is impossible with God."

Mary understood fully the extent of her honor. She was to be Mother to the Son of God. She did not know how or why, but she would not ask. She had been raised in an atmosphere of filial piety, and in deep reverence for all things holy: she knew how to accept and how to obey.

"Regard me as the humble servant of the Lord," she said. "May all that you have said be fulfilled in me."

There was one way in which Mary could prove to herself that what she had heard was not a dream. She left almost at once for a mountain town in Judea to visit her kinswoman Elizabeth, wife of a priest named Zachary. Elizabeth was old, and in spite of many entreaties to God, no baby had been cradled against her warm breast. Unknown to Mary, the same angel had appeared to Elizabeth and she was indeed in her sixth month. In June, she would give birth to a baby called John, who would someday be referred to as the Baptist, and who would go ahead of the Messiah and preach to the multitudes, baptizing as he went.

As Mary came up the walk, her kinswoman stood in the doorway and the young one shouted a greeting. Elizabeth felt her baby move sharply and was moved to tears and said: "Blessed are you beyond all women! And blessed is the fruit of your womb!" Mary was dumbstruck. Elizabeth, apparently, knew more about this than she. "How privileged am I," Elizabeth said gravely, "to have the mother of my Lord come to visit me!

Hear me now: as the sound of your greeting fell upon my ears, the babe in my womb leaped for joy! Happy is she who believed that what was told her on behalf of the Lord would be fulfilled!''

In the shading of difference between believing something and being convinced of it, Mary had believed: that is, she had listened well to Gabriel's words, and she understood them and placed credence in them. But every time that she thought, ''I am to be the Mother of God,'' the eight words sounded to her like blasphemous presumption. Now, hearing the words of the graying Elizabeth who had known little Mary almost from the moment of her birth, she was convinced; doubly convinced because her kinswoman understood more about the divine interposition than Mary did.

In reply to Elizabeth's words of welcome, Mary became lyrical with joy. She held out both hands, standing before the doorstep, and almost sang:

> My soul extols the Lord;
> and my spirit leaps for joy in God my Saviour.
> How graciously he looked upon his lowly maid!
> Oh, behold, from this hour onward
> age after age will call me blessed!
> How sublime is what he has done for me—
> the Mighty One, whose name is 'Holy'!
> From age to age he visits those
> who worship him in reverence.
> His arm achieves the mastery:
> he routs the haughty and proud of heart;
> he puts down princes from their thrones,
> and exalts the lowly;
> he fills the hungry with blessings,
> and sends away the rich with empty hands.
> He has taken by the hand his servant Israel,
> and mercifully kept his faith
> —as he had promised our fathers—
> with Abraham and his posterity
> forever and evermore.

Mary remained with her old aunt for three months, almost until the day of the birth of John. Then the betrothed girl went home. She was now three months pregnant and the time of her wedding was close. Then Mary told Joseph that she was with child, but told him nothing else. The shock to the carpenter was incalculable. He had grown to love Mary deeply, and he was as positive as any young bridegroom-to-be that the object of his affections was as innocent as a day-old lamb. Mary had been away three months; she returned three months pregnant.

She could have told Joseph the whole story. There was no reason for not telling him. The baby was going to need a foster father and who better than the gentle and pious Joseph? This woman could keep locked within her breast the greatest announcement God ever made to the world! So Joseph went about, thinking about it, worrying about it, asking himself questions. He could marry her and hope that, in a small town like Nazareth, the gossips would not think that a six-month baby was remarkable. Or he could divorce her, in which case he would have to tell the reason and, if she was found to be with child and he swore that he was "without knowledge of her," she would be adjudged an adulteress and the penalty was stoning. Or he could put her away privately; pay to have her sent off to some remote place, there to have her baby and not return to Nazareth.

The carpenter thought these things over again and again. At last he made up his mind. He would put her away privately. This, he felt, was the merciful thing. He was certain that he would never give his heart to another; his heart was broken.

When Joseph had made his decision, sleep came. And in sleep he was visited by an angel who said: "Joseph, son of David, do not scruple to take Mary, your wife, into your home. Her conception was wrought by the Holy Spirit. She will bear a Son and you are to name him Jesus; for he will save his people from their sins." This would fulfill a prophecy with which Joseph was familiar: "Behold! The virgin will be pregnant and give birth to a Son, who will be called 'Emmanuel'—which means 'God with us.'"

Joseph believed. When he awakened, he felt refreshed and it is reasonable to assume that he told Mary that he now understood. He was bewildered and happy and also afraid of all that was going to happen to them. He took Mary into his home and he had no relations with her before or after the baby was born.

If all of this was to fulfill the words of the prophecy, then something was amiss. All Jews knew that the promised King of Kings was to be born in the town of Bethlehem—the City of David. In the autumn Mary was in advanced pregnancy and had no intention of going anywhere. Life with Joseph had been sweet. She was an obedient wife and his business was in Nazareth. She was in secret trembling joy. She could feel life move within her as she lay alongside Joseph waiting for sleep to come. The older women had long since warned her not to travel at this time, and no one could coax the young bride to go beyond her little house and the homes of her neighbors.

At that time, Caesar Augustus in Rome decided, after holding a council, that an Emperor could not get an accurate count of his taxes unless he knew how many subjects he had and where they came from. So he issued an imperial rescript that in his domains all subjects were to return to the city of the father of the family, there to be counted. He knew that this would work hardship on many; he knew that the economic balance would be upset, but his reply to such criticism was that, to prevent people from being counted twice, or not at all in the case of transients, each would go to the abode of the fathers at the beginning of winter, and then the census could be made.

Mary did not want to make the trip. The normal maternal instinct within her was opposed to this. Joseph told her that they would have to go to Bethlehem; that it was not a matter for discussion; it was the law. By road, they would go south about ninety miles and would pass through the Holy City of Jerusalem on their way. This may have mollified Mary a little. It is doubtful that she had ever seen Jerusalem, or Solomon's temple.

She sat sideward on the little gray ass that Joseph used to deliver finished work. Jews seldom took the direct route through Samaria because they believed the entire country was defiled! They traveled by way of the Jordan Valley, along the banks of the river to Jericho and then turned west to Jerusalem. Families averaged about ten miles per day; at night they paid for a little space in the public rooms of the various inns.

When they arrived in Bethlehem, Mary was in labor. Joseph hurried to the inn, which was on top of a cliff facing the shepherd's hills to the east, and, while Mary waited outside with the animal, he explained his urgent need. Under Jewish law, cases of this type require the immediate services of a midwife, but Mary had made it plain that she was not worried about this. What she wanted more than anything else was privacy.

Joseph discussed the matter with the proprietor of the inn. The owner threw up his hands. Did the carpenter understand that this town was bulging with people? Did he know that all the people of the family of David had returned, and they had filled all the homes in the city, had jammed the inn, were sleeping in streets and out in the hills? A room? Privacy? Impossible.

The carpenter was a silent man. He asked, quietly, where a man could go with his wife to have a baby. The proprietor consulted his wife. The night was chill; the stars were cold. The shepherds dozed with their cloaks over their noses. Where? The stable below! It was hardly a fit place to deliver an infant, but it would be warmer than outside, and no more guests could be admitted. Even the stable was full of animals on this night, but Joseph and Mary were welcome to the space.

The young bride stood outside, in the chill dark, holding the donkey. She was tired. The chalk of the road whitened still further her wan face, her hands, her feet. Her bones ached, and she knew that her time had come. When her husband came from the Hospice of Chamaan, he brought news which, to him, was humiliating; to her it was a relief.

The cliff on which the inn stood was shaped like the rounded bow of a huge ship. Two trails led down the sides, like dark bow waves, and met halfway down the hill. There Joseph led Mary. He apologized; he said that he was sorry he had not been able to find better lodging; he was ashamed that, as a husband, he had failed her in her time of need. He had not even found a midwife.

And so, at the age of fifteen, the singularly blessed young woman would have to undergo this trial alone, just as, thirty-four years from now, her son would have to undergo a trial alone.

Mary had been told, almost from babyhood, that the ways of Yahweh are mysterious indeed, not to be plumbed or weighed by humans, and if it was His will that the Son of God was to be born in a cave under an inn, Mary would not question the wisdom of it, although she might permit herself the small hope that the place was clean.

The discouraged bridegroom led his spouse into the stable. He fixed and hung lamps, looked at the staring, blinking animals, and collected sufficient straw for a pallet. He took the water bucket from the ass and went out and filled it. He wanted to build a fire, but there was no dry wood in the hills and he went back up to the innkeeper and bought some charcoal. The fire was built outside the entrance to the cave. When their big goatskin bag had been emptied of pots and dishes and cups, he led the donkey inside.

Then, after a whispered conversation with Mary, he went outside and left Mary alone. In the ruddy light of the fire he heated water and mumbled prayers which begged for mercy. He tried to keep busy. When an animal snorted, Joseph jumped. He crouched beside the fire, moving the coals, and when they had stopped smoking he edged them toward the cave.

The proprietor's wife might have come down to see whether Mary needed help. No one came. Time was slow and contained infinite loneliness: the pendulum of it was in the systolic and diastolic pulse of two hearts—one beating slowly and with heavy effort, the other swift and shallow as that of a baby rabbit held in the hand. Time would not be hurried. Nor would it be slowed further than its own steady pace. It went on and on, and Joseph, crouching by the gray-furred embers, saw a new and bright star over the Mountains of Moab.

She called him. He went inside timidly, noting the plumes of breath from the animals, and he saw Mary crouching beside a manger. In it were the broad bolts of the white swaddling cloths she had brought. And, bending far over, he could look inside the little tent of cloth and see the red face of a tiny infant.

This, Joseph said to himself, is the one of whom the angel spoke. He dropped to his knees. This was the Messiah.

Escaping the wrath of Herod by means of a brief flight into Egypt, Mary and Joseph brought the infant "home" to a normal life. Jesus grew up in Nazareth, where the neighbors thought of him as the son of Joseph. His Mother taught the law to him long before he went to school to learn to read and write. He "advanced in wisdom and age and grace" but not out of proportion to his years. He had neighborhood playmates, and if we can guess the child from what we know of the man, he was a serious child. He would not be given to pranks, although he was probably imaginative enough to want to play in sand piles and dream.

The Greek city of Sepphoris was a few miles over the hill, and the Jews of this part of Galilee did much of their "big" shopping in the markets there. Joseph went there many times, holding Jesus by the hand and listening to the swift Greek words of the shopkeepers. There was a government arsenal in the town, and soldiers. When his father bought a new cutting tool, a shopkeeper may have offered the child a sweet—a sugared spice from a jar—but, if so, the child was taught, as all Jewish children were, not to accept the gift from a Gentile but to bow his deepest and thank his loudest.

Nazareth was, among towns in Palestine, a cipher in the northern hills. A nothing. In Judea, they made jokes about Nazareth. The old Scripture mentioned many places in the land of the Israelites, but Nazareth was not among them. The name comes from the Hebrew: Nazar, a rod. In the old Scripture, Isaias had said that the Messiah would be a rod of Jesse.

Every year in the month of Nisan, Joseph went up to Jerusalem for the Pasch. He left his wife and his foster son at home until the boy was twelve. From that time Jesus was an adult male Jew, as responsible as his foster father in religious duties. Mary was not obliged to go to Jerusalem, but her piety was as close to her as the next breath, and she accompanied her men. It was she who taught Jesus the precepts of his faith and it was she who enrolled him in a rabbinic school so that he would learn to read and to write and to study more and more of the law.

Study did not come easily to Jesus simply because of the divine side of his nature. When he assumed the nature of a human, he became, in a sense, vulnerable as a human. If a knife slipped in his fingers he bled like any other boy. If his Mother rebuked him, he felt sorrow. If, in

Joseph's shop, he planed a piece of pine to exact thickness and Joseph complimented him, Jesus reddened with pride and tried harder to please.

The annual trip to Jerusalem was always exciting. It was a festive occasion. Neighbors banded together in little caravans, and the men joked and felt a deep joy in this pilgrimage. The little caravans blended into other little caravans, and the roads were choked with pilgrims, all happy, bowing and smiling and exchanging godly greetings. Little sons often sat astride their fathers' shoulders for the entire trip.

Often they stopped at sundown in good warm weather and slept in the fields. If the night air was cold or rainy they would seek an inn, and these were usually shaped like a hollow square, with a courtyard in the middle where the animals were tethered. Around the sides were a few small rooms reserved for the rich, and one public room reserved for the poor.

In the public room the Jews always asserted their freedom and their independence. No man would tell another when to go to sleep or when to stop talking. Some debated questions of the law, or the market for produce, until the late hours. Some prayed loudly and long. Some huddled in groups, sitting against a wall, singing psalms until the morning hours. Children huddled on the floor between parents and slept through the din.

Most families arrived in the Holy City a day or two before the 14th Nisan. Some left the day after the Feast of the Pasch, but the pious ones stayed inside or outside Jerusalem for the entire week of the Passover, until the 21st Nisan. When Jesus was twelve years of age, a youngster perhaps a litle taller than the average and more serious than most, Joseph and Mary left the Holy City with their Nazareth caravan for home and discovered, after a day's journey, that their son was nowhere to be found.

They were frantic with worry, and said farewell to their friends and hurried back to the temple. When they got to Jerusalem, they did not find him. They searched in the place where they had spent the week. He was not there. Their worry was intense beyond words. This child was more than their son. He had a sacred mission, and only they knew about it. He was a special charge from God, and they had lost him. They hurried through the narrow streets, looking in shops, running to catch up with each tall, slender boy ahead of them—only to find that it was not Jesus— asking authorities if a boy without parents had been found, or reported. Everywhere the answer was the same: no one had seen him.

On the third day, fatigued beyond tears, they walked into the temple to appeal to his true Father for help. There, on one of the porticoes, they saw their boy seated among rabbis, listening to them propound the intricacies of the law, asking questions and answering questions. The rabbis seemed to be charmed with the intellect and the knowledge of the youth.

The mother who has lost a child will weep and worry and think only of the tragic things which might happen, but the moment her eyes rest on the child and she sees that he is unhurt, her automatic reflex is anger.

"Child," Mary said to Jesus sternly, "why did you behave toward us in this way? Oh, our hearts were heavy—your father's and mine—as we searched for you."

Jesus looked up at his Mother. He seemed to be surprised at the anguish he saw in her face and in Joseph's. "Why did you search for me?" he said softly, placatingly. "I had to answer my Father's call, and did you not know it?" No doubt the rabbis around him were mystified by this answer, and there is reason to believe that neither Mary nor Joseph understood. His true Father was God the Father, and his Father lived here.

Still, he was an obedient son. He stood and thanked the rabbis, and he left with his parents for Nazareth. From that time until Jesus was thirty-two years of age, a matter of twenty years, he lived in Nazareth, known only to his own family, his kinfolk and his friends.

There he was part of two large families—Joseph's and Mary's. He had many relatives, and the custom of the Orient was to cherish all of them, even the outermost branch of cousins. In fact, cousins of the first and second order were called *ab* (brother) and *aboth* (sister) so that Jesus was said to have many brothers and sisters although in the strict sense, he had none. They loved him, as he loved them, and at weddings and circumcisions he was part of a great gathering of his clan.

None of these thought that Jesus was in any way remarkable. A little more thoughtful, perhaps, than the other boys of his age; disinclined to joke or to flirt with the pretty ones among the cousins; more inclined to sit with the older men and listen, or to dip into the outer edge of the conversation.

It is understandable that he was not considered to be holier than the others, because piety, to the Jews, was such an all-pervading part of daily life that religion invaded their eating, drinking, thinking, talking and even their sleeping habits. The only way in which one good person might seem to be more religious than another would be if he showed signs of being a prophet. Jesus showed none.

He helped his foster father in the shop, and as Jesus grew tall and strong he assumed more and more of Joseph's work, especially when Joseph's health declined. And when that quiet, faithful man died, there were the thoughts of the son as he stood over all that was left of the man who had given him "legality" and—much more than that—his love. The first adult tears of the human Jesus were shed at this time. But of course in this grief he was not alone. The boy and his Mother were together.

The public life—the ministry to redeem mankind—began in the latter part of A.D. 27. Jesus was thirty-two years of age, a mature man whose eyes seemed to reflect a secret sorrow. He spent less time in the shop and more time among the people, teaching and listening. Many in the Galilean country knew him, and he knew many, but they did not know his mission, nor did he speak of it. He was acquainted with their problems and their pleasures and they knew him as one of their people, the true Galilean with the soft, slurring, sibilating tongue.

Jesus must have known that this accent was a source of laughter and mockery in Judea. A favorite joke was the one about the Galilean farmer who wanted to buy wool in Jerusalem, and he asked where he could find "amar." A shopkeeper said: "Stupid Galilean, what are you looking for—hamor [an ass], hamar [wine], immar [a lamb] or amar [wool]?"

The farmers in the north knew Jesus on sight. He walked the roads alone, and barefooted unless the journey was to be long; he wore a plain white outer garment with no stripes along the hem and he wore no phylacteries. Sometimes the farmers stopped work to cross the fields and talk to Jesus. They sought him as one seeks a learned, sympathetic man—a teacher—and they told him their problems and were astonished at the shrewd solutions he offered.

He was now almost ready to begin his work of salvation, but he knew that, according to Scripture, someone would precede him. "Look!" Isaias had said, "I am sending ahead of you a messenger, who is to prepare your road; a herald's voice rings out in the desert; make ready the road of the Lord; make straight his path." Jesus knew that the one ahead of him would be the one who had preceded him in birth: John, son of the aged Elizabeth.

The cousin of Jesus was now in the desert. He had grown to be a fierce ascetic, given to long, rolling phrases of denunciation. When God gave him his apostolate, John came out into the rich, green country on both sides of the River Jordan and he baptized all whom he could convince. He wore a long shirt of camel's hair and a raw leather girdle; he ate locusts and wild honey and his weapon was anger. The people came to him from all over the country, including Jerusalem. He stood shin deep in the Jordan and they confessed their sins and he poured water over them for the remission of sins.

Once, when he saw Sadducees and Pharisees among the ordinary people of the country, he turned to them and roared: "Brood of vipers! Who advised you to flee before the gathering storm of anger? Well, then, let your conduct show your change of heart." His face showed contempt. "And do not presume to say to yourselves: 'We have Abraham for our father!' I tell you, God is able to raise up children to Abraham out of these very stones." They moved toward him timidly, ready for contrition. "Besides," he said shrilly, "from now on the axe lies ready to strike at the root of the trees; any tree, therefore, that does not produce sound fruit is cut down and thrown into the fire.

"I baptize you with water to help you make a change of heart; but One shall come after me who is mightier than I and whose sandals I am not worthy to take off his feet. He for his part will baptize you with the Holy Spirit—or else with fire." John threw both hands into the air. "His winnowing fan in hand," he warned, "he will thoroughly cleanse his threshing floor; the wheat he will store in his barn, and the chaff he will burn in unquenchable fire."

He baptized the people in great crowds and they asked him what they should do to attain salvation. And John shouted: "He who has two coats should give one to him that has none; and he who has food should do likewise." Tax collectors asked, and he said: "Exact nothing in excess of the rate prescribed to you." Policemen came with the question and John said: "Browbeat no one; blackmail no one; and be content with your pay."

And the day came when they asked John who he was. The Baptist understood them, and knew that their question really was: "Are you the Messiah?" He shook his head vigorously and said: "I am not the Messiah."

"Who, then? Are you Elias?"

"I am not."

"Are you then the Prophet?"

"No."

"Who are you? We have to give an answer to those who sent us. What do you say about yourself?"

"I am a herald's voice which rings out upon the desert: 'Make straight the road of the Lord,' as the Prophet Isaias has said."

The Pharisees, who felt a delicious tremor of suspicion run through their minds, said: "Why, then, do you baptize, if you are not the Messiah or Elias or the Prophet?"

"I baptize with water," John roared. "There is already one in your midst whom you do not know—the one who is to follow me, the strap of whose sandal I am not fit to untie."

The next day, John was exhorting a crowd on the banks of the Jordan when he saw his tall cousin walking toward him. "Look," said John, "there is the lamb of God who takes away the sin of the world. This is he of whom I said: 'There is a man to follow me who takes precedence over me because he existed before me.' I, too, had not known him; but he had to be made known to Israel, and it is for this purpose that I came to baptize with water." John did not recognize his cousin. He had not seen him since childhood.[15]

Jesus lifted the hem of his garment with one hand and stepped into the Jordan. John shook his head negatively. "It is I who should be baptized by you." The Messiah kept walking into the water. "And you come to me?" John said.

"Let me have my way for the present," Jesus said, and he bowed his head for the water. "After all, it is only so that we fulfill, as is proper for us, all just demands."

When he was baptized, Jesus walked out onto the embankment of the brown stream and the heavens opened and the Spirit of God descended in the form of a dove. It alighted on him and a voice from afar cried:

"This is my Son, the beloved, with whom I am well pleased."

The service which John had rendered to his cousin was in apprising the people of the coming of the Messiah, and then in pointing him out. Jesus, as the Son of God, did not need baptism, and accepted it only as an example to the people of the world. On the next afternoon, John performed the final loving service for Jesus.

It was 4 P.M. and crowds lined both banks of the River Jordan and listened to the Baptist. He stood knee deep in water, flanked by a disciple, Andrew. The Baptist was shouting and waving his arms, denouncing sin and exhorting the people to repent, when he paused and saw one standing a little apart.

"Look," he said softly, so that only Andrew heard. "There is the lamb of God."

He must have known that this would cause the defection of his own follower. All along he had preached that he was the precursor of the Messiah; now he had pointed to a stranger and called him the lamb of God, which is to say, the servant of God and also the sacrifice of God. Andrew did not even pause to say good-bye to the Baptist. He just hiked his garment and waded through the water to the far shore. Andrew's reasoning was that if this was the Messiah for whom the world had waited so many hundreds of years, then the multitudes were foolish indeed to be listening to a shouting Baptist when the Son of God was standing among them.

Andrew climbed the tawny bank and saw that Jesus had turned away and was walking down the Jericho road. The fields were deep in rising grain and, here and there, a thatched hut poked its top above the deep waves the wind rolled through the barley. Jesus saw that Andrew was following him, and he stopped and half turned toward him.

"What is your wish?" he said.

"Teacher," he said, "where are you staying?"

The expression means more than it says. It means who are you and what manner of person are you?

Jesus smiled a little and crooked his finger. "Come," he said, "and you will see."

Thus, he acquired the first of his twelve apostles. He did not inquire into his character, probe his heart, or even ask his name. It is possible that the twelve had been picked in advance by God the Father, and if this is so, it explains why Jesus had among them a traitor. The others, with their human weaknesses, small amount of formal education and wavering faith, were far from the highest type of men Jesus might have found in the land. He accepted them as they came to him.

One by one—Peter, Philip, Jude, and the others—were recruited. The nearest thing to a witticism in the story of Jesus occurred when Philip saw his friend Bartholomew sitting under a fig tree in the noon sun and said, with some excitement: "The One about whom Moses has written in the Law, and the Prophets, too—we have found him!—Jesus of Nazareth, the son of Joseph!" Bartholomew (also known as Nathanael) looked up drowsily and murmured: "Can any good come out of Nazareth?"

"Well," said Philip, "come and see."

After some thought, Bartholomew got to his feet and, still yawning, followed down the road to where a little knot of people surrounded Jesus.

"Look!" said the Messiah. "Here is a true Israelite. A good and honest soul."

"How do you know me?" Bartholomew said.

"Before Philip called you," said Jesus, "when you were still under the fig tree, I saw you."

This moved Bartholomew deeply because the fig tree was not in sight from where Jesus stood. "Rabbi,"[16] he said fervently, "you *are* the Son of God! You are the King of Israel!"

Jesus shook his head sadly. "Because I told you that I saw you under the fig tree," he said, "is that why you believe? You will see greater things than that." He turned to the others, as though he was mildly disappointed in Bartholomew's type of faith. "Yes," Jesus said, "so it really is! I tell you all, you will see heaven opened and the angels of God going up and coming down upon the Son of Man."

The Baptist did nothing more for Jesus. He knew that his Messiah had begun his public life by acquiring some disciples, and by going into the wilderness to fast and to be tempted by Satan. It was shortly after the baptism of Jesus that John the Baptist was imprisoned by Herod and, at the whim of the Tetrarch's women, was beheaded. All of his impatient zeal was in the eight words he shouted most frequently: "Repent! The kingdom of heaven is at hand!"

The two years and two or three months between the day of baptism for Jesus and the day of his death are, in a breath, known and unknown. They have been detailed by his apostles and touched upon by some who were almost contemporary with him; still, the portrait is like one seen with brilliant sunshine pouring on it through bars. In some features, the definition is complete—what he did, what he said, where and often why. Others are vague, some scenes are barely mentioned in passing; whole weeks and sometimes months seem to drop out of the life of Jesus. None of the chroniclers ever looked upon him as a man—a person of blood and sinew and bone and brain with a stupendous mission to accomplish in a very short time and in a place where the powers were alien to his cause. They saw him as God, and they longed to be present when he exterminated his enemies with fire and the swords of many legions of angels.

The first act of his public life occurred at Cana, in Galilee. A friend of his family was being married and Mary, the Mother of Jesus, was invited, as were her son and his friends. The hosts were not rich. They ran out of wine. Mary felt a maternal sympathy for the bridal party in their embarrassment.

She looked at her son, and said: "They have no wine."

"What would you have me do?" he whispered at table. "My time has not yet come!" He was telling her that he was not prepared to start his public career at this moment. Mothers who are certain of the unqualified love of their sons do not change with the centuries. Without a further glance at him, she knew that he would do something about this matter because she had brought it to his attention.

She nodded to the nervous steward and said: "No matter what he tells you, be sure you do it!"

Against the wall behind the dining couches were six huge stone jars. They were empty. Each had a capacity of twenty gallons and each was to be used, at the conclusion of the reception, for religious purification.

Jesus looked at his new apostles in discomfort. Then he said to the servants: "Fill the jars with water." The servants looked at one another and shrugged. They brought small stone jugs inside and ostentatiously poured water into the huge jars. When they were filled to the brim, the young Messiah held up a hand.

"Now draw off some," he said, "and bring it to the steward in charge."

They did as he ordered, and the master of the feast tasted it and found it to be the finest wine. He was so surprised that he did not go to Jesus, but went instead to the bridegroom and said: "Everybody serves his good wine first, and only when the guests have their fill of it does he put out the poorer sort. But you have kept back the good wine till now!"

When his apostles saw this, they believed in Jesus. His Mother, of course, needed no miracle to be certain of his divinity. The object lesson of this miracle is not that he turned water into wine, but the more potent fact that even the God-man was bound by the rules of obedience. The wish of his Mother was imperative.

After the wedding, Jesus and his Mother, his cousins and his disciples walked to Capharnaum, a fishing town on the north side of the Sea of Galilee. The journey was about thirty miles and required two days. One of the dark bands across the life of Jesus is this trip. Nothing has been written about it except that it occurred, and that the Galilean decided to make Capharnaum his center of operations, instead of Nazareth.

These blank episodes are, to the student of history, disappointing for several important reasons: the Jews used long foot journeys for excellent conversation and especially for the interchange of ideas; Jesus had just embarked upon his public life and was at that moment with the people closest to him—his Mother, his cousins and his first apostles—on that journey he probably explained the goal of glory to them, and may have hinted, in parables, of the hardships ahead.

The transfer of abode from Nazareth to Capharnaum is logical. The town of his adolescence would be poor ground in which to begin announcing that he was the Messiah. He had scores of relatives in Nazareth who knew him as an average child. His late foster father and his Mother had many friends in Nazareth, and to these Jesus was one more youngster whom they had watched with slight interest grow from the cradle into slender manhood, with less promise, maybe, than some of the other boys who were already in the exporting business, running caravans to Syria, or working on farms. They, of course, knew nothing of the special circumstances of his birth, and therefore, of his divinity.

Jesus knew—and his knowledge was borne out well—that when accounts of his more dramatic works in Jerusalem and in Capharnaum got back to Nazareth, the people would say: "Is this not the son of Joseph the carpenter whom we all knew? Is his Mother not Mary, a woman of character to whom we bid the time of day? Then where did he acquire his learning to become a doctor of the law? Miracles? What miracles? Is it not probable that the people elsewhere are more easily impressed by his words than we, who know him?"

The Nazarenes would not be impressed.

Some of his neighbors would, in time, stand before Jesus and accuse him of performing miracles everywhere but in his own town. He dreaded to hear the word *miracle*. He understood the weaknesses of man—he had promised his Father to give his life in expiation of these weaknesses—but it was an almost horrifying thing to learn that they preferred the working of miracles to being told the road to heaven. They were children, and everywhere he went they grinned and rubbed their hands together and nodded their heads and asked for "a sign."

They had asked the same thing of John the Baptist and he had had no patience with them. He had roared back that the time of the Messiah was growing shorter and that they had better repent here and now. Signs, he warned them, could come from Satan. But Jesus could not answer in that manner. With all of his heart he loved the people. Their childishness seldom moved him to anger; his response was pity, and more love. Over and over, he would repeat the same lessons to the youthful minds in mature bodies and they would listen, or debate the lessons with him, but, when they warmed to the task of looking fairly upon his face, they would always ask for "a sign." And, no matter how many times he bowed to their whims, and effected a miracle, they would ask again for "a sign." Without proof, they would have no part of him. And it grieved him to see that his chosen twelve needed many miracles too.

At the Passover of A.D. 28 Jesus and his followers went up to Jerusalem. As his first public act had been for his Mother, now his second would be for his true Father—Yahweh. He stood among the jostling mobs in the Court of the Gentiles and he heard the cries of the money-changers quoting the price for transferring Gentile coins into temple shekels, and he smelled the dung from the sheep and the oxen, and he heard their lowing across the court.

How could his people make of his Father's abode a gigantic stinking stable; how could such a mundane thing as money have anything to do with the proper worship of his Father? Jesus the man was shocked. His brown eyes opened wide and he knew that there was no end to the way in which man can, by slow degrees, pervert a beautiful concept. The piercing cries, the odors, penetrated the Holy of Holies and this, to Jesus, was sacrilege.

Anger in this man was rare. When it came, it had the dark silent quality of an oncoming thunderstorm; it could be seen before it broke. He reached to the ground without a word and picked up some pieces of rope. Of these he made a whip with knotted ends. His apostles watched and they looked at each other but asked nothing.

Then he walked across the big marble court, flailing before him with the cords in his big right hand. He saw the surprised faces of the money-changers, and then he saw fear as they jumped from their tables and ran. He kicked the tables over, and the stacks of burnished coins tinkled and rolled over the big slabs of marble.

The pilgrims were in an uproar as they watched him turn from the money-changers to the market of Annas. He loosed the oxen and the sheep and set the pigeons free. Jesus was breathing deeply and his face was flushed as he came upon the men of the market. "Get these things out of the way!" he shouted. "Do not turn my Father's house into a market place!"

The animals were running all over the court. The money-changers and market men did not dare attack Jesus because by now some of the pilgrims were shouting encouragement to him. They did not know who he was, but they agreed with his sentiments.

"What proof do you give us," some of the market men said, "to show your right to do these things?"

Jesus, still angry, tapped his chest with cold scorn. "If you destroy this sanctuary," he said, "I will build it up again in three days." He knew that they wanted to kill him for what he had done; and he was telling them that if they did, he would raise himself in three days. But they misunderstood. They thought he referred to the great temple.

"Six and forty years this sanctuary was in building," they said in astonishment, "and you will build it up again in three days?"

He turned away from them and he strode back to his apostles, who huddled in fear on the perimeter of the crowd. Jesus then arranged for the ritual sacrifice to be made. In the outer court it was argued that the stranger with the Galilean accent must indeed be insane and dangerous, because his violent act was a challenge to the most powerful man in Palestine—Annas. Besides, anyone who claimed he could rebuild the whole temple in three days was clearly not responsible for his words.

When the Passover had been concluded, Jesus led the way home. It felt good to be among the more simple people, and he spent the warm sunny days strolling along the sand of the Sea of Galilee, meditating and preaching. In his walks, he recruited more apostles, and he did this casually, almost carelessly. Simon, for example, was pulling in a net when Jesus asked him to follow, telling him he would make of him a fisher of men. It was then that he changed the man's name to Cephas—Peter—the Rock. James and John, the sons of Zebedee, were working with their father in a prosperous fishing business when Jesus called to them. They dropped nets, fish, security and future to follow him at once. And so with the others—each looked upon the sorrowful face and beckoning finger, and almost as though hypnotized into submission, followed without question.

The moment he began to preach, the fame of Jesus spread quickly. The candor in his eyes matched the truth on his tongue and the people believed. Whole families left their homes and farms and some tried to carry a part of their possessions with them in his roadside retinue. Jesus had to admonish them that their worldly possessions meant nothing in the kingdom where he would lead them. A week or two after the beginning of his mission one could stand on a hill and see Jesus, on a pale scar of a trail below, leading hundreds of men, women and children as he moved from town to town.

Many of his most valued followers were not of the Amé-Haaretz, but rather from among the intellectuals. Nicodemus, one of the leaders of the Pharisees, came to Jesus in the stealth of night and said:

"Rabbi, we know that you have a mission from God to teach. Surely, no one can give such striking proofs of his claims as you are giving, unless God is with him."

Jesus looked at the man who represented the power opposed to the new Scripture. He saw a man of good heart and he said with honest kindness: "If one is not born anew, he cannot see the kingdom of God." He meant, of course, that one must renounce the old life, be baptized of the Holy Spirit, and begin anew under the precepts of love.

Up to this time, the Galilean had not used the word "Messiah."[17] Now the time had come to use it, and the one whom he selected for the revelation was a poor woman, a Samaritan who was a half-Jew. She was an adulteress.

He was sitting alone at the well outside Sichar. In the lavender haze of the early afternoon, he could see Mount Garizim, where the Samaritans had built their own temple, competitive with that of Solomon's in Jerusalem. Nearby also was the tomb of the prophet Joseph, and Jacob's well. The disciples had been sent on an errand into town, and Jesus sat on stones near the cool wetness of the well, and flexed the fatigue from his toes.

A woman came by to draw water and Jesus engaged her in a conversation in the course of which he, a total stranger, showed a remarkable knowledge of her sin. "You had five husbands," he had said, "and the man with whom you are now living is not your husband."

The Samaritan woman raised her head and looked directly at Jesus. "I see, sir," she said, "you are a prophet! Our fathers worshiped on this mountain, and your people say that Jerusalem is the place for worshiping."

"A time is coming," said Jesus, "when you will worship the Father neither on this mountain nor in Jerusalem. You worship what you do not know; we worship what we do know." He allowed a moment for the woman to dwell on this. "Salvation comes from the Jews. And yet a time is coming, in fact, it is now here, when true worshipers will worship the Father in spirit and in truth. Such are the worshipers the Father demands. God is Spirit, and his worshipers must worship in spirit and in truth."

The woman became animated with understanding. "I know very well," she said, "that the Messiah—the Christ, as he is called—is to come, and when he comes, will tell us everything."

Jesus smiled. "I am he," he said simply, "I who now speak to you."

The apostles returned to Galilee with the master for a few days and, if Jesus was ever surprised, it was that the people of his own country gave him a welcome. He had already said in the synagogue that a prophet was without honor in his own country, and the people welcomed him as though they revered him. They formed in clusters on the road into Cana, bowing and smiling and following in his train. Jesus found out why. Many of them had been to the Passover in Jerusalem and they had heard how he had shown his power by kicking over the tables of the money-changers. Their enthusiasm for the neighborhood youngster lasted several days.

They went down through Perea to the Mount of Olives and there, one quiet evening, the apostles saw Jesus on his knees, motionless, his eyes upon the stars. They had seen him this way before, but no one had asked what it meant. They knew that, in some way, he was in communication with his Father. When he had finished, one said timidly, "Master, teach us to pray as John taught his disciples."

In a way, the request is ironic because the Jews had many formulae for prayer. They had special prayers for before meals and others for after meals, for confronting certain situations, for the receipt of news good or bad, for daily worship, for the dawn of new days at sundown, for death, for birth, for Sabbath, for sacrifice, for atonement, for thanksgiving, for crops, for business, for dear ones. They had the shema, a profession of faith, and the eighteen blessings which constituted their official prayer.

"When you pray," Jesus said, "pray thus." He dropped to his knees again, and they did too. This was a novelty to them because most Jews prayed standing. They listened and he said:

> Our Father who art in heaven,
> Hallowed be thy name;
> thy kingdom come,
> thy will be done on earth, as it is in heaven.
> Give us this day our daily bread
> and forgive us our debts
> as we also forgive our debtors,
> and lead us not into temptation,
> but deliver us from evil.

Jesus did not intend them to follow this as the only prayer. It was given as an example containing the required elements of homage, humility, and petition. A blueprint. They remembered this particular prayer (although two of them disagreed on the phrasing) and they devised their own prayers.

One time when Jesus was going home to Capharnaum, a royal official—in all probability a ranking member of the retinue of Herod

Antipas—met the Messiah on the outskirts of town and begged him to come at once to see his little boy, who was dying. The official was not a follower of Jesus; as a member of the royal family he was, in all likelihood, a Sadducee. The man wept as he pleaded.

Jesus looked at him with a mixture of pity and resignation. "If you do not see striking exhibitions of power," he said, "you will not believe."

The man would not deny it. "Come down, sir," he urged, "before my child dies."

Again, the request for a miracle. The people would if they could, have had him use his godlike prerogative to sustain and continue life every day and many times a day, if he did not turn his face away from their pleas.

"Go," he said, waving a hand at the man. "Your son is safe and sound."

The man did not know whether to leave or stay. He had assumed that the worker of miracles had to be at the bedside for results. After a moment he mumbled his gratitude and hurried off to his home. It was a long journey, and the next day, as he drew near his city, the slaves of his household met him on the road.

"Your son is safe and sound," they chanted.

The official was overcome with joy. When his voice returned he asked when the boy showed signs of recovering.

"Yesterday," the slaves said, "at one in the afternoon the fever left him."

The man knew this was the hour when Jesus had said to him: "Go. Your son is safe and sound." He and his family became followers of Jesus. But this was not the kind of faith the Messiah was looking for.

In October Jesus returned to Jerusalem for the Feast of the Tabernacles. This time, his followers numbered into the hundreds and they covered the road in a long awkward march. There were many hundreds more already waiting in Jerusalem, and these Jews too believed that Jesus was the Messiah. There were so many of them, in fact, that the Sadducees and Pharisees of the temple were worried, and asked questions about the Galilean. To their way of thinking, he was inaugurating a separate sect of religious Jews who, like the old Essenes, would make their own laws without regard to the temple. Long ago, the Sadducees and the Pharisees had agreed that if defections did not stop, all Israel would be broken into groups, none of which would be beholden to the temple. Therefore, if the might and the glory of the temple were to be upheld, the splinter groups would have to be discredited.

Jesus took a few apostles with him and went to the pool of Bethesda near the Sheepgate. The spot was a few rods north of Fortress Antonia and here, under five porticoes, were the helplessly ill and maimed. Here were the blind, the crippled, and the senile. Each patient had the same hope. Each had been given up by the physicians of the city, and each had come to Bethesda because he knew of the legend of the water. The story went that, on rare occasions, an angel of the Lord descended into the pool and stirred the water. Whoever among the ill was the first to immerse himself after the water began to move would be cured of whatever ailed him.

One of the patients had been on his back under a portico for thirty-eight years; since before Jesus was born. The Messiah walked through the place and saw the man lying on his mat. The man saw Jesus, and asked nothing.

The Messiah leaned over him and said gently: "Would you like to get well?"

The invalid smiled. "Why, sir," he said, "I have nobody to put me into the pool the moment the water is stirred up, and by the time I get there, someone else has gone down ahead of me."

Jesus nodded and looked on the man with compassion. "Stand up," he said. "Take your mat and walk." The startled man leaned on an elbow, then he stood. He picked up his mat, and walked away.

Some Pharisees met him and said to the former cripple: "Today is a Sabbath. You are not allowed to carry the mat."

"But he who made me well," he replied, "also told me: 'Take up your mat and walk.'"

"Who is the man," they asked him, "who told you to take up your mat and walk?"

He looked puzzled. He did not know. The cured man looked around to point to his benefactor, but he could no longer see him. The man walked on to the temple to give thanks, and there he saw Jesus again.

"You are now well and strong," said Jesus. "Do not sin any more, or something worse may happen to you." The man bowed his thanks humbly, and when he saw the Pharisees again he said that he had been cured by someone named Jesus of Nazareth.

When the Pharisees charged Jesus with breaking the Sabbath by making sick people well, he said: "My Father has been working to this hour; and so I, too, am working." They realized then that Jesus was more dangerous than they had supposed, not only because he worked wonders beyond the understanding of man, but because, in his reference to Yahweh as "my Father," he was asserting equality with God.

It is an irony of enormous proportions that the closer Jesus came to success in redeeming man for the heavenly kingdom, the more the religious leaders feared him and plotted against him. The ratio of his success was in direct proportion to the imminence of his death. In this first year, a few talked of plotting death against the Galilean, but the wise ones of the temple counseled prudence, and they remembered that there had been other "Egyptian magicians" and spurious Messiahs. These, when they had been permitted sufficient latitude, had eventually been stoned by the people.

In early March of A.D. 29, the Messiah went to the far side of the Sea of Galilee, and on this journey even his apostles remarked on the size of the crowds which followed. Some went by boat; many led asses around from Capharnaum into Gaulanitis. There, where the cocoa-colored mountains thrust their foothills into the sea, Jesus sat on a mountain in the midst of his disciples.

The people were as numerous and as dark as locusts in a grain field as they stood below him. Their desire was to meet him, to exchange a word with the man who would strike the fetters from the ankles of Israel; who would lead them, they were certain, to a great earthly kingdom in which the Jews would rule the world, and then on to a heavenly kingdom which would be sublime for all eternity. They wanted to meet him, but they were bashful and they would not come forth unbidden. They glanced up at him cautiously and, when they found the full charge of his eyes upon them, they turned away and whispered.

Jesus said to Philip: "Where shall we buy bread enough for these people to have a meal?" This was not Philip's problem because, even if he had had sufficient money for it, there was no place near the mountain where bread could be purchased, and even if that difficulty could be overcome, what baker would keep enough bread on hand for thousands of people? No, this was a problem for Jesus.

"Bread for two hundred denarii is not enough for each of them to get even a little." Andrew, trying to be helpful, said: "There is a lad here who has five barley loaves and two fish; but what is that for so many?"

Jesus nodded and studied the crowd. As one who could read hearts, Jesus must have been discouraged, because most of these people did not understand him, nor their relationship to him. They hungered for honor and glory and triumph; if he pointed a hard road to heaven, they would scorn him.

"Have the people recline on the ground," Jesus said. The apostles went among the people at once, shouting for everyone to lie on the grass. The Messiah asked for the five loaves of bread and the two fishes. They were given to him. He blessed the food and gave thanks to his Father for it. Then he told the apostles to pass it to the people. They did, taking the baskets and permitting the people to break off pieces of bread and fish. The further they proceeded, the more the fragments seemed to increase, and they called for help from among the boys in the crowd. More baskets were requisitioned and more help was required, and the apostles said that the men in the crowd alone numbered five thousand.

When each one had eaten all that he wanted, Jesus said to his men: "Gather up the pieces that are left over; nothing must be wasted." This was done and the apostles returned to their master with twelve full baskets.

The people noted all this and some of the men began to shout: "This is really the Prophet who is to come into the world!" The shouting increased and the women shrilled hosanna. Jesus was troubled. He knew that they would now want to make him their king. Amid a scene of mass joy, he disappeared farther up the mountain. He retreated alone. Nor did he return that afternoon to the crowd ready to acclaim him.

In the evening, when the crowds had dispersed, the apostles were confused. Jesus still had not returned, and a fresh and chill northwester was blowing across the lake, so that they would have to launch their big boat through heavy waves. No one knew where Jesus had gone, and they did not want to leave him, but when dusk dropped a lid over the sun, they tucked their garments high into their girdles and pushed their boat out to sea.

The trip back to Capharnaum was about five miles due west, so they bent their oars into the wind. There were whitecaps on the water, and in the darkness aboard the small craft these loomed large and ghostly. They had gone halfway across when in the darkness behind them they saw a luminescence and the apostles became frightened. Some wanted to turn back; some began to pray.

When the luminescence resolved itself, they saw Jesus walking on the water toward them. He said: "It is I. Do not be afraid." They were struck with awe and joy, and they uttered fervent thanks that he had quieted the waters when he stepped into the boat. The apostles exchanged greetings with the Messiah, and when they turned around to look forward, they saw the land of the opposite shore. Most of these men in the boat were fishermen; they knew piloting and they knew the waters of Palestine both from personal experience and by hearsay; they could not understand how their boat had covered the remaining distance so quickly. And then they realized that once more on this day Christ had performed a miracle.

Sometimes Jesus conducted the services in the synagogue at Capharnaum and, when this was known in advance, many of his neighbors from Nazareth and Cana made the trip to sit and to listen to his discourses. They were puzzled and envious. Some had sons of the same age who had had more diligent rabbinical schooling than Jesus, and they asked themselves from whence he acquired the right to teach. In private discussion, they conceded that he was indeed learned, but where did that come from? Not from the Nazareth local school. This was a provincial school. The only other who taught Jesus was his Mother, and what woman in all Israel could show the wisdom that this young man displayed from behind the little lectern? None.

Often, they came away angered at his words because, when he spoke in parables, they laid his words down like separate tiles and took them literally.

Many of his followers left him. So many, in fact, that Jesus called the twelve, and said: "Are you, too, minded to go away?"

Peter answered for all. "Lord, to whom shall we go? You have a message of eternal life; we firmly believe and are fully convinced that you are the Holy One of God."

The recording of harsh judgments and somber warnings tells very little of the personality of Jesus. It does not permit one to see the man. This is akin to assessing the heart of a judge by consulting his judicial opinions. If love—which is a perpetual act of selfless devotion—could be molded into arms and legs and sinew and features and brain, the result would be Jesus of Nazareth. Many who did not believe in him or in his mission saw in him a deep affection for all mankind.

Nor does this tell it.

He was a giver. And the tenderness, the mercy which he held in his hands and offered to strangers was struck from those hands with sneers. He offered solace and comfort and would be given nails and a spear. He wept over Jerusalem, which he loved, but he went back to the city which he knew would kill him. He unlocked his heart to the twelve whom his Father had given to him, and they would give back to him weakness, lack of understanding and cowardice.

Had he not had a mission to perform and a short time in which to perform it, he might have spent almost all of his days curing afflictions—making the blind to see, the lame to walk, dying children to arise and run off in glee. At times, when there was not enough food to go around the little circle, he excused himself and went off to pray.

The mind of Jesus could look into the heart of Judas and see every scar, every soiled tissue, but he would say nothing hurtful to this man even when he knew that Judas was stealing from the common purse, even when he knew that Iscariot no longer believed in Jesus. Love? It required a unique devotion to continue to address this person as an apostle, to refrain at all times from showing a mark of disfavor, to be able to do it so well that, at the Last Supper, the others could not guess the name of the traitor and had to ask, one after another: "Is it I, Lord? Is it I?"

He did it. And all the time, he knew.

"Love ye one another," Jesus said, "as I love you." He not only loved them, but he would prove it by doing something that none would do: he would crouch on his knees and wash their feet. There was love in the brown eyes as he listened to the shrewd people of the towns ask him for a "sign." They could not believe in him unless he performed a work which would be beyond their comprehension—a miracle. If he had less love for them, could he not have asked them for a "sign" before it would be possible for him to believe in man?

Man betrayed Jesus almost every time he was given a choice. He called Jesus a faker; he lied about him; he bunched his lips and spat in the face of his redeemer; he beat him and spent time devising cruelties to vent upon the one who held out hands laden with tenderness.

Except in one case, no one cared to mark the numberless times that Jesus sat by a road with children. It was of no significance to anyone, including the apostles, that the little ones brought the full, ripe, unguarded smile to the face of Jesus. These were the times when the man who was never known to laugh, laughed; this was the time for the sharing of innocent secrets, the time when a small pudgy hand could pull through the brown beard with impunity; the time when a weary heart sang as it saw, in a rare dream, love coming back in full measure to him who had offered it.

Has any journalist remarked on the expression he wore when he looked from the face of a young mother to the tiny blue-eyed face inside the bundle she carried at her breast? It was not of consequence. It had no bearing on the grim mission of saving man from himself. Did Jesus long, for a fraction of an instant, to take the little bundle into his own arms, to feel the warmth and goodness of innocence encompassed in a toothless smile? Of course he did. He came here as man with all of the limitations of man—the joys as well as the sorrows, the affections as well as the pains.

These limitations hindered and hurt Jesus at all times because they hobbled his divine nature; these were self-imposed fetters which held his feet to earth while his soul yearned to soar. At times, the shackles chafed him and he became exasperated with the men around him who tried hard to understand, but couldn't.

His little band of warriors could not even remain awake on his last night on earth. At one time or another, almost everyone failed him except his Mother. She alone comprehended without understanding. It was enough that she knew who he really was; it was enough to know that he was devoted to her and would prove it by beginning his public ministry before he was quite ready; it was sufficient for her to know that he did many wondrous things without understanding how he did them, or even why.

Love? He showed that he preferred to sit with sinners rather than with saints. The saint was already pleasing to his Father. He needed no further cultivation, for he had borne the fruit which was so necessary to salvation. But the sinner was just as human as the saint—perhaps, ironically, more so—and the sinner was swimming in dark joys. Only Jesus knew that, at some time, the swimmer would become fatigued and would drown. And so Jesus was willing—nay, eager—to sit and sup with the sinners.

What he had to offer was not recrimination. Not condemnation. Not a recital of errors. Love . . . Mercy . . . Forgiveness . . . No one understood the weaknesses of the human heart as well as Jesus, and no one was as willing to spend time trying to save one contaminated soul while the healthy and righteous ones grumbled outside the door.

And when the time came to die he flinched from it and worried and sweat blood and felt a convulsive agony even before the busy little man came to the garden to kiss him. Men have gone to death more stoically than this. From the time of the caves on down, the wind-whipped pages of history are replete with the faces of men who looked directly into the face of death and who had a smile for a superior enemy.

Jesus did not come here to be brave. He came to be tested as a human being. He came to suffer and to feel pain beyond the power to endure, to be humiliated, and to die.

What was needed—in human form—was one who was sensitive and hypersensitive; one whose mind could be made prey to all the horrors ahead before each one arrived; one who had lived long enough to learn to love all men and who was willing to undergo torture at the hands of those to whom he gave his heart.

There was no other way. The pain had to be magnified in a man who could weep. This too was Jesus.

Indecisiveness is not compatible with the character of God, even when God imposes upon himself the limitations of human mentality. Once Jesus seemed indecisive. This occurred at the Feast of the Tabernacles. His "brothers" in Galilee urged him to go to Jerusalem for the feast: "Since you are having such success," they said, "let your light shine before the world."

Jesus said he would not go. The world, he said, hated him because he exposed its wickedness. "I am not going up to this feast; my time has not quite come as yet."

After everyone had left for the feast, Jesus remained in Galilee and he was alone. He knew that, in Jerusalem, the politicians were aready plotting against his life and now, in a sense, he was pitting himself against his own creatures because he had to weigh the amount of good he might do with his preachments in Galilee against the amount of harm which might be done by the crowing questions of the Pharisees in Jerusalem, who would demand of the disciples why the Messiah was not in the temple at this high holy time. In spite of risk, Jesus should be in the temple.

He was in a dilemma. He was here to save man, but man was plotting to kill him; Jesus was pointing the road to eternal life; man was leading Jesus to death. Suppose he appeared at the temple and the Pharisees stirred up the crowds and the plot against his life came to a quick boil? Too much had yet to be done; too many words had yet to be uttered; too many lessons had yet to be drilled into those poor twelve who would carry the New Testament in their hearts and on their tongues.

Of a sudden, he decided to go. He went up to the Holy City alone, shunning the crowds en route and arriving incognito. Along the marble flagstones of the courts, the Pharisees loudly asked: "Where is this man? Why isn't he here, in the house of his so-called Father?" The people listened to the questions and some said: "He is a good man." Others said: "Not at all. He leads the masses astray."

The feast was half over when Jesus stood on the temple steps to teach. He carried some written tracts in his hand and some of the temple priests watched and said: "How is it that this man is able to read? He has had no regular schooling." This proves that, at this early date, Jesus had been investigated by the temple authorities, who must have sent investigators all the way to Galilee to inquire about his past.

Standing there, Jesus looked older than he was. His public life, short as it had been, had begun to chisel little lines of worry about his eyes, little skeins of fatigue lines around the mouth. He was thinner than he had been at the marriage feast of Cana. His voice was as strong as ever, and the arms made large masculine sweeps for emphasis as he spoke. But the strain of being man, and being spurned by man, was beginning to chip the sides of this sturdy oak.

"My teaching is not my own invention," he said, looking over the heads of the people to the priests. "It is his whose ambassador I am. Anyone in earnest about doing his will can form a judgment of my teaching, to decide whether it originates with God, or whether I speak my own mind. He who speaks his own mind is looking for his personal glory; but he who looks for the glory of him whose ambassador he is, is truthful and not given to deception."

The faces, like so many evenly spaced eggs in a crate and just as neutral in expression, stared up at him. The human side of Jesus was pleading for understanding. "Did not Moses give you the Law?" he shouted. "And yet, not one of you lives up to the Law! Why are you so anxious to kill me?"

The people smiled. And some cupped their hands and yelled: "You are not in your right mind; who is anxious to kill you?" He knew that the plot had its origin when he had cured the sick man on the Sabbath. The common people who stood before him knew nothing about this. Only the few Levites, standing in a group to the rear, knew that the great temple was beginning to gird itself against the blasphemer.

"One deed I have done," said Jesus, holding up one finger, "and you are all surprised at this. Moses gave you the rite of circumcision—not that it originates with Moses, but with the fathers—and you practice circumcision on the Sabbath. If a man may be circumcised on a Sabbath to prevent the Law of Moses from being broken, why are you enraged at me for restoring a whole man to health on a Sabbath? Do not judge according to appearances, but form your judgments on just grounds."

On the last day of the feast, the authorities of the temple sent guards to arrest Jesus, and this was the calculated risk which the Galilean had weighed before coming up to Jerusalem. He was not prepared to be arrested yet. While the guards were threading their way through the crowds, their ears could not blunt his words and they listened. They heard him talk of living water and belief in Jesus and his Father and the guards were muted and they stood quietly.

When Jesus had finished, they heard many say: "This is really the prophet!" "This is the Messiah!" Some dissented and said that, according to Scripture, the Messiah could not come from Galilee and this man came from Nazareth in Galilee. The Messiah would have to come of the family line of David and he would come out of David's city, Bethlehem.

The temple police returned to the high priests who said: "Why did you not bring him?" The guards shook their heads with disbelief. "Never," they said, "has man spoken as this man speaks!"

The Pharisees exchanged glances. One said: "Have you, too, perhaps, been led astray? Has anyone of the authorities or of the Pharisees ever believed in him?" The unnamed Pharisee uttered the sentence which would ring hollowly down the corridors of time. "Oh," he said in exasperation, "this rabble which does not know the Law is a damnable pack!"

Nicodemus was present. He who sneaked at night to interview Jesus stood and listened. Now his conscience pried his mouth open. "Does our Law condemn a man," he said timidly, "without first hearing what he has to say and inquiring what he is doing?"

The Pharisee glanced at the member of the Great Sanhedrin and he chuckled. "Are you, too, perhaps from Galilee?" he said. "Search the Scriptures and see for yourself that prophets are not raised in Galilee."

In the morning, Jesus was again at the temple and now the Feast of the Tabernacles was over and only the cosmopolites of Jerusalem remained. They came to him in crowds because he was now a controversial figure. He was a topic. A man should know something about the Galilean Messiah and be able to say: "I saw him. I heard him. Let me tell you what I think. . . ." The people stood before the steps leading from the Court of the Gentiles to the Court of the Women and he stood a few steps above them.

As always, he was teaching, and what he was teaching was that the relationship between God and man was far simpler than all of the trappings which they attached to it. He was opposed to all displays of piety; he opposed the use of external boasts; likewise, he denounced all the formalistic stages of worship; he had spoken out against the building of tombs to the dead. He espoused charity and brotherhood and love with no hope of reward. His Father, he said, expected glory from the people and, in return, would glorify them. Baptism, to him, meant a renunciation of the old and an embracing of the new with a disavowal of all past sins; the way to heaven was not crowded with those who counted their goodnesses, but rather with those who felt that they were the poorest and least of all people.

He was still talking when the Scribes and the Pharisees led a shrinking, frightened woman to him. She was in shame. She was a wife who had been caught in an act of adultery. This morning they were going to catch Jesus in his trap of love and pity and commiseration. The law about adultery was explicit; it had come down from Moses, whose words could not be contravened: the penalty was stoning.

"Rabbi," the leader said loudly, because he wanted to expose Jesus before the people, "this woman has been caught in the act of committing adultery." They held her by the wrists and she tried to shrink to the ground. Her head hung down and her dark hair covered her face. One of the Pharisees reached down and lifted a huge skein of hair from her features, so that all the men in the court could look at her. "Now in the Law, Moses has commanded us to stone women of this kind. What, then, do you say?"

Jesus did not glance at the woman. He walked down the two steps onto a little square of sand and stooped, in silence. With his index finger, he drew little circles in the earth. If he upheld the law, the woman would die just as though he—and not the law—had condemned her. This was not consistent with his preachment of love and forgiveness. If he ordered her to be freed, he would thereby oppose the revered judgment of the great Moses, who had led the Jews out of bondage and had made the pact with God which led to the gift of the Ten Commandments.

At last he raised his head, as though in assent to the law, and said: "If there is one among you free from sin, let him be the first to throw a stone at her." He crouched again and drew more figures in the sand. The Pharisees and the Scribes thought about his words, and they looked at one another. Then, one by one, so that it would not be noticeable to the crowd, they stole away.

The people waited, but nothing was said. They shifted from foot to foot and Jesus continued to draw the odd little figures with his finger. At last only the woman, shaking and sobbing, was left on the steps. Then Jesus raised his head and looked at her for the first time. He said quietly, "Where are they? Has no one condemned you?"

"No one," she whispered.

"Neither do I condemn you," he said, standing erect. "Go, and from now on, sin no more."

In the evening, he sat with his apostles on top of the Mount of Olives. The sun was like a red ball on top of the cypresses fringing the hills behind the walled city of Jerusalem, and it tipped the golden spires of the temple and traced blue patterns on the near side of the great wall. He sat looking at the lovely jewel of Jerusalem which he loved, but he knew that she would never be his. He longed for Jerusalem, and she would treat him not as a bridegroom but as a murderer.

When the twelve saw him sitting like this, thinking, they did not break in on his thoughts. They busied themselves with the many followers and with the feeding of families and the bedding down of groups for the night. The dark little man Judas used the early evening to balance his accounts; to count the money which had been contributed by the sympathetic people that day; to dole out money for food for all the followers of Jesus; to complain to the other apostles about excessive expenditures; to secure the purse inside his girdle. Sometimes, he took a donkey and went into Jerusalem to bargain for vegetables and marrow and bread.

The gates of Jerusalem were always jammed with beggars. There were eight big gates and the blind, the limbless, the chronically sick sat—each at his appointed place—holding out dry, fleshless hands to passing pilgrims, crying piteously for a piece of silver. They were filthy and scabby and they begged mercy in the name of Yahweh.

One day, coming through the Probatic Gate, the apostles noticed one who was blind and who was trying to feel his way along the wall to the temple. He had been born blind. They knew this because he had no eyes and the lids were, it seemed, sewed together.

"Rabbi," they said to Jesus, "who has sinned, this man or his parents to account for his being born blind?"

The Messiah turned to look. "Neither this man has sinned," he said quietly, so that the blind man would not hear him, "nor his parents. No.

God simply wants to make use of him to reveal his ways." He stopped. A few feet away, leaning against the wall, the blind one stopped.

"Our duty," said Jesus to the twelve, "is, while it is day, to conform to the ways of him whose ambassador I am. Night is coming on, when no man can do anything. As long as I am in the world, I am the light of the world." He pursed his lips and spat upon the ground. Then he stooped and with his fingers turned the clay over in the spittle and made a lump of it. By this time, much of the traffic through the gate had stopped and pilgrims were standing by to watch.

Jesus took the wet clay and walked over to the sightless man and began to spread the soil over the soft emptiness of the sockets. "Go," he said to the man, "and wash in the pool of Siloam." The beggar started off nervously, murmuring to himself and spreading his fingers against the cool stone of the wall. The Messiah went on to the north side of the Court of Gentiles to teach.

He was there about an hour and the sun was getting high when the blind man came back, hysterically pawing at his face and screaming that he could see. He was followed by a crowd who had seen him washing his eyes in the pool down near the Fountain Gate, and who were scarcely less ecstatic about the miracle. The noise and general tumult brought out some of the Levites and priests. Others, who had been listening to Jesus, looked at the man, whose eyes were now weeping real tears, and they said: "Is this not the fellow who used to sit and beg?"

Many nodded and said: "This is the man." Others said: "Not at all, he only looks like him." The man with the new eyes went through the crowd shouting: "I am the man; I am the man!" The Levites said to him: "How, then, were your eyes opened?" He said happily: "The man called Jesus made a lump of clay and spread it over my eyes and said to me: 'Go to Siloam and wash.' So I went and washed, and got my sight."

The news spread swiftly and people hurried from all over the city. The priests took the former blind man into the temple and said: "Where is this man?" He looked about and shrugged. "I do not know." They took him before the Pharisees and, the moment they heard the story, they reminded their listeners that today was the Sabbath.

"That man has no authority from God," they told the former blind man. "He does not observe the Sabbath." Others among the Pharisees began to argue: "How can a sinner give such proofs of power!" They fell to disputing the case among themselves, and that there was any argument at all proved that Jesus had friends, even among the powers of the temple. One of them turned to the beggar and said: "What do you say about him, because he opened your eyes?" The man said simply: "He is a prophet!"

The high priests and some of the members of the Sanhedrin became excited about the case, and they hoped to prove to the people of the city that the man who could see was not the blind beggar they knew. They held an extraordinary hearing on the matter in the temple and summoned the parents of the beggar.

"Is this your son?" they said, pointing to the man who could see.

"Yes," the old couple said.

"And do you say that he was born blind?"

"Yes."

"How then is he at present able to see?"

The old couple were afraid. They had heard that the authorities were opposed to the man of miracles and they had threatened to put out of the temple anyone who espoused him. The father of the blind man stammered in the august presences: "We know that this is our son, and that he was born blind," he said, "but how he is now able to see we do not know, nor do we know who opened his eyes. Ask him yourself; he is old enough, he will give his own account."

Later in the day the high priests summoned the man who had been blind. As he entered, the priests said: "Give glory to God!" Then, referring to Jesus, they said: "We know that this man is a sinner."

The beggar was not afraid. "Whether or not he is a sinner," he said, "I do not know; one thing I do know: I was blind and now I see."

"What did he do to you?" they asked. "How did he open your eyes?"

"I told you already," he said, "and you did not listen. Why do you want to hear it again? Do you, too, perhaps want to become his disciples?"

A tumult arose in the room. The priests beat their breasts and abused the cured man. "You are a disciple of that man," they shrieked with venom; "we are disciples of Moses. We know that Moses is God's spokesman, but whose mouthpiece this man is we do not know."

"Why," the beggar said, "the strange thing is that you do not know whose mouthpiece he is when, as a matter of fact, he has opened my eyes! We know that God does not listen to sinners; but when one is God-fearing and does his will, he does listen to him. Since the world began, it is unheard of that anyone opened the eyes of one *born* blind! If this man had no mission from God, he could do nothing."

In disgust, the priests said: "You were wholly born in sin and you mean to teach us?" They ordered the guards to throw the beggar from the temple.

The news reached Jesus and he sought the beggar.

"Do you believe in the Son of God?" Jesus said.

"Well," the beggar said cautiously, "who is he, sir? I want to believe in him."

"You are now looking in his face," Jesus said. "Yes, it is he who is now speaking to you!"

In the days and weeks and months after the Feast of the Tabernacles in A.D. 28, the name of Jesus was a prime topic in Jerusalem. The miracles of the restoration of the old cripple and the blind beggar had set the tongues to wagging in high places and low.

With each passing day, the number of his followers among the Jews increased, although the number of plotters remained small—probably less than a hundred men. But this small group was, of course, powerful. Even so, no one dared to take a chance with the temper of the people, because rioting led to Roman intervention and that, in turn, led to a lessening of the temporal powers of the priests. So nothing was done.

The Messiah retired from Jerusalem and went into the country. It was time for the new gospel to be preached by many voices in many cities. When he first arrived in Galilee, Jesus said nothing about the organization of missionaries. He first went into the synagogue to teach. These edifices, throughout Palestine, had a uniformity of design. They consisted of one large rectangular room. The steps leading to the synagogue were almost always on the side of the building facing Jerusalem (in Galilee, the southern) and, inside, the congregation faced the door. It was common to have the room divided by rows of columns. In the back there was a matroneum, or women's balcony. In front of the building there was a stone basin on a pedestal for the washing of hands.

Sometimes, when the congregation was rich, paintings and mosaics adorned the walls, but these were always of flowers or trees or bodies of water because the Jews would not reproduce the image of an animate object. Small rooms flanked the main one, and these were used to teach the children of the town. In the front of the big room, near a small pulpit, stood the sacred cabinet ('aron) facing Jerusalem and, within it, the scrolls of holy Scripture. A perpetual lamp was kept burning before this cabinet, or ark.

Round stools were scattered about the room and the men sat on these. Those in the first row were reserved, and individuals of the congregation aspired to these places of honor. At services, the texts of the Torah to be read were uttered in Hebrew but, as very few understood the language, each portion had to be read a second time in Aramaic.

When Jesus stopped in at the local synagogue in Capharnaum, it was the Sabbath and he was duty-bound to be there in the morning and again in the afternoon. At the morning session, he walked in with a great crowd following. Among them were some Pharisees from Jerusalem, and these became interested when they saw a man standing inside the door with a withered hand. He looked imploringly at Jesus. The Messiah stopped.

Would he cure again on the Sabbath? He would. Jesus looked at the crowd of men and said: "What man shall there be among you who has one sheep and, if he falls into a pit on the Sabbath, will not take hold of him and lift him up?" No one answered. "How much better is a man than a sheep? Therefore, it is lawful to do a good deed on the Sabbath days." He ordered the man to hold the withered hand out in front of him. Jesus made a sign over it and it became a healthy hand.

The Pharisees whispered among the congregation, saying that Jesus was evil and should be destroyed. The Messiah left the place and walked to the edge of the Sea of Galilee. But now, added to all the people who normally followed wherever he went, were many Galileans who had heard that he was now performing miracles in his own neighborhood, and they brought with them all the lame and the sick and the blind and the withered that they could find.

They pressed so close to him that Jesus stood with his back to the breaking waves and quietly asked his apostles to have a boat waiting for him "lest they throng me." He healed many, and many asked him merely to touch them, and he did. The sinners in the crowd fell to their knees and cried: "You are the Son of God!" He then asked them, with rare asperity, not to make him known and not to discuss the work that he had done that day. His heart and mind were full, for shortly he would define, in a single sermon, a great many of the basic tenets of what would later be known as the Christian Church.

He went up on the side of the mountain, and with him trudged the twelve. There he gave them power to heal the sick, the lame, the crippled, the blind, and he gave them power to cast out devils. He charged the twelve with their responsibility in having this power, and there on the mountain he gave them their first and most important lesson as men who would carry his word to the ends of the earth. Below, the multitude listened.

They sat about him on rocks and he spoke slowly and feelingly, so that they would understand, and most of all, remember. They sat in silence, listening and, at times, nodding with understanding.[18]

"Blessed are the poor in spirit," Jesus said, "for theirs is the kingdom of heaven. Blessed are the meek and gentle for they will inherit the land. Blessed are the sorrowing, for they will be consoled. Blessed are those who hunger and thirst after holiness, for they will be fully satisfied. Blessed are the merciful, for they willl have mercy shown to them. Blessed are the singlehearted, for they will see God."

Sometimes he paused, as though thinking, and then he continued. "Blessed are the promoters of peace, for they will rank as children of God.

Blessed are the victims of persecution for conscience' sake, for theirs is the kingdom of heaven. Blessed are you when you are reviled, or persecuted, or made a target for nothing but malicious lies—for my sake. Rejoice; yes, leap for joy; a rich reward awaits you in heaven. So, too, were the prophets persecuted who preceded you.

"You are the salt of the earth. But suppose salt should lose its savor, what is there to restore its nature? It is no longer good for anything except to be thrown out of doors and trampled upon by passersby.

"You are the light of the world. It is impossible for a city to escape notice when built on a mountaintop. Nor do people light a lamp and then hide it under a bushel-basket. No, it is set on a lampstand that it may give light to all in the house. Just so let your light shine before your fellowmen, that they may see your good example and praise your Father who is in heaven."

The high cirrus were standing still. The afternoon was dozing its way into dusk. Below, a moored boat was slapped by little waves. Still, the great crowd below stood hushed. The apostles sat in several attitudes of listening. The eyes of Jesus were on the apostles and he laced his fingers together as he told them the basic rules for attaining eternal life.

"Do not think it is my mission to annul the Law or the Prophets," he said, looking up. "It is not my mission to annul, but to fulfill. I assure you emphatically: before heaven and earth pass away, not a single letter or one small detail will be expunged from the Law—no, not until all is accomplished. Whoever, therefore, breaks one of these least commandments and instructs his fellowmen to do likewise, will be of lowest rank in the kingdom of heaven. He, on the contrary, who both observes and inculcates them will win high distinction in the kingdom of heaven. Yes, let me tell you: if your religion is not very much better than that of the Scribes and Pharisees, you will not enter the kingdom of heaven."

This, to the apostles, was most important. They sat enraptured because as Jesus had moved more deeply into his mission on earth, they began to fear for their old faith: the faith of Israel. Each of them had been born a Jew—as had Jesus—and the faith of the fathers is important to all good men of every age. Now he was telling them that he too subscribed to the faith of Abraham and Moses; his criticism of it lay in the observance of the covenant. Without changing the law, he proposed to observe the spirit of it, while the Pharisees and Sadducees observed only the letter of it. He proposed to take the old law and to modernize it with the teachings of the Father, the Son and the Holy Ghost.

"You have heard that it was said to the men of old," he continued, "'Do not murder' and 'He who commits murder is answerable to the court.' I, on the contrary, declare to you: anyone who is angry with his brother is answerable to the court; anyone who says to his brother, 'You imbecile' is answerable to the Supreme Council; anyone who says 'You fool' must answer for it in the fiery pit. Suppose, then, you are about to offer your gift at the altar, and there remember that your brother holds something against you; leave your gift there before the altar, and first go and make up your quarrel with your brother; and then come back and offer your gift."

This was almost too subtle even for the apostles. The incisive criticism of worship, as practiced in Judea, is pointed up here by negation; many pilgrims paid homage to Yahweh with hatred in their hearts. Jesus was laying down as law (note the use of "I declare to you . . .") that no sacrifice was good in the eyes of God unless the worshiper was clean of heart. Better to leave the sacrifice on the altar and go out and purify the heart with love, and then come back.

"Show a kindly disposition toward your opponent in good time," he said, "while you are on the way to court with him; otherwise, your opponent hands you over to the judge, and the judge to the jailer, and you are thrown into prison. And mark my words: you will not be released from that place until you have paid the last penny."

"You have heard it said: 'Do not commit adultery.' I, on the contrary, declare to you: anyone who glances at a woman with a lustful intention has already committed adultery with her in his heart. If your right eye tempts you to sin, pluck it out and throw it away; it is better for you that one of your members should perish than that, body and all, you should be thrown into the infernal pit. And if your right hand tempts you to sin, cut it off and throw it away; it is better you that one of your limbs should perish than that you should be thrown, body and all, into the infernal pit.

"It has been said: 'To effect a divorce, let a man give his wife a writ of separation.' I, on the contrary, declare to you: anyone who divorces his wife—except on the score of lewdness—makes her a party to adultery; and so, too, he who marries a divorced woman is an adulterer.

"Again, you have heard it was said of old: 'Do not swear falsely, but you must redeem your promises made under oath to the Lord.' I, on the contrary, declare to you: do not swear at all, whether by heaven, for it is God's throne; or by the earth, for it is his footstool; or by Jerusalem, for it is the city of the Great King; nor should you swear by your own head, for you cannot make a single hair white or black. Let your speech be 'yes,' when you mean yes, and 'no,' when you mean no. Whatever is in excess of these expressions is due to the evil in the world.

"You have heard it said: 'An eye for an eye, and a tooth for a tooth.' I, on the contrary, declare to you, do not meet evil with evil. No, if someone strikes you on your right cheek, turn to him the other as well. And if a man intends by process of law to rob you of your coat, let him have your cloak as well. And if someone forces you to go one mile with him, go two miles with him. Give to anyone who asks you, and if someone would borrow from you, do not turn away.''

Jesus was now forging the essence of a new testament and the hammer blows of his words were striking hard against the harsh instrument of the existing scriptures, which permitted revenge and extermination of enemies. In effect, he was remodeling a worn tool.

''You have heard it said: 'Love your neighbor, and hate your enemy.' I, on the contrary, declare to you: love your enemies and pray for your persecutors, and thus prove yourselves children of your Father in heaven. He, certainly, lets his sun rise upon bad and good alike, and makes the rain fall on sinners as well as saints. Really, if you love those that love you, what reward do you deserve? Do not tax collectors do as much? And if you have a friendly greeting for your brothers only, are you doing anything out of the common? Do not the heathen do as much? Be perfect, then, as your heavenly Father is perfect.

''Take care not to practice your religion before your fellowmen just to catch their eyes; otherwise, you will have no reward with your Father in heaven. For example: when you are about to give alms, do not send a trumpeter ahead of you as the hypocrites do in the synagogues and streets to win the applause of their fellowmen. I tell you plainly, they have their reward already. When you give alms, your left hand should not know what your right is doing. Thus your alms is given in secrecy, and your Father, who sees what is secret, will reward you.

''Again, when you pray do not be like the hypocrites, for they love to pray standing in the synagogues or at street corners to attract the attention of their fellowmen. I tell you plainly, they have their reward already. When you pray, retire to your private room and bolt the door, and then pray to your Father in secrecy. And your father, who sees what is secret, will reward you.

''Moreover, when you pray, do not use many and idle words, as the heathen do; for they think that their glibness will win them a hearing. So do not imitate them. Surely, your Father is acquainted with your needs before you ask him. . . .

''Again, when you fast, do not imitate the gloomy-looking hypocrites. They go about unkempt and unwashed, so that their fasting may be noticed by their fellowmen. I tell you plainly: they have their reward already. When you fast, anoint your head and wash your face; thus your fasting will be noticed, not by your fellowmen, but by your Father in secrecy; and then your Father, who sees what is secret, will reward you.

"Do not lay up treasures for yourselves on earth, where moth devours and rust consumes, and where thieves break in and steal; but lay up treasures for yourselves in heaven, where neither moth devours nor rust consumes, nor thieves break in and steal. After all, where your treasure is, there, too, your heart is bound to be.

"The eye serves your person as a lamp; so long, then, as your eye is sound, your whole person will have light; but when your eye is defective, your whole person will grope in the dark. Consequently, if your inward lamp is darkened, how dense will that darkness be!

"A man cannot be the slave of two masters. He will either hate the one and love the other, or, at least, be attentive to the one and neglectful of the other. You cannot have money and God for masters.

"I tell you, therefore: do not fret about what to eat, or what to drink, to sustain your life, or about what to wear on your bodies. Is not life more precious than food, and the body more precious than clothing? Look at the birds of the air: they do not sow, or reap, or store up provisions in barns, and yet your heavenly Father feeds them. Are not you more precious than they? And which of you can by fretting add one minute to his span of life? And as for clothing, why do you fret? Observe the lilies of the field! How they grow! They do not toil or spin; and yet, I tell you, even Solomon in all his glory did not dress like one of these. Now if God so clothes the grass in the field, which is there today and is thrown into the furnace tomorrow, will he not much more readily clothe you?" Jesus shook his head from side to side, slowly. "What little faith you have!

"Therefore, have done with fretting, and do not constantly be asking: 'What are we going to eat?' or, 'What are we going to drink?' or, 'What are we going to wear?' Why, the heathen make all these things an object of eager search; besides, your heavenly Father knows that you need all these things. No, let your first concern be the kingdom of God and what he requires of you; then you will have all these things thrown in for good measure. In short, have done with fretting about the morrow. The morrow, surely, can do its own fretting. One evil a day is burden enough."

The crowd was taken with the beauty of the words which came from Jesus' lips so slowly and so distinctly. But their minds were filled to overflowing as the Messiah moved to the close of his discourses.

"Do not judge, that so you may not be judged; for the sentence you pass will be passed upon you, and the measure you use in measuring will be used to measure out your share. Strange that you see the splinter in your brother's eye and do not notice the log in your own! Or, how can you say to your brother, 'Let me take the splinter out of your eye,' when, think of it, there is a log in your own eye? Hypocrite! First, take the log out of your own eye, and then you will see clearly enough to take the splinter out of your brother's eye.

"Do not give to dogs what is sacred. And do not throw your pearls before pigs; otherwise, they may trample them underfoot, and then turn around and tear you to pieces.

"Ask, and you will receive; seek, and you will find; knock, and you will gain admission. In fact, only he who asks receives; only he who seeks finds; only he who knocks will gain admission. Really, will anyone among you give a stone to his son that asks him for bread? or a snake, when he asks for a fish? Well, then, if you, bad as you are, choose to give useful gifts to your children, how much more will your Father in heaven give what is good to those that ask him!

"In short, in all respects do by your fellowmen exactly as you wish them to do by you. This, surely, is the gist of the Law and the Prophets.

"Enter by the narrow gate, for wide and spacious is the gateway that leads to destruction; and many there are who enter by it! But oh, how narrow and obstructed is the gateway that leads to life, and few there are that find it!

"Beware of false prophets—people that come to you in sheep's clothing, but inwardly are ravenous wolves. By their conduct you can tell them. Are grapes picked from thornbushes? or figs from thistles? In the same way, as every good tree bears healthy fruit, so a sickly tree bears fruit that is bad. As a good tree cannot bear fruit that is bad, so a sickly tree cannot bear healthy fruit. Any tree that does not produce healthy fruit is cut down and thrown into the fire. Evidently, then, by their conduct you can tell them.

"Not everyone that says to me, 'Lord, Lord,' will enter the kingdom of heaven, but only he that does the will of my Father who is in heaven. Many will say to me on that Day: 'Lord, Lord, did we not prophesy in your name, and in your name drive out demons, and perform many miracles in your name?' But I will tell them plainly: 'I have never had anything to do with you! Leave my presence, you inveterate evildoers!'

"In short, whoever hears these words of mine and acts accordingly is like a sensible man who built his house upon rock: the rain poured down and the floods came and the winds blew and beat against that house; but it did not collapse. It was founded upon rock. And whoever hears these words of mine and does not act accordingly is like a foolish man who built his house upon sand: and the rain poured and the floods came and the winds blew and beat against that house, and it collapsed. In fact, the collapse of it was complete."

Jesus stood; he must have been tired, but, at the same time, exalted. He had finished his Sermon on the Mount. Below, the people were

stunned for a moment. Then they shouted their hosannas to him and
the apostles stood and smiled. Some said that there was enough food in
what the Messiah had said to last a man a lifetime. Others said that they
detected a new authority in the way he handed down the revised law. The
story of the wonders of Jesus was carried on every vagrant breeze over the
land, and in places where he had never been, Jews wept with joy and dared
to hope that this, for certain, was the true Messiah at last.

There were the miracles in Galilee—a leper cured; likewise, the servant
of a Roman centurion afflicted with palsy; a few others. But the work of
organizing the apostles proceeded, and was the most important work to
be concluded before the final assault on Jerusalem.

"The harvest is indeed great," Jesus said with sorrow to the twelve,
"but the laborers are few." His heart's desire was to save Israel first, before
spreading his gospel to the rest of the world, but there weren't enough
missionaries even for his own people. "Therefore, pray the owner of the
harvest to send out laborers to do the harvesting."

He sent the apostles on the first missionary tour—a small one into the
neighboring provinces; a human test—and, before they left, he admonished
them about many things:

"Do not turn aside into Gentile territory, and enter no Samaritan
town. Instead, go to the lost sheep of the house of Israel. As you go along,
preach on this text: 'The kingdom of heaven is close at hand.'

"Listen!" he said. "I am sending you like sheep among a pack of
wolves. Be prudent, then, like serpents; yet, for all that, as innocent as
doves. Beware of your fellowmen: they will try to hand you over to courts
of justice and to flog you in their synagogues; you will even be brought
before governors and kings for my sake.

"It will be your chance to testify to Jew and Gentile. But once handed
over, do not be uneasy about how or what to speak; for at that moment
the words will be put into your mouth. In fact, not you are then the
speakers; no, the Spirit of your Father is then the Speaker inspiring
you. . . . You will be the scorn of all because you profess my name. But
he who holds out to the end will be saved.

"When you are persecuted in one city, flee to another; and when
you are persecuted in the other, flee to still another. . . .

"What I tell you in the dark you have to speak out in broad daylight;
and what you hear in a whisper you have to proclaim from the housetops.
And do not fear people that kill the body, but have no power to kill
the soul; rather, fear him who has power to ruin both body and soul in
the infernal pit. Do not two sparrows sell for a penny? And yet, not

one of them can drop dead to the ground without the consent of your Father. As for yourselves, the very hairs on your head have all been numbered. Away then, with all fear; you are more precious than whole flocks of sparrows."

Still once more he summed up the meaning and the importance of faith. "Everyone who acknowledges me before the world will, in turn, be acknowledged by me before my Father in heaven; but he who disowns me before the world will himself be disowned by me before my Father in heaven.

"Do not suppose that it is my mission to shed peace upon the earth; it is not my mission to shed peace but to unsheath the sword. . . . He who freely parts with his life for my sake will win it in the end."

This was startling to the apostles because it represented a departure from the meekness of the lamb to the violence of the militant. But, in spite of their shock, the twelve were learning that the doctrine of Jesus had facets, sides which, to the undiscerning, had no relation to one another.

"He who befriends you befriends me," he said in conclusion, "and he who befriends me befriends him whose ambassador I am. He who befriends a prophet on the ground that he is a prophet will get the reward of a prophet; and he who befriends a holy man on the ground that he is holy and will get the reward of a holy man. And whoever gives only a refreshing drink to one of these little ones, doing so because he is a disciple, will not, I tell you truly, go without his reward."

After his disciples had gone, two by two, to range the countryside, Jesus roamed Galilee, preaching and curing and raising the dead. He spoke many parables, and the Jews understood this subtle form of storytelling because they were given to it themselves.

Sometimes, he dined with tax collectors and sinners and they reclined together on the dinner couches. The Pharisees made much of this, and Jesus, hearing of it, said: "The sick have need of a physician, not the healthy. Make off, and learn what is meant by the words: 'Compassion is what I desire, and not sacrifice.' Indeed, it is my mission to call sinners, not saints. . . ."

Once, Jesus said, in almost lyrical prose, to the poor who were all about him: "O come to me, all you who are weary and overburdened, and I will refresh you. Take my yoke upon you and master my lessons, for I am gentle and humble of heart. Thus you will find refreshment for your souls. My yoke is easy and my burden light."

The mission of the twelve turned out well. So, from the many, Jesus picked seventy-two disciples and also sent them in pairs ahead of him to preach in the places he intended to visit.

When they returned, the seventy-two were joyful. "Lord," they sang, "even the demons are subject to us because we use your name!"

One afternoon, Jesus motioned to Peter and James and John to join him, and they went up the hill to pray. The three watched over Christ, standing a little distance away as they had done before. Suddenly they noticed that his face was radiant with light and that his clothes had changed to a luminescent white. And, while they watched, Moses and Elias came from above and conversed with Jesus. They were in halos of glory, and the three apostles looked and shut their blinded eyes and looked again.

Peter and James and John were overcome with awe, and they felt a drowsiness descend on them. When they awakened, they still saw Moses and Elias, but they were about to leave. Peter said: "Master, it is well that we are here. . . ." As he spoke, a cloud enveloped the apostles like a warm mist. They heard a voice ring out from above: "This is my son, the chosen one. Listen to him!"

The cloud dissipated. The voice ceased. The three apostles looked around. They were alone with Jesus. For a long time afterward, they told no one of what they had seen.

On still another day, the people of a town not only came to the road to meet Jesus, but they brought with them their babies and their children. The apostles, who tried to surround Jesus with a proprietary air, walked ahead and scolded the parents for all the noise the children made. Jesus hurried toward the center of the disturbance, and stopped the apostles. Then he looked at all of the infants and children, some of whom were shy, some of whom held his garment, and some of whom took a look at him and burst into tears.

Jesus' broadest smile of all appeared at this moment. Gently, his voice husky with emotion, he said: "Let the little children come to me, and do not stop them. The kingdom of God belongs to such as these. Yes, I assure you: he who does not accept the kingdom of God as a little child does will never enter it."

It was in December of A.D. 29 that Jesus arrived in Jerusalem for the Feast of Dedication. In the latter part of this month, he passed his thirty-fourth birthday with no observance of it. Whatever work had to be done, he had less than four months left in which to do it.

This was a cold day—a rare thing for Jerusalem—and the fresh winds came down from the Mount of Olives and across the Cedron and burst surflike over the temple walls. Jesus was walking up and down the Porch of Solomon, apparently in thought. The apostles stood in a group near the rail, watching him as always for a sign that he needed them, and watching also the Scribes and the Pharisees who paced with Jesus, and in front of him, with their questions.

"How long will you keep us in suspense?" they asked in pleading tones. "If you are the Messiah, tell us outright!"

Jesus looked at them with infinite patience. "I told you," he said, "but you refuse to believe. The things I am doing in the name of my Father testify in my behalf. The pity is, you refuse to believe because you do not belong to my sheep. My sheep listen to my voice. I know them, and they follow me, and I give them eternal life. They will not be lost in eternity, for no one can snatch them out of my hand. The Father, who has entrusted them to me, is all-powerful, and no one can snatch anything out of my Father's hand. The Father and I are one."

The last part of this reply—about the followers of Jesus remaining with him—might seem unrelated to the question. The Pharisees had asked him to proclaim himself the Messiah. This would be blasphemy, and they knew that if he admitted it, he would lay himself open to trial and death by stoning. However, Jesus realized that the main concern of the temple priests at this time was not his death, but the loss of Jews to the temple. So he told them, in effect, that no matter what happened to him, the temple would not be able to reclaim the sheep which it had lost to him. This, culminating in the final words "The Father and I are one," was too much for the Scribes and Pharisees and they ran off the portico and out into the courts to pick up stones.

When they returned, he had not fled. They stood, holding their rocks, glaring at him, and Jesus said to them, "Many a kindly deed have I performed under your eyes, with power from my Father. For which particular deed do you mean to stone me?"

"Not for a kindly deed do we mean to stone you," they shouted, "but for blasphemy, and because you, a man, make yourself God."

Jesus held out both hands. "Is it not written in your law that in the sight of the Lord you are gods? If it called gods those to whom the word of God was addressed—and the scripture cannot be annulled—will you then say 'You are a blasphemer' to him whom the Father has consecrated to his service . . . ?

"If I do not act as my Father does, then do not believe me. But if I do, then believe in the strength of my actions, even if you do not believe my words. Thus, the truth will dawn on you, and you will understand that the Father is in me and that I am in the Father."

They thought about his words. A few were placated but many insisted that the blasphemy had been repeated. They argued, and by the time they agreed to arrest Jesus he was gone.

He left after the Feast of Dedication, and this happened shortly after the 25th day of Kislew. This was the height of the rainy season (November–December) and, as Jesus and the apostles left Jerusalem at night to hide from the plotters, the temple behind them was lighted to its most dazzling. In the gusty winds and swirl of mist, the little group made its retreat to Perea.

Again the Holy City had defeated Jesus, and again so that he would not die before his time, he turned his back on the temple and departed. They went as far as Bethany on the first night, there to repose in the home of Jesus' good friend Lazarus, and of his sisters, Martha and Mary. He had stayed here often, when it was too cold or too wet to remain at the gethsemane, and as it was only two miles or a little more from the walls of Jerusalem, it was, in effect, part of the metropolitan area. So much confidence did Jesus repose in Lazarus and his sisters that often he left his Mother there when he was not certain of a good reception in Jerusalem.

In the morning, they started off through the wilderness, a stretch of twenty-three miles of ugly beige mountains between Jerusalem and Jericho. This was a bandit-infested road. Travelers feared it by day as well as by night, and many would not use it unless they joined a large caravan. From the wilderness, on the third day, Jesus and the apostles walked down out of the mountains into the lush green valley of Jericho, which appeared to lie like a sprig of parsley in the bottom of a bowl.

From Jericho they continued west across the River Jordan, and up into the tall forbidding Mountains of Moab. There they rested. There they hid. There Jesus told them about his impending death and what he expected of each of them before and after it happened. He stayed for some weeks, doing good works among the people of Bethabara and Mount Nebo. For a time, he went up to Ephrem, in Samaria, and there he rejoiced as he listened to reports from the seventy-two disciples he had sent out through the land. But, as a man and as a friend, he was saddened because he knew that, in the spring, he must die.

In the early part of March, a message came to Jesus from Martha and Mary, the sisters in Bethany. It said: "Please, Lord, your dear friend is ill."

The Messiah, who was teaching, said: "This illness will not result in death. No, it is to promote the glory of God. Through it the Son of God is to be glorified." So, unworried about his dear friend, Jesus continued to work in the same little town. Two days later, in the company of his apostles, Jesus stopped talking, looked pale, and said: "Let us go back into Judea."

"Master," his men said, "only recently the people of Jerusalem wanted to stone you to death, and you mean to go back there again?"

The Messiah appeared angry. "Are there not twelve hours to the day?" he said. "As long as a man walks in the day, he does not stumble, because he sees the light of this world. But when a man walks in the night, he stumbles, because he has no light to guide him."

They did not answer. They did not understand the decision, but they would abide by it. "Lazarus, our friend," Jesus said sadly, "has fallen asleep. Well, then, I will go and wake him from his sleep."

"Lord," the apostles said, "if he has fallen asleep, he will be all right."

The look of sadness deepened in the eyes of Jesus. "Lazarus is dead," he said. "For your sake I am glad I was not there, so that you may believe. Come now, let us go to him."

All of them believed that it would be fatal to go near Jerusalem. And all looked frightened except Thomas, who said: "Let us go also that we may die with him."

It was several hard days of journeying to get to Bethany, and when they arrived, it was learned that Lazarus had been in the tomb four days. The house, which was a little east of the tomb, was full of people who had come from Jerusalem to commiserate with the sisters.

Someone said that Jesus and the twelve were coming. Martha hurried out to meet them. Mary remained in the house with the mourners. When Martha saw Jesus coming up the road, his followers spread fanwise behind him, she could not restrain herself. "Lord," she wept, "if you had been here, my brother would not have died. And even now I know that whatever you ask of God, God will grant you."

Jesus studied the tear-stained face. "Your brother will rise again," he said, and started to walk toward the house.

"I know," said Martha sorrowfully, "he will rise again at the resurrection on the last day."

The Messiah put his hand to his chest. "I am the resurrection and the life," he said. "He who believes in me will live even if he dies; and no one who lives and believes in me shall be dead forever. Do you believe this?" he said to Martha.

"Yes, Lord," she said. "I firmly believe that you are the Messiah, the Son of God, who was to come into the world."

She hurried on ahead of him and called Mary aside. "The Master is here," she said, "and asks for you." At once, Mary excused herself and hurried through the mourners, who jammed every part of the house. The Pharisees and others who were indoors saw Lazarus' sister Mary hurry out, and assumed that she was on her way to the tomb up the street. They went to mourn with her, and followed. She ran to Jesus, and the Pharisees saw her drop to her knees at his feet and cry as her sister had: "Lord, if you had been here, my brother would not have died."

The Pharisees began to weep too. They had known Lazarus as a good man and a good friend. The sight of the girl in the dust, sobbing, was too much. The Messiah looked around and was moved by the sight of so many people in tears. (John said later that it shook Jesus' inmost soul.)

"Where have you laid him to rest?" the Galilean asked.

"Come and see, Lord," several people said. They started off, up the hilly street, and everyone was surprised to see Jesus suddenly pass his hand over his eyes and begin to weep. The tears were flowing down his face as he walked behind the leaders up to the tomb.

"Look," said some, "how dearly he loved Lazarus."

Others said: "He opened the eyes of the blind man; was he not able to prevent this man's death?"

A slab of stone lay tilted against the entrance of the underground tomb. "Remove the slab of stone," Jesus said softly.

Martha came running up, and she looked frightened. "Lord," she said, "the body is decayed by this time. He has been dead four days."

"Did I not tell you," Jesus said gently, "that, if you have faith, you will see the glory of God?"

The slab was lifted and turned away. Now they could look down into the dark interior, where water dripped from slimy rocks. Jesus folded his hands and, lifting his eyes up to the clouds, said: "Father, I thank you for giving ear to me. For myself, I know that you always hear me; but I said it for the sake of the people surrounding me, that they might believe that I am your ambassador."

He spread both arms out before him. His eyes were now fixed on the entrance to the tomb. "Lazarus!" he shouted, "come forth!" The people looked at the Messiah and then at the tomb. Nothing happened. Jesus stood with his arms out straight, staring ahead. The people were silent, and their hearts beat loudly with trepidation. They waited. They stared fixedly at the mouth of the tomb, and suddenly they saw a white ball, then a long white garment, and then the tottering feet, bound so as to be almost immobile.

It was Lazarus. The mouths of the people hung open in ghastly surprise as they saw him, wrapped in big broad muslin strips, his head covered, his hands bound to his sides. Over the head bandage was a white scarf.

"Unwrap him," Jesus said, "and let him go."

Many of the Pharisees believed for the first time. They acknowledged Jesus to be the Messiah. Others hurried back to Jerusalem, running most of the way, to tell the story of the great miracle to the high priests in the temple. When the news spread, Caiphas called a special session of the Great Sanhedrin at once.

They met in an atmosphere of worry. In the silent struggle between them and Jesus, these men had been losing. Now they had not only lost thousands of temple worshipers to him, but some of their own Pharisees were defecting. This was a grave matter. Whatever the decision might be, it could not be postponed any longer.

"This man," they testified, "is giving many proofs of power. What then are we to do? If we let him go without interference, all the world will believe in him. And then the Romans will come and put an end to our rank and race alike."

These words were well spoken. The problem had been stated succinctly. He was now raising the dead in the outskirts of Jerusalem. Tomorrow he might walk into the city and raise a prophet from the dead. And, as the member of the Sanhedrin had said, if Jesus continued without interference, soon the whole world would be impelled to believe in him; one could not restrain people from believing in a man who could, at will, accomplish the impossible. If that happened, the Roman legionnaires would move in and take the temple and abolish the rank and income of the high priests.

Something had to be done. What?

"You are not men of vision," Caiphas said calmly, almost sarcastically. "Can even you not understand that it is to our advantage that one man should die for the people so that the whole nation may be saved from ruin?"

The design of Caiphas was malice. He wanted to kill Jesus to save his own position. Still, unknown to him, Caiphas was part of a much larger design fashioned by God himself. Jesus had to die to redeem the sins of mankind, and it was necessary for someone to decree that he perish.

That day, the Great Sanhedrin passed a resolution to put Jesus to death. All that remained was for the high priest to determine the best way of carrying out the plan. The restraints placed upon Caiphas were that the will of the Sanhedrin must be carried out expeditiously; it must be done in a manner compatible with the law; most important of all, *it should be done without arousing the followers of the Galilean*. Thus, Caiphas was obliged to move with extreme caution; he could not arrest Jesus during daylight hours.

Jesus and the apostles left Bethany the same day and returned to Ephrem. They remained there two weeks and left in the last week of March. The pilgrims from all over the land had already started up toward Jerusalem for the Feast of the Passover, and Jesus and his group might have joined any caravan moving south. Instead, he and his apostles walked southeast to Jericho. There is a reason for this, as there is a reason for everything that Jesus did. He knew that this was to be his last journey.

Ephrem was on the road between Galilee and Jerusalem and he did not want to join a Nazareth or Capharnaum caravan and thus enter the Holy City with a show of neighborhood strength.

In Jerusalem, an order went out to all priests of the temple and all guards that, if anyone knew the whereabouts of Jesus, he should report it at once to Caiphas.

Early in the month of Nisan—the last week of March—Jesus led his little band out of Jericho on the final trip to Jerusalem. The apostles were afraid and there was a slowness in their feet. They tarried behind the master, seeking for further delay. He stopped and called them around him.

"We are going up to Jerusalem," he said, "and the Son of Man will be betrayed to the high priests and the Scribes, and they will condemn him to death and hand him over to the Gentiles. And they will mock him and spit on him and scourge him and put him to death. But after three days he will rise again."

They started to walk again, this time on a note of hope. The apostles could only bear the impending tragedy so long as they were repeatedly reminded that the Messiah would rise again and be with them three days after his death. They could make themselves forget the unbearable to concentrate on a single good aspect of a bad situation.

They were walking along, in good order, when James and John, the sons of thunder, walked ahead of the others and drew up beside Jesus. "Rabbi," they said, "we would like you to do for us whatever we ask of you."

"What would you like me to do for you?"

"Give us a seat, one at your right, the other at your left, in your glory."

His glory was in his death. He was to be remembered by man for a painful and degrading death. The brothers wanted to sit beside him in heaven.

"You do not realize what you are asking," he said to the bright young ones. "Can you drink the cup that I am to drink, and be baptized with the baptism with which I am to be baptized?"

"We can," they said.

"Yes," he said, looking far into the future. "You will drink the cup that I am to drink, and be baptized with the baptism with which I am to be baptized, but as for a seat at my right or left, that is not in my power to assign except to those for whom it has been reserved."

When the remaining ten heard what had happened, they became angry at James and John and quarreled with them. Jesus called them all together again and said: "You know that the distinguished rulers of the Gentiles lord it over their subjects, and that their princes tyrannize over them. That is not your way! On the contrary, he who would be a prince among you must be your servant, and he who would be a leader among you must be the slave of everyone. Why, even the Son of Man did not come into the world to be served but to serve and to give his life as a ransom for many."

One more afternoon and they were within sight of the eastern slope of the Mount of Olives. Jesus was now ready to begin his Passion. This was the year A.D. 30 by the Gregorian calendar, 784 by the Roman calendar, and 3790 by the Hebrew calendar. The day was March 31.

When he and his party reached Bethany, Jesus was received in triumph. He was a hero, and much more than a hero—he was one who could save all. Lazarus greeted the Messiah with tears; Simon the Leper, a rich man cured of his disease, greeted Jesus with awe; Mary and Martha met him with adoration; the people of Bethany shouted hosanna and the visitors from Jerusalem bowed low before him.

There was a dinner—a big dinner—given by Simon the Leper for all who would attend. Lazarus reclined on a couch beside Jesus, and Martha insisted on preparing the food and serving it. This was a gay dinner, and there was much happiness and Jesus was relaxed, almost carefree, among his followers. Outside the building multitudes waited to catch a glimpse of Jesus. Everyone paid homage to him, and again and again neighbors wanted to look at and touch and talk to Lazarus, whom they had seen dead.

The gaiety of the dinner was infectious, and Mary, sister of the practical Martha, left the room for a moment and returned with a pound of costly spikenard, a perfumed ointment from the East Indies. Intending to show love for the Messiah, she poured some of it over his head. Then, while the entire company gasped at her extravagance, Mary went to the foot of the couch and anointed the feet of her Saviour with the rest of it.

The lavender-like odor pervaded the house. The guests looked in astonishment on Mary who, smiling happily, finished rubbing the ointment into the feet of Jesus and now wiped the excess off with her long hair. Jesus said nothing. His eyes roamed the room, looking from one to another of the guests. All knew that the spikenard cost more than the entire dinner.

Still, there was no word of reproach until Judas, who reclined to the right of Jesus, sat up and said loudly enough for all to hear: "Why was not this perfume sold for three hundred denarii and the money given to the poor?" It was a good question, uttered a little late.

"Let her have her way," Jesus said, making a placating gesture to Judas. "It will turn out that she has reserved this perfume for the day of my embalmment." Indignation was on the face of Judas. "Besides," Jesus said softly, "the poor you always have with you, but you do not always have me."

The deed was done, and Jesus, who knew that he would be dead a week from this night, would not have it undone. The human side of him seemed to need additional marks of love, and this tribute by an impetuous girl was welcome.

By Sunday morning, the news of the arrival of Jesus was known in every alley in the Holy City. The people, not bound by the Sabbath, which expired the evening prior, came down the sloping road from the temple toward Bethany to greet him. They came in festive flocks, and the high priests, watching from the great height of Solomon's Porch, were vexed and passed a resolution condemning Lazarus to death. They knew that the raising of Lazarus from the dead had excited the people of Jerusalem to a pitch of frenzy for the Messiah; even some who had argued most vehemently that Jesus was not the elect of God were now admitting that he was, and were in the procession which set out to meet him.

It was a clear, cool, lustrous morning, with the spring sun spangling the dewy leaves, and the sky over the white marble of the temple spires was china blue. It was a day to drug the senses with goodness, and soon the road to Bethany was jammed with families, all of whom had their backs to the temple. Some of the pilgrims from Galilee joined their brethren from Judea and many began to pick branches of palm to lay down before the feet of the anointed.

In Bethany, Jesus thanked his hosts, and with his party of apostles and disciples was ready to leave. They walked out to the crossroads, and Jesus pointed to a village nestling against the slope of the Mount of Olives. He said to two of his disciples: "Go into the village directly in front of you, and as you enter you will find hitched a foal on which no man has ever sat. Unhitch it and bring it here.

"And, in case anybody asks you: 'Why do you unhitch it?' just say: 'Because the Lord has need of it.'"

The two went to the little village and found a young donkey, hardly more than three feet tall, tethered to a public post. They looked around and, seeing no one, untied the line. Two men walked up and, studying the apostles suspiciously, said: "Why do you unhitch the foal?" The chosen ones looked worried and said: "Because the Lord has need of it." The owners bowed low and turned away.

When the two apostles returned leading the donkey—it was gray, with dainty hoofs, as was common to the country—the others tossed their cloaks onto its back and Jesus, turning his back to the animal, jumped off his toes and sat sideward on the cloaks.

Some started to lead the animal by a halter, but the crowd pressed in heavily on both sides and there was no need to guide it. The road was so thick with people that many families were forced higher into the hills, to ensure a look at the Messiah. Those close to the side of the road threw their cloaks before the hoofs of the donkey and the owners of the capes counted themselves fortunate that the weight of the Saviour had pressed on their apparel. Others threw palms and early spring flowers.

The Messiah went up the eastern slope of the Mount of Olives, and, when he started down the western side, those who called themselves disciples of Jesus gasped as a panorama of people spread below them all the way to the northeastern gate of the temple. At once, the disciples burst into song:

A blessing on the King
who comes in the name of the Lord!
Peace in heaven
and glory in the heights above!

The donkey moved slowly, and the crowds pressed from all sides, crying, "Hosanna to the son of David!" and the people threw the palm branches out and made a pliant green road for him all the way to the city. The Pharisees cupped their hands above the din and said: "Rabbi, reprove your disciples!" But Jesus, moved by the demonstration, shook his head and said: "I tell you, if these are dumb, the stones will cry out."

The procession moved down the Mount of Olives and close to the garden of the gethsemane, then across the Brook Cedron and up the far side, past the cemetery of white stones and ossuaries, and into the northeastern gate, between the temple and the Fortress Antonia.

The Roman sentries looked down on the scene, and they called to their superiors to come look at the Jews in a happy mood. The hosannas rang to the sky and fathers held infants as high as possible to permit them to look up on the face of the Lord. A group of Sadducean priests tried to use this gate to the temple and were forced by the press of the mob to go around to the western side. They were frightened at what Jesus had done to the people of Jerusalem, and some reported to Caiphas that not only had the people acknowledged Jesus as the Messiah, but that some Pharisees and elders had been seen bending the knee to the faker. Unless something was done quickly, the temple would have no authority.

When Jesus reached the gate of the temple, he stopped the donkey.[19] The press of people on three sides of him was now augmented by pilgrims running from the Gentile court toward him.

Jesus broke down. Tears shimmered on his lids and then he sobbed. He bowed his head and murmured:

Oh, if you, too, did know,
at least on this your day,
what makes for peace!
But alas it is hidden from your eyes!
Days are coming upon you
when your enemies
will throw a rampart round you,
and encircle you,
and press hard upon you on every side;
and they will dash to the ground
both you and your children within,
nor will they leave stone upon stone
within your walls;
because you did not recognize
the time of your visitation.[20]

Only a few of his disciples, jammed tight against the foal, heard the words and saw the tears. Jesus dismounted and walked into the temple grounds. At once he saw that the money-changers and the animal sellers were back in business.

From the north side of the Porch of Solomon, the high priests watched him leave the multitude and again chase the merchants from the grounds. Jesus shouted: "The Scripture says: my house shall be a house of prayer; but you have turned it into a den of robbers."

He walked over to the place where some of the chief priests were standing. A group of little children who had been running up and down the courts stopped and turned their sunniest smiles on Jesus. "Hosanna to the son of David," they shrilled. "Blessed is he who comes in the name of the Lord!"

"Do you hear what these are saying?" the high priests said in tones of shock.

Jesus wiped his eyes and smiled at the young. "Yes," he said, "have you never read: 'Out of the mouths of infants and sucklings you have perfect praise'?"

The priests were in such a state of rage that they could no longer bear to watch the triumph of Jesus. He was anathema. It was beyond their comprehension to entertain, even for a moment, the thought that he might be the true Messiah, and it was equally beyond their comprehension to fathom the stupidity of a people who, in effect, were worshiping false gods by bowing the knee to Jesus on the temple grounds.

Jesus walked around in the outer court, the people making way for him and shouting praises to God for sending him to them. Some Greeks in the Court of the Gentiles approached the dark, good-looking Philip. "Sir," they said, "we would like to see Jesus."

This was an agreeable notion to Philip, and like the other apostles he was beside himself with happiness because this was a day of triumph for the Saviour. Jesus had predicted dire things—even death—and look, the people called him their Messiah! This indeed was the first day of Jesus' coming into his true kingdom on earth.

But in spite of his joyous excitement, Philip did not dare approach Jesus directly. He went to Andrew and pointed to the Greeks, telling the muscular fisherman that they would like to meet Jesus. Andrew thought about it and asked Philip to join him in speaking to Jesus.

The Messiah listened, and paused in his pacing. The Greeks came over in time to hear Jesus begin a dissertation and the populace crowded closely to hear his words. The radiance of his glance was reflected in the faces around him.

"Come at last is the hour for the Son of Man to be glorified!" he said. "I tell you the plain truth: unless the grain of wheat falls into the earth and dies, it remains just one grain; but once it has died, it bears abundant fruit." He made a small, graceful gesture with his hands. "He who holds his life dear destroys it; he who sets no store by his life in this world will preserve it for eternal life. Whoever would be in my personal service must follow me: and then, wherever I am, there, too, my servant will be. Whoever is in my personal service will be honored by the Father."

He paused and looked at the earth at his feet. The Greeks and the apostles and the people looked at one another to better understand the words of Jesus. Most of them had understood him to mean that, in the service of the Messiah, one should hold one's life cheaply and in that way save one's soul for eternal life and honor by God the Father.

The tall Galilean looked over the heads of the crowd and, instead of rejoicing, he seemed to be saddened. "Now is my soul shaken in its inmost depths," Jesus said, "and what shall I say: 'Father, save me from this ordeal'?" He shook his head negatively. "No, no," he said. "For this very purpose I am facing this ordeal." He sighed and in a tone of resignation and softly: "Father, glorify your name!"

Then a voice came from afar like thunder rolling through the hills. "I have glorified it and I will continue to glorify it." Some in the crowd began to pull their cloaks tighter and many said: "It has thundered." Others said: "No, an angel has spoken to him."

"Not for my sake," Jesus said, "has this voice rung out, but for yours. Now is the sentence of condemnation being passed upon this world; now is the prince of this world being evicted; and I, once I have been lifted up from the earth, will draw all men to myself."

The people were confused. The men stroked their beards and looked from one to another. They had heard the term "lifted up." It was an idiom of the times, like "to carry a tree." Both meant the same thing: crucifixion. But what did this have to do with the Son of Man or the prince of the world? How could the Son of Man be lifted up? By whom? And why? The Messiah had been promised to them for many hundreds of years and he was to come in honored glory, maybe on a cloud surrounded by legions of angels—maybe unknown out of Bethlehem, the city of David.

"We have been taught by the Law," they said respectfully, "that the Messiah is to remain forever. How, then, can you say that the Son of Man must be lifted up? Who is this Son of Man?"

"A little while longer," said Jesus, "will the light be among you. Walk while you have the light, or darkness will overtake you." Meaning: move swiftly toward acceptance of the Messiah while he is still here, or he will leave and, spiritually, you will be in darkness. But they did not understand.

In the higher recesses of the temple, some Pharisees watched the scene below. "Look, the whole world is running after him!" they said.

Jesus left and walked back toward Bethany with his apostles. They were elated; on the road their steps were light and they recollected happily the details of the great triumph for Jesus on this Sunday of palms. They hardly noticed that the Messiah was walking with his eyes downcast, focused on the stones of the road. He felt no sense of triumph.

For this was not the full triumph of God's truth. This was a day in the life of Jesus when his recognition was at its height, when the people tried hard to understand him and when they paid homage to him; but they did not truly understand his mission, and their questions proved it.

As the group left the walled city, one of the apostles marveled at the huge stones and the glittering white of the temple. "Look, Rabbi!" he said, moving in front of Jesus and pointing back. "What wonderful slabs of stone! What a wonderful edifice!" In an oblique manner, the apostle was questioning the prophecy about the destruction of the city.

The Master looked at him sorrowfully. "You admire this mighty edifice?" he said. "Not one stone will here be left upon another, but all will crumble to pieces."

A few of the others stopped their lighthearted progress to listen. And they pondered his words among themselves. They could not imagine the stones being reduced by siege—which is what was to happen—and the more they thought about the words, the more convinced they became that Jesus was talking about the end of the world.

This, too, was a topic which perpetually excited the people, because they had been taught, as part of the law, that it would come, although no man knew when. The apostles said nothing to Jesus about it at the time, but they waited until he had reached a big rock near the summit of the Mount of Olives. When he had sat down, Peter, James, John and Andrew asked him, as friend to friend:

"Tell us, when will this catastrophe take place? And what is the sign to indicate that the whole world is coming to an end?"

The Messiah sat facing the setting sun. In silhouette stood the Holy City. The air was cooling. On the slopes below, thousands of families set up their Passover abodes. In an hour the twenty-four gates of the temple would be closed and white smoke would bloom from the temple as the priests washed down the rock on the altar of sacrifice and stoked the fires for the night.

"See to it," Jesus said, "that no one leads you astray. Many will come and, assuming my title, say: 'I am he!' and many will they lead astray! And when you hear of wars or rumors of wars, do not be alarmed. These things must happen, but the end is not yet. . . ." He went on to tell them of flood, famine and personal agonies, and said: "You will be the scorn of all because you profess my name. But he who holds out to the end will be saved. . . ."

Still they wanted to know more of the world's end, and again he warned them of false prophets and told them of awful cataclysms. But, most important, he told them to be ready, to be prepared.

"Regarding that day or hour no one knows," Jesus said, looking at the four faces before him, "not even the angels in heaven, nor yet the Son, but only the Father. Look out, be wide awake! You do not know when the moment arrives. It is as when a man goes abroad: on leaving his house he gives his servants their authority, assigning to each his special task, but he directs the doorkeeper, in particular, to keep awake. Remain awake, therefore, for you do not know when the master of the house returns, whether late in the evening or about midnight, whether at cock-crow or in the small hours of the day. Otherwise he returns unexpectedly and finds you sleeping. What I say to you, I mean for all. Remain awake!"

Having spoken his dreadful warning, Jesus allowed his face to soften as he looked with affection upon his followers.

Jesus stood for a moment. Behind the city, the sky was outrageous in lavender bands and on the low fat clouds there were red stains. The wall of Jerusalem reflected a blue blanket down on the Cedron, and behind Jesus the young moon hung over Jericho. The fig trees on the hillside were silent eavesdroppers. Below, fires fought the darkness with little yellow ellipses. It was, if one had the time to look, a lovely evening.

Jesus turned toward Bethany and now the silver of the moon made his face look tired.

The Messiah was now only a few days from his death, and he spent those days in the temple, healing the sick and comforting the sick in heart.

On two of these nights he rested in Bethany at the home of Lazarus, where he saw his Mother and sat with her and tried to prepare her for something which would wrench her soul. He also spent the late hours talking to the disciples, telling them the scriptural story of the good news of his coming, and admonishing them to be charitable to all in his name. He called the twelve together for many lessons and he repeated some of the old lessons for them. Toward the middle of the week he and the chosen ones began to go at night to the little garden of gethsemane and at times Jesus surrendered to fatigue and slept; at others he was agitated and worried and his hands clasped and unclasped as he walked in the garden under the little lacy trees.

He was pacing his cell.

On Tuesday evening, April 4, he sat with the twelve so that they might understand what the judgment was going to be like. He squatted on a stone, elbows on knees, his hands making small gestures to accentuate the words, his head nodding in punctuation of the lessons to be learned from the discourse.

"When the Son of Man returns in his glory," he said, "and escorted by all the angels, he will seat himself on a throne befitting his glory. All the nations will assemble in his presence, and he will part mankind into two groups just as a shepherd parts the sheep from the goats. The sheep he will range at his right, and the goats at the left.

"Then the King will say to those at his right: 'Come, the elect of my Father! Take possession of the kingdom prepared for you at the beginning of the world. For I was hungry, and you gave me to eat; I was thirsty, and you gave me to drink; I was a stranger, and you took me into your homes; I was naked, and you covered me; I was sick, and you visited me; I was in prison, and you came to see me.' Then the saints will be surprised and say to him: 'Lord, when did we see you hungry and feed you? or thirsty and give you to drink? And when did we see you a stranger and take you into our homes? or naked and cover you? When did we see you sick or in prison, and come to visit you?' And in explanation the King will say to them: 'I tell you the plain truth, inasmuch as you did this to one of these least brethren of mine, you did it to me.'

"Next he will say to those at his left: 'Out of my sight, you cursed ones! Off into the everlasting fire prepared for the devil and his ministers! For I was hungry and you did not give me to eat; I was thirsty and you did not give me to drink; I was a stranger and you did not take me into your homes; naked, and you did not cover me; sick, and in prison, and you did not visit me.' Then they, in turn, will be surprised and say to him: 'Lord, when did we see you hungry or thirsty or a stranger or naked or sick or in prison and did not minister to your wants?' Then will he hurl back at them this answer: 'I tell you the plain truth: insofar as you failed to render these services to one of those least ones, you also failed to render them to me.' And so the latter will be consigned to everlasting punishment, while the saints will enter into everlasting life.''

The apostles nodded to each other. They understood this lesson. Jesus was speaking plainly. The Messiah stood and looked down at his weak army. ''You know that in two days the Passover is kept. On that occasion,'' he said, ''the Son of Man will be delivered up to be crucified.''

On one of the mornings toward the end—perhaps Wednesday—Jesus entered the temple enclosure for the final time. And once more the people shouted the good news to one another that the prophet from Galilee was back, and they hurried to the Court of the Gentiles to see him and to listen to his words. The priests also heard and they came too, out of the holy places and down ten feet to the Court of the Priests and then down again to the Court of the Women and once again down to the Court of the Gentiles.

There they confronted him. ''By what authority,'' they said, ''do you engage in this activity?''

If he said by the authority of God, he would be proclaiming himself the Messiah, and they could have made out a case against him before the huge crowd. So Jesus countered their wrath by answering a question with a question.

''Let me ask you one question,'' he said, ''and I will tell you by what authority I engage in this activity. John's baptism—was it from heaven or from men? Answer me.''

The priests glanced furtively at one another. The Galilean they were trying to trap in blasphemy had caught them in dilemma. They turned away in private consultation and they agreed that if they said the baptism of John was authorized by heaven, then the foundations of the temple would be cracked, because baptism by water was a new teaching alien to the law of Moses. If, on the other hand, they said that John's power to baptize had come from men, they would alienate the multitude now waiting for an answer because, almost to a man, the people believed that John the Baptist was a true prophet.

They turned back to Jesus and said frankly: ''We do not know.''

Then Jesus said: ''Neither will I tell you by what authority I am acting the way I am.''

A number of the sick were now carried to his presence while the crowd watched. At this time the priests returned. They were smiling as though they too were surrendering to the power of Jesus. In truth, they were going to try once more to ensnare him, and this time, on the advice of Annas and the council, they would try to make him guilty of preaching against the power of Caesar.

"Rabbi," they said in humility, "we know that in all your teaching you speak straightforwardly, and who a person is never worries you; on the contrary, you teach the way of God truthfully. Is it right for us to pay the poll tax to Caesar, or is it not?"

The crowd sighed. This indeed was a good question, a clever interrogation worthy of the old Hebrew schools of rabbinical argument. Like those ancient conundrums, it was designed so that a reply was impossible. If Jesus said that the payment of tax to the Gentile King was just, he would lose the affections of the Jews, who despised Caesar and his Roman legions. If he said that such a tax was unjust and should not be paid, the priests would report the matter to the Procurator, who would be bound to arrest and crucify Jesus for preaching insurrection to the people.

"Show me a denarius," he said, holding out the palm of his hand. One of the priests reached into his garment and, although it was against the law to carry a coin with an image, produced it. Jesus turned it over slowly in his fingers.

"Whose head is this?" he said, holding up the coin so that, in the glint of silver, all could see. "And whose title is here inscribed?"

"Caesar's," the priests replied.

"Therefore," he said, sending the coin back to them spinning in air, "render to Caesar what is Caesar's, and to God what is God's."

The priests, who hated him, were forced to smile in admiration at his answer.

As they walked away, Jesus said to his disciples: "Beware of the Scribes who fancy fine robes for outdoor wear, and crave ceremonious greetings in public places, and front seats in the synagogues, and places of honor at meals. These men who devour the fortunes of widows and recite long prayers for show will receive a more than ordinary punishment."

When Jesus and the disciples left the temple grounds in the evening, Judas remained. He complained that he had work to do; the Pasch was approaching and the money-keeper had much responsibility. Jesus looked at the busy one and said nothing. He turned and led the others from the temple for the night. Then he went to Bethany and said good-bye to his Mother.

Judas was now alone. He did nothing. He stood in the outer court thinking.[21] He was standing astride a crossroads of history, and he had the power to force events this way or that, depending on his pleasure. There was a tickle of apprehension in the belly of the bright money-tender.

He could go to the priests and hand Jesus over. Or he could remain silent, and watch Jesus die as he had said he would on several occasions. Which way should he go? Which turn should he take? The Messiah—if he was the Messiah—had been good to Judas, but this was not a strong factor in the thinking of a man who had been brought up in a family of nonbelievers. And, even if Jesus was merely man and not the Messiah, loyalty was not a consideration to one who set a higher premium on riches than on righteousness.

The other eleven would call it a betrayal; this Judas understood. But their scorn could not hurt a man whom they had treated as an alien all along. The vein of miracles had been worked out anyway. If Jesus had remained quiet in Galilee; if he had not insisted on flaunting his power before the temple priests, everyone could have become rich in time from the donations. But no. He had tried to smash the power of the high priest, and now the streets were filled with whispers of the plot against Jesus.

Besides, even before the plot came to full flower, Jesus had conceded that he would have to die. That being so, the high priest would be the winner. A man of sense owed it to himself to think of the future. Surely when Jesus died, Caiphas would round up the apostles and have them stoned. That being so, would it not be practical to go before Caiphas and offer to deliver Jesus? For a good price perhaps? But, good price or not, the mere act of offering to cooperate with the properly constituted authorities would be a mark in favor of Judas for the future. Instead of being a fugitive, like the other eleven, he would have Caiphas in his debt. Caiphas would owe him the equivalent of a life.

The word that had seeped to Judas was that the priests were now afraid to arrest Jesus. When the temple was crowded, Jesus appeared quite openly. And Caiphas did not dare to lay hands on him. At night the Galilean disappeared outside the environs of the Holy City and no one knew exactly where to find him.

Judas understood the high priest's quandary. If Jesus were permitted in the temple enclosure during the Passover, the pilgrims from the diaspora would be present, and the wonderworks of Jesus would be told in all parts of the world when the pilgrims went home. The temple would then have only half of its authority left. Or less. Who would listen to the lawful interpretations of Caiphas when Jesus could stand in a court and make a man whole, give sight to the blind, or raise the dead before the gaze of many? Could Caiphas do these things?

Therefore, Caiphas was desperate to arrest Jesus; but there were two absolutely imperative conditions—that it be done before the feast, and that it be done without arousing the people. Jesus, on the other hand, was waiting to be arrested and killed. The apprehensive tickle in Judas' stomach stopped. He saw himself as a catalyst: one who hurries natural events.

He gathered his cloak about him, and just before sundown the busy little man hurried across the court and up the steps and inside the next enclosure. He hurried across it and up more steps until he came to the quarters of the priests. There he said that he wanted to be taken to Caiphas. This must have been greeted with derision, because the priests were accustomed to the pleas of hundreds of loose-witted people who insisted upon seeing none other than Caiphas. They made fun of the man and asked if Judas had an appointment. They asked, mockingly, if he would prefer that the high priest come to him in the temple, or would Judas deign to walk across the city to the home of Caiphas?

Emotionally, these priests were harsh people. To their inferiors they seldom displayed good manners. They tried to push Judas out before the gates were closed, but when he said that he wanted to see Caiphas about the Galilean, that he could furnish information for a price, the collective attitude of the priests changed.

They became serious. And when Judas, still afraid of what might happen to him, timidly admitted that he was one of the chosen men of Jesus, the priests asked at once how it came about that Judas spoke in the Judean manner and not the Galilean? He convinced them that, of all the twelve, he was the only one from this province.

Now they became deferential, and they surrounded him so that he could not change his mind and break and run. They agreed to escort him to the home of the high priest, and sent one of their number ahead to acquaint Caiphas with the great news. The priests danced attendance upon their new friend and inquired about his family and his friends, and they cursed Jesus to test the reaction of his apostle.

In a dusk the color of purple grapes they walked the informer across the city and into the courtyard of the high priest. There they waited, and there Judas wondered if the trapper was now trapped. He had admitted that he was a disciple of the man they sought. This constituted a crime in itself, so Judas was no longer in a position to bargain. He could be stoned to death on the testimony of any two of the priests, who had heard him say that he was one of the twelve.

His fear returned. He waited, and, looking around at the grandeur of the court in the bright moonlight, he saw the priests whisper to the servants and point to him, and he knew by the way they spat on the marble flagstones that they despised him for being what he was. This did not hurt his feelings though, because if he won the favor of powerful Caiphas these smaller candles would glow upon him.

There was some commotion on the porch, and then the high priest, accompanied by elders, came down the long steps into the court. He walked over to where Judas stood. Judas could not remember ever having been privileged to look upon the high priest before. And it is certain that Caiphas had never seen Judas Iscariot before. The most contemptible of creatures studied one of the most powerful; the high priest looked down on the sniveling traitor.

These two then struck a bargain. "What are you willing to give me?" Judas said, putting the money first. "I, for one, am ready to deliver him to you."

The high priest had some questions to ask. When he was satisfied that this man was, beyond argument, one of the closest of the followers of Jesus, a thrilling hope ran through his being. He might have promised to pay Judas half of all the treasure in the temple for the delivery of Jesus in secret, and he could not have felt that he would have overpaid this man. But Caiphas too understood the law, and Judas was now a confessed accomplice to blasphemy.

So he dryly told the apostle that he would be given "thirty pieces of silver" for the job, and that it was worthy work to be done in the service of Yahweh. The treasurer nodded agreement. Caiphas then explained the danger of arresting Jesus in daylight anywhere. If the matter had to be put off until after the Feast of the Passover, that too would be all right because it might not be propitious to arrest him in the presence of so many of his followers among the Jews.

Judas understood. He promised Caiphas that he would return to the side of Jesus and await a proper time. When the job could be done at night, without danger of arousing anyone, he would return and let the high priest know the circumstances.

It was agreed. Both smiled and nodded acknowledgment of the bargain. The guards parted to permit Judas to leave in peace. He walked out of the courtyard and out of the city toward the Mount of Olives.

NARRATIVE

April 7, A.D. 30

12 Midnight

Never had the apostles known Jesus to talk so much. And with such finality. They would walk a little way and he would stop and they would cluster around, looking almost sinister in the faint silver, and he would talk forcefully for a moment or two, his head moving slowly to encompass the semicircle of faces, and when he had finished they would open the way for him to lead again.

It was after midnight when Jesus and the eleven passed the Lower Pool and moved toward the Fountain Gate. Some pilgrims were coming through the gate from the hill country to the east and Jesus turned left and walked along the chalky road which hugs the base of the great east wall of the city.

"Do not let your heart be troubled," he said at one pause in the journey. "Do not let your heart despair. You heard me say to you: 'I am going home and I am coming back to you.' If you loved me, you would rejoice that I am going to the Father, because the Father is greater than I.[22] I have told you this now, before it takes place, so that when it does take place, you may revive your faith."

It may be that he sensed that they were tiring of so many things to remember. "I am not going to converse with you much longer, for already the prince of this world is on his way. Not that he can claim anything in me as his own; no, but then, the world must come to know that I love the Father and am acting strictly according to the Father's instructions." The group had been resting by the side of the road; the gentle one followed these words with: "Rise, we must be going on our way."

The moon had passed the zenith, and it threw the shadow of the high east wall across the little road they followed. The road itself was only six or eight feet above the Brook Cedron which, in the month of Nisan, was a fading freshet.

On the left, they passed the village of Gihon, which hugged the bottom edge of the wall. Farther along, they passed the little hilly village of Siloam on the opposite side of the brook. Along here, thousands of families camped outside the holy city and the embers of their fires were ruddy in the night breeze. From here, the walk toward the Mount of Olives was on a slight curving grade.

The road moved a little bit away from the wall and now they could see the real beauty of the great temple. It was after midnight and the lamps were lighted all along the Porch of Solomon. From far below, the city walls rose majestic and brown, with their immense thirty-seven-foot stones and, above them, the Porch of Solomon stood cool and august in the glow of a thousand man-made fireflies. Above that rose the great east façade of the temple, its four-story solid-gold cluster of grapes and the gold-pointed spires glistening in the white light of the Nisan moon.

Jesus saw the glittering cluster of grapes and soon after he stopped the party and said: "I am the real vine, and my Father is the vinedresser. He prunes away any branch of mine that bears no fruit, and cleans any branch that does bear fruit, that I may bear yet more abundant fruit.

"By now you are clean, thanks to the lessons I have given you. Remain united with me, and I will remain united with you. A branch can bear no fruit of itself, that is, when it is not united with the vine; no more can you, if you do not remain united with me. I am the vine, you are the branches. One bears abundant fruit only when he and I are mutually united; severed from me, you can do nothing. If one does not remain united with me, he is simply thrown away like a branch, and dries up.

"Such branches are gathered and thrown into the fire to be burned. As long as you remain united with me, and my teachings remain your rule of life, you may ask for anything you wish, and you shall have it. This is what glorifies my Father—your bearing abundant fruit and thus proving yourselves my disciples."

The party moved on, and the apostles were fatigued to the bone. It had been a long day; they had been up by dawn in Bethany, where Jesus had left his Mother in the care of Mary and Martha. It was past midnight now, and the eyes of the fishermen were heavy and their feet were slow. Besides, their Lord had said so much that their brains ached with remembering. They did not complain because they sensed that this night they might receive the last of many lessons from the Messiah and they knew that they would have to remember, before they could apply the word. These men were very human. Grief for the suffering and impending death of his beloved Jesus must have stunned young John, just as the humility of his brother James surely prevented appreciation of his own adequacy for the job ahead.

"Just as the Father loves me, so I love you. Be sure to hold my love. If you treasure my commandments, you will hold my love, just as I treasure my Father's commandments and thus secure his love. I have told you this, that my joy may be yours, and your joy may be perfect."

They walked on awhile, and now they were underneath the cemetery outside the wall, and in the darkness the sepulchers and the little ossuaries looked like so many broken teeth. Near here they crossed the stone bridge over the Brook Cedron and took the road on the far side toward the little gethsemane where they would sleep.

When they came abreast of the three great mausoleums—one of which was built to the memory of Absalom—which had been standing gaunt and friendless for five hundred years, Jesus glanced briefly at them; he had condemned memorials to the dead a long time ago. Now he stopped again.

"This is my commandment." Again he said, "Love one another as I love you. No one can give greater proof of his love than by laying down his life for his friends. You are my friends"—he looked around at the wan, bearded faces—"provided you do what I command you.

"No longer do I call you servants for a servant is not in his master's confidence. But I have called you friends, because I have made known to you all that I have heard from my Father. Not that you chose me; no, I have chosen you, and the task I imposed upon you is to go forward steadfastly in bearing fruit; and your fruit is to be lasting. Thus the Father will grant you any petition you may present to Him in my name. This is all I command you: love one another."

Surely, this often-repeated commandment to love had now taken root in the apostles' hearts. It would not only sustain them during the hours that lay just ahead, but, of course, become the central theme and identification of Christians throughout the ages.

They were two hundred yards from the little olive press in the miniature valley which separates Jerusalem from the Mount of Olives. For some time now, since they had crossed the brook, they had been bearing away from the city. At the gethsemane, the wall and the temple are a quarter of a mile to the west.

He made no more pronouncements until he reached the stone caves with the big rotary presses, full of the odor of old oil. During this whole walk, he had been concerned, in the main, with imparting to his leaders the few basic fundamentals of his new testament. These eleven would, with proper roots, produce new branches for the teachings of their master, and they would impart his blessings and his sacraments. They would cultivate newer roots in young men as yet unknown and begin the course of the most marvelous spiritual movement in the history of man. It was necessary, it was urgent, that they understand all the truths about God the Father, God the Son and, as they had learned only this evening, the paraclete who would visit them and who was God the Holy Ghost.

It was complex and burdensome for these simple, believing men to try to understand these truths, and they were comforted to know that after Jesus had gone, the Holy Ghost would come to them and repose within them without their knowledge; that He would reveal many things to them and even sharpen their memories so that the words of Jesus would come back truly and clearly.

They turned off the little road near the juncture of the highway to Jericho, and moved easily in the moonlight among the little olive trees at the base of the mountain. Jesus knew that he had a further task. He must tell them something of the future. They were innocent of the trials ahead; they were human reeds easily bent and broken; some, he knew, would not pass the first trial tonight. And yet he had to tell them so that, in remembering his words, they would, in the days ahead, be armed with his prophecies.

"If the world hates you," he said as they moved into a big cave cut in the limestone, "bear in mind that it has hated me first. If you were children of the world, the world would cherish its own flesh and blood. But you are not children of the world; on the contrary, I have singled you out from the world, and therefore the world hates you."

None of this fitted with the notions of the Messiah that they had been taught as children. He was speaking of the hatred of the world as though it were axiomatic. But it was contrary to everything they knew; the triumph of being at his side during the judgment was being transmuted into fear, and a warning of the future animosity of the world. They would not be kings, sitting on thrones flanking his: they were to take his word out to people who would not listen; not only would they not listen but they would scorn and revile, and often kill cruelly the men sent to them with the word of God. Now, for a time, they must have lost their vision of victory. With good courage a man such as Peter could make an impetuous offer of his life, but here for a moment he lost his religious (and gallant) sense of victory in death. The apostle Thomas was most easily reconciled to the brutal truth of future martyrdom. He would be the first to welcome such a role.

"Remember what I told you: a slave is not better off than his master. If they persecuted me, they will persecute you also; if they took my teaching to heart, they will take to heart yours also. Not only that: it is because you profess my name that they will treat you in all these ways; for they do not know him whose ambassador I am. Had I not come with a message to them, they would have no sin: as it is, they have no excuse for their sin.

"He who hates me hates my Father also. Had I not done in their midst what no one else has ever done, they would have no sin; as it is, they have seen and hated both me and my Father. How pitiful that this saying in their Law must needs be fulfilled 'They have hated me without cause!' "

One by one, the apostles sat. A little light filtered from the moon through the olive trees into the cave. One stood and lit a few old lamps along the wall and now they could see Jesus plainly in the feeble saffron glow. He looked taller, broader, and some noticed for the first time that his feet were bare. A few stood leaning against the cave wall, understanding that this was the moment to chisel into their minds every feature, every aspect, every attitude and every word so that someday soon, when he would be no longer with them, they could say to the new disciples of

Jesus: "This is how he looked. This is how he talked. This is what he told us to tell you. . . ."

No one knows what they thought of his most recent discourse, especially of the *two* references to "they would have no sin." Jesus had told the people, and more especially the Pharisees and the Sadducees, that the external signs of obedience to the law of God were as nothing: rubbish. They were as worthless as the rich, heavy bark of a tree which conceals the rot inside. He had come with a message of love, a command to love, from his Father, and they had been appalled. They had, for many centuries, been busy following the forms of religion, mouthing the words which should be spoken, doing the things which had been commanded by Yahweh, and now a country man from the north wanted to discard the outer trappings, the phylacteries and the ritualistic prayers, for a wellspring of love coming from the heart and pouring out to God and to all men.

"When the Advocate whom I am going to send you with a mission from the Father—the Spirit of truth, who proceeds from the Father—has come, he will witness in my behalf. And you, too, will witness, because you have been with me from the beginning."

This was the second time, within the hour, that he had assured the eleven that they would not be alone after he had gone.

"I have told you this, that you may not waver in your faith. You will be put out of the synagogue," he said quietly, and he looked about to see whether the fear which he sensed was apparent. It wasn't, and Jesus continued: "Not only that: a time is coming when anyone who kills you will think he is offering to God an act of supreme worship." Those who had been leaning against the wall sat upright and listened. "And they will do this because they know neither the Father nor me." Now human fear began to show in lines around the eyes of the men who listened. "But enough!" the Messiah said. "I have told you this, so that, when the time comes for it to happen, you may recall that I told you so. I did not tell you all this at the outset, because I was still with you."

They were not comforted. They had accepted sudden death as a daily risk in their business of fishing the Sea of Galilee, but to have the Messiah predict violent death for some of them because of the work they would do for love of him was almost too much to bear. They looked at one another and some swallowed hard.

"But now I am going home to him whose ambassador I am. Yet none of you asks me: 'Where are you going?' Well, because I told you this, sorrow fills your hearts! But I tell you the truth: it is to your advantage that I depart. Unless I depart, the Advocate will not come to you; whereas, if I depart, I will send him to you. And when he comes, he will prove the world wrong about guilt, about innocence, and about condemnation;

about guilt: they do not believe in me; about innocence: I am going home to the Father and you will see me no longer; about condemnation: the prince of this world stands condemned.

"There is still much that I might say to you; but you are not strong enough to bear it at present. But when he, the Spirit of truth, has come, he will conduct you through the whole range of truth. What he will tell does not originate with him; no, he will tell only what he is told. Besides, he will announce to you the future. He is to glorify me, for he will draw upon what is mine and announce it to you. Whatever the Father possesses is mine; that is why I said that he will draw on what is mine and announce it to you."

Jesus had been their advocate in the flesh; now they would have a spiritual one who would never leave them. The sleepy apostles joined the ones who were standing, and some walked around the cave to induce greater wakefulness. Here again was solace; when they did not have Jesus, the paraclete would guide them. And the paraclete was also a divine spirit like the Father and the Son.

The eleven men closest to Jesus in his ministry to the world were beginning to have a slight understanding of the divine Trinity. They may not have comprehended the separate sides of the mystery—as, indeed, no man would ever understand it except, perhaps to illustrate it with a figure of speech likening it to fog over an icy lake and pointing to the fact that the ice, the water and the fog are separate entities, but that each one is water. But, for what he told them, they had progressed from the point of thinking of Yahweh as God one and alone, to God the Father and God the Son, and now, this evening, to God the Father, God the Son and God the Holy Ghost, equal and indivisible.

They were, in any case, not expected to understand, but rather to accept, to believe. If anything, the phrase "the Father is greater than I" would tend to deepen the mystery. This, coupled with the several statements that "the Father is in me, and I am in him" would baffle a prophet. The Holy Ghost, as far as the eleven were concerned, was to be the repository of truth, the consoler, the unseen witness.

"A little while and you see me no longer," Jesus said, "and again a little while, and you will see me." This too mystified those who stood in the little gethsemane, because they did not relate it to his death—the words, to them, described a man going on a journey. They began to ask one another what was meant, and Jesus now was patient with them, fatigued as he was.

"Is this what you are discussing among yourselves, my saying: 'A little while, and you do not see me; and again a little while, and you will see me'? I must be perfectly frank with you: you will weep and lament, while the world rejoices. You will be plunged in sorrow, but your sorrow will be turned into joy.

"When a woman is about to give birth, she is in sorrow because her hour has come; but when she has brought forth her child, she no longer remembers her pangs for sheer joy that a human being has been born into the world. So you, too: at present you are in sorrow; but I shall see you again, and then your hearts will rejoice, and no one will take your joy away from you. That will be the time when you ask me no more questions. . . . If you make any request of my Father, he will grant it to you in my name. Up to the present you made no requests in my name. Make them, and they will be granted. Thus nothing will be wanting to your joy."

This was not only the story of his death and of his resurrection from a new grave, but it was more than that—it was a direct challenge to doubters (if any existed among the eleven) to prove the divinity of Jesus by asking the Father for something in his name. In the final fifteen hours of his life, Jesus was prepared to have his apostles put him to the test.

"Thus far," he said, in his final discourse to them, "I have spoken to you in figures. A time is coming when I no longer speak to you in figures, but tell you about the Father in plain language. That will be the time when you make requests in my name; and I do not tell you that I shall petition the Father in your behalf. Of his own accord the Father loves you dearly, because you are settled in your love for me and in your conviction that I come from the Father. I come from the Father and have come into the world.

"And now I am leaving the world and going home to the Father."

The eleven were so pleased with the little speech that they interrupted the discourse and, with happiness in their eyes, began to say: "There now. You are speaking plainly and avoid all figures of speech. Now we know that you know everything and need not wait till someone asks you. And that is why we believe that you come from God."

Jesus nodded in understanding, partly pleased, partly in sorrow. "You now believe?" he said. "Mark well: a time is coming, in fact, it is at hand, when you will scatter, each going back to his home, and leave me all alone! Not that I am really alone, for the Father is with me. I have forewarned you of this event, that you may find peace of soul in union with me. In the world, afflictions are in store for you. But have courage; I have overcome the world."

Once, on top of this mountain, the twelve had asked Jesus how to pray, and he had lifted his eyes to pale and serene skies and, as they had listened, he began the words "Our Father, who art in heaven . . ." and the fisherfolk had been impressed. Now, having finished all of the discourses, he looked at each of them tenderly and, clasping his hands together, again raised his eyes heavenward and began his final public prayer.

"Father," he said loudly, "the hour is come!

Glorify your Son,
that your Son may glorify you.
You have given him authority over all mankind,
that he might give eternal life
to all you have entrusted to him.
And this is the sum of eternal life—
their knowing you, the only true God,
and your ambassador Jesus Christ.

I have glorified you on earth
by completing the work you gave me to do.
And now, for your part, Father,
glorify me in your bosom
with the glory I possessed in your bosom
before the world existed.

The apostles were entranced. They stood in reverence and they could not conceal their amazement that the privilege of listening to their Messiah address his Father had been extended to them. Nor were the nuances of the prayer lost to them because Jesus was still speaking "plain." He was giving an account of his earthly works to his Father, and, having finished, having pointed the way to eternal life to the apostles and through them to the world, Jesus wanted to be returned to the bosom of his Father.

Almost without pause, he began part two of his prayer, which was for the eleven men who were left to him:

I have made your name known to the men
whom you singled out from the world
and entrusted to me.

Yours they were,
and to me you have entrusted them;
and they cherish your message.
Now they know
that whatever you have given me
really comes from you;
for the message you have delivered to me
I have delivered to them;

and they have accepted it.
They really understand
that I come from you,
and they believe that I am your ambassador.

I am offering a prayer for them;
not for the world do I pray,
but for those whom you have entrusted to me;
for yours they are.
All that is mine is yours,
and yours is mine;
and they are my crowning glory.

I am not long for this world;
but they remain in the world;
while I am about to return to you.
Holy Father!
Keep them loyal to your name
which you have given me.
May they be one as we are one!
As long as I was with them,
I kept them loyal to your name.
I shielded and sheltered the men
whom you have entrusted to me;
and none of them is lost
except the one who chooses his own doom.
And thus the Scripture was to be fulfilled!
But now I return to you,
and I say this before I leave the world
that they may taste my joy
made perfect within their souls.

I have delivered to them your message;
and the world hates them,
because the world finds nothing kin in them,
just as the world finds nothing kin in me.

I do not pray you
to take them out of the world,
but only to preserve them from its evil influence.
The world finds nothing kin in them,
just as the world finds nothing kin in me.

Consecrate them to the service of the truth.
Your message is truth.
As you have made me your ambassador to the world,
so I am making them my ambassadors to the world;
and for their sake I consecrate myself,
that they, in turn, may in reality be consecrated.

This, too, the followers of Jesus understood. They were awed to think that only they and God the Father were listening to these words and they were surprised to note that Jesus seemed to make it plain that it was the Father who had chosen them to be his apostles—including Judas, the twelfth man. That would explain why, when he recruited them, he did not pause to investigate their characters or even to question them. He had merely glanced at most of them, beckoned, and said, "Follow me." Jesus closed his petition by praying for all true believers.

However, I do not pray for them alone,
I also pray for those
who through their preaching will believe in me.
All are to be one;
just as you, Father, are in me and I am in you,
so they, too, are to be one in us.
The world must come to believe
that I am your ambassador.
The glory you have bestowed on me
I have bestowed on them,
that they may be one as we are one—
I in them and you in me.
Thus their oneness will be perfected.
The world must come to acknowledge
that I am your ambassador,
and that you love them as you love me.

O Father!
I will that those whom you have entrusted to me
shall be at my side where I am:
I want them to behold my glory,
the glory you bestowed on me
because You loved me
before the world was founded.

Just Father!
The world does not know you,

but I know you,
and thus these men have come to know
that I am your ambassador.
I have made known to them your name,
and will continue to make it known.
May the love with which You love me
dwell in them
as I dwell in them myself."

Nowhere has Jesus stated with greater clarity the single purpose of his earthly birth, growing up, public ministry and death than in the line "that they may be one as we are one." His credo was encompassed in these few words. It was not oversimplification. Everything Jesus hoped to do on earth was bound and wrapped in that one neat package of words.

He said no more. He motioned to Peter and to James and to John and he left the cave.

1 A.M.

The work was finished. There was an end to the preaching; an end to the miracles; an end to the instruction of the apostles; an end to prophecy. The time for waiting had come. There were about ninety minutes left of freedom, and there was nothing of consequence to do with them. Jesus had publicly audited his accounts to the Father in the presence of the chosen ones, and in these prayers he had prayed for himself first— as all good priests should do—and then he had prayed for the men who would carry his story of love to the people. He had closed with a prayer for all the faithful of all times.

There was nothing of importance that had not been said, or done, several times; some to the point of redundancy for the sake of emphasis. Jesus had offered himself to the world, and that part of it which had the best culture and the best understanding of a monotheistic universe had spurned him. If Jesus failed here, in Palestine, how much more quickly he would have failed in Rome, the world of many marble gods. Or in Greece, where man often had a better intellect than the gods he worshiped—or in Alexandria, or in Gaul or in Carthage or anywhere where men were afraid to die in everlasting darkness.

And, as he knew when he had told the Father that he would consent to be born and to live as a man, and to die *as a man,* the moment of trial would be slow and terrifying and his God side would not be able to save him a bit of pain, a shred of shame, or even shield him from the horror of anticipating the awful things that were to come.

It was a time for waiting. He might have walked through the little grove in the full light of the waning moon; he might have sat in the cave with the eleven and talked of the time when they had first met, of the time when many Jews up and down the land had come forward convinced that this was indeed the Messiah; he might have talked about the time, only last Sunday,[23] when hundreds of his people in a festive mood had acclaimed him as the son of David, and their hosannas had rung up and down the road from Bethany to Jerusalem, the echoes dying against the gleaming pillars of the temple. They might have talked of triumphs.

Instead, Jesus motioned to Peter and James and John. These three, in whom Jesus reposed special trust, walked with him out of the cave and across the little road of gray steps which stretched all the way from the Temple down to the Cedron and up to the top of Olivet. They crossed these steps and walked into the shadows of the little olive garden.

It was, it seemed, always warm there. The heights of the walled city were cool and breeze-swept and, even now, one could see cloaked pilgrims walking in and out of the Golden Gate to the temple. It was cool on top of the Mount of Olives too, but the valley places near the Cedron were warm and moist and the last to see the sun.

The three followed him. He stopped under the trees. In the pattern of foliage which blotted part of the moonlight, they saw the face of Jesus and it held fear and horror. The long slender hands shook. The features seemed to be gray, tinged with blue. The mouth was slack. The eyes were huge with a vision the others could not see.

Peter and James and John tried to help; they wished to console. But the Messiah merely shook his head. He was beyond any help of man, precisely because he was now more man than god. *As a man* he was able to sustain the fullness of suffering. And, as man, Jesus had not only the nervous structure of all other humans, plus the emotional capacity for great joy in addition to a great sensitivity, but as the Son of God he had a knowledge of what was to come.

To them, he seemed to be immeasurably weary, and this was strange because, only a few minutes ago, he had been expounding the last of the lessons of the missionaries to them. And he had finished the work with vigor. They fell mute and turned their eyes away because they did not think that it was right to look upon the face of the Messiah in weakness and fear.

He doubled his hands into fists and held them against his breast. "I am plunged in sorrow," he said loudly and bitterly, "enough to break my heart!" The three glanced at him, sadly. Jesus looked up through the branches at the miniature beauty of a thousand other worlds, and then he glanced once more at the temple, so near across the valley.

"Stay here and keep awake," he said with entreaty. They nodded in silence and watched him make his way through the low-branched trees for a short distance. There, he paused beside a big flat rock. He knelt for a few moments. Then, abandoning himself to overwhelming mortal fear, he threw himself full length on the rock, face down. In a loud voice he said: "My Father, if it is possible, let this cup be spared me!" The lament came, almost involuntarily, from the lips. "And yet," he said, as though afraid to be afraid, "not as I will, but as You will."

No one knew better than Jesus that if he died as the Son of God the gesture would be small, the sacrifice negligible. From this moment until the hour when he expired he knew that he would have to suffer much more than anyone else who might travel the same path and endure the same things; the mere waiting was almost beyond him. Every minute of every hour must now be borne as a man with extraordinary courage in order to achieve the victory of a God, the one God.

It was at this time that young Mark—about seventeen years of age— ran into the gethsemane. He was panting and he was in his night clothes. He went to the side of the road where the cave was and, with excitement, told the eight who had been sleeping that there had been a raid on his father's house and that there had been a great mob of men armed with clubs, led by Roman soldiers and temple guards as well as some elders of the temple, Scribes and Pharisees, and they had searched the premises looking for Jesus and demanding to know where he had gone. The neighborhood had been in an uproar and many were seen carrying torches and some carried lanterns on top of long staffs.

The Tribune and some of the elders had questioned his father and then they had left. Some said that they were going to the temple. At this news, one of the eight hurried across the road to tell Jesus and, not finding him, told it in whispers to Peter and the others who waited. No one, with the exception of the boy who brought the news, seemed alarmed. The apostles apparently felt that, if the raid had failed at Mark's home, then that was the end of it. Their lack of concern could hardly have shown itself better than in the fact that the eight on the other side of the road and the three who reclined against olive trees in the garden fell asleep.

Now and then, John awakened and listened to the loud and fearful voice of Jesus but, in spite of his love for the Messiah, and his natural compassion, the heavy lids of his eyes refused to obey his will and shut again. Thus in the little grove was the incongruous sound of the Son of Man beseeching mercy and, mingled with it, the sleep-born noises of healthy men whose faculties had been short-circuited by fatigue.

And so, in a real sense, Jesus was alone in the garden. As he prayed, his anguish deepened and became unbearable. He stood. He was close to a stupor of fright at the visions he had seen and he came back to the three, perhaps to seek human solace. His agitation was pronounced. His body seemed older and bent forward. The hair, which usually hung smoothly to below his shoulders, was awry and some of it was plastered to the sweat on his forehead.

He looked down and his heart ached as he saw the three sleeping. John stirred and awakened, and jostled the others.

"How can you be sleeping?" Jesus asked. "Rouse yourselves and pray, that you may not succumb to temptation."

He was dismayed at the sight of his defenders grunting apologies and trying to get to their feet. The twelve may have been originally chosen by his Father, but he had granted these three special honors—only Peter and James and John had been privileged to see his transfiguration on the mountain; only these three had been present when he had raised the daughter of Jairus from the dead.

Jesus went back to pray, now even further into the realm of agony than before. The three had fallen asleep again almost before he had returned to the rock. This time he knelt, and his forehead touched the rock and, as he prayed, he rocked back and forth as though in deep physical pain.

This, he knew, was the hard road to his Father. There was no other, easier route. The nature of man is such that he must shrink from thoughts of his own death, more so when the body is well and not close to death. The man side of his nature became more and more pronounced as he dwelt upon the imminent dissolution of the bonds between this miraculously fashioned body with its sinews and blood and its bone structure and its mind imprisoned by an inverted cup of bone and yet free by the God-given power to think and to will. He considered the soul which would cling to this body until, in dreadful agony, the body died.

The man side of his nature was not reconciled to death. Thoughts of it, after thirty-four years of living within the body, were sickening. And yet, this had been his choice. He would come here and die for man.

Once he called out "My Father!" He prayed, sometimes in rapid murmuring; sometimes slowly, distinctly and loudly. Once, he looked up above the rock and, for a moment, fell silent. He saw an angel. The sight was luminous, but he was not encouraged. The angel said nothing. The silence probably meant that his Father would do nothing to lessen the suffering of Jesus.

He got to his feet, slowly and with the aid of his hands, and he went back to the men who were eager to lay down their lives for him. They were again sleeping and, as Peter half opened his eyes, Jesus half whispered: "Simon, are you sleeping? Were you not able to stay awake one hour? Keep awake and pray, all of you, that you may not succumb to temptation." He sighed. "The spirit is willing, but the flesh is weak."

This was, at the moment, as true of him as it was of them. His flesh was so weak that all the strength of his soul could not keep it from betraying the will which made it function. The Lord, said Isaias, would lay down upon him all the iniquities of mankind, and now, the weight of countless sins pressed upon his shoulders as he knelt again to tell his Father that he would accept the cup.

The salty sweat, gleaming on his face and forehead, began to change color. It reddened and deepened in hue until, in his agony, he knew that it was blood. It clung to his face and moved slowly down to his chin. Some of it dropped off in clots onto the rock and some of it congealed in his beard.

Medically, this is called haematidrosis. It occurs when fear is piled upon fear, when an agony of suffering is laid upon an older suffering until the highly sensitized person can no longer sustain the pain. At that moment, the patient ordinarily loses consciousness. When that does not happen, the subcutaneous capillaries sometimes dilate so broadly that, when they come into contact with the sweat glands the little capillaries burst. The blood is exuded with the perspiration and, usually, this occurs over the entire body.

Luke, who was a physician, later wrote: "And his sweat became as clots of blood, trickling down upon the ground."

2 A.M.

The night air was still. In the garden of the gethsemane, the leaves of the twisted little trees hung quietly. All along, there had been some sounds coming from the early worshipers walking the Bethany road to the temple; now there was no sound. If Jesus had looked up from the rock, he would have noted that the traffic in and out of the Golden Gate to and from the temple had stopped.

The insects in the fields had ceased their monotonous monologue. The moon was now far over in the west and the temple was hung in mourning silhouette. A shepherd's whistle in the hills sounded lonesome and far off. Even the Brook Cedron, black and cold, moved silently over the round stones on the bottom on its way to the Valley of Hinnom. This was the breathless hush of anticipation.

Inside the walls, Jerusalem began to come to life. On this night, it was common for families to sleep four hours or less so that the joy of the Passover could be savored in sweet consciousness.

The Seder meal was over and, in homes all over the land, the closing words of the grace had been pronounced slowly, solemnly, fervently: "May the All-Merciful make us worthy of the days of the Messiah and of the life of the world to come."

The early worshipers hurried to Solomon's Porch because here the senses could be made intoxicated with beauty. The fluted colonnades stood tall and majestic and the sound of many sandals clopped on the marble underfoot. The view to the east on a clear night like this stretched over the top of Olivet all the way to the Mountains of Moab on the far side of the Dead Sea. Below were the city walls and Cedron and on the far side was the road to Bethany, etched like silver crayon in the darkness, and the deep green grove of olive trees around the little gethsemane at the bottom.

Somewhere behind the portico, musicians in snowy garments sat to many harps and played the favorite psalms from now until the first pink shaft of daylight. In another part of the temple, a kind of organ called a magraphah was playing softly as the crowds moved from court to court under thousands of yellow lanterns. Many a pious Jew stood on the porch that night and whispered: "God is indeed good to us!"

Unless he was one who knew Jesus, his joy would not have been clouded if someone had told him that, within his vision, in that clump of small trees on the opposite side of the Cedron, one who called himself the Son of God lay on a rock, sweating blood. It would not have stirred any interest in the pilgrim because, if the sufferer was really the Messiah, why was he not sitting inside the Holy of Holies in this very temple, instead of weeping alone on a rock? Besides, was it reasonable to suppose that the chief priests—who have knowledge of such things—would permit the Messiah to weep in a tiny gethsemane when they should be prostrate before him?

No. The pilgrim would have said wisely: "Let him split the temple veil. Then I will believe." And that would have closed the conversation because everyone knew that the temple veil was the biggest, the heaviest, the most beautiful in the world and a true Messiah would perform such a symbolic act.

From the great portico, many of the pious, looking down, must have seen Judas and his party leave. They left by way of the Golden Gate. It was a big, double-arched exit at the bottom of the wall below the temple, and the marchers, with torches and lanterns and swords and staves, must have attracted the attention of those above.

More than that, there was certainly some speculation from the wall because this was a strange party to be leaving the city. No one had ever seen Pharisees marching with Roman legionnaires. And it is beyond dispute that the legionnaires had never marched with Sadducean elders. Each of these three groups had reason to distrust the other two. And all three were being led by Judas Iscariot, one of the chosen disciples of the blasphemer. The party, kept in line by the Chiliarch, left the walls and walked down the steep steps leading into the valley and up the far side.

These were momentary allies. The Pharisees (Separatists) were adorned with phylacteries, and in their radical piety they would ordinarily have had nothing to do with this adventure on this day for they seldom agreed to the law's being suspended, no matter what the situation. But they, the "separated," were agreed that Jesus was a grave menace to the temple, and they were willing, for this once, to forswear their natural abhorrence for the violation of even the punctuation of the law.

In itself, this alignment is not so very strange because, in the practical politics of administering the affairs of Palestine, the Pharisees had often voted along with the Sadducees. What was strange to the onlookers from the porch above was to see Pharisees in company with Gentile Romans, since the Pharisees proclaimed religious purity above all other matters. In the world, as they saw it, there was a Jewishness and a non-Jewishness, and they would have nothing to do with the sight, smell, sound of anything or anyone non-Jewish.

The feelings of Jesus toward the Pharisees and Scribes were condensed into two deadly sentences: "The Scribes and the Pharisees have sat on the chair of Moses. All things that they shall say to you, observe and do, but according to their works, do ye not."

In the group marching on the gethsemane there may also have been some Herodians because Herod had spies everywhere and trusted neither the priests nor the Romans to tell him of current events. They were not a political group, nor did they have any prestige among the political parties. They were merely lax Jews who supported Herod Antipas, who was, of course, Tetrarch of Galilee and a half-Jew who believed in himself.

The big ungainly band marched down into the valley, and, when the head of the column was near the bottom, Judas called for a halt and drew the chief Scribes and Romans to him. He had an idea that, when they reached the oil press, they might see nothing in dim light except fleeing figures in white clothes.

"The one I kiss," said Judas, "that is he. Arrest him and lead him away, carefully." The leaders of the raiders nodded. It was a good idea and it simplified matters. They need not be troubled with running apostles. All they had to do was to let Judas lead everyone to the man whom he would kiss.

In the garden, Jesus got to his feet. His face was again serene in dignity. He walked back to the three apostles and at once they sat up. Now, after his agony of human loneliness, he revealed a Godlike compassion. "Sleep on now," he said. "Take your rest." He turned to walk away and, through the foliage, he could see the many torches and lanterns. He could hear the clank of metal shields and the murmur of many voices.

After a time, Jesus turned back to Peter and James and John. "The hour has struck," he said. "Look, the Son of Man is being betrayed into the hands of sinful men." They looked up at him dumbfounded. "Rise! Let us go. Look, my betrayer is close at hand."

3 A.M.

The three got to their feet quickly. James and John ran across the road to warn the others. Peter, as was fitting, remained at the side of his master. These things had barely been done when the garden became filled with light and sound and men moving among small trees and shrubs and flowers. The eight who had been sleeping in the cave and young Mark could have fled to the Bethany road, only a hundred yards to the north, but they were half hypnotized, half fascinated by the alarm. And so, instead of running away, they walked over to the garden, not so much to see what the law would do to Jesus, but rather to see what the Messiah would do to the raiders.

The scene was chaotic. The face and figure of Jesus were well lighted by the torches. Peter stood nearby, trembling. The remaining apostles came up and it seemed to them, even though the grove was full of men, that no one was hurrying to approach Jesus. Men were stumbling about, and calling to one another, and soldiers could be seen among them, but there was a reluctance to be first to step into the little clearing where Jesus stood.

At last Judas walked into the little open space and looked at Jesus. His eyes opened with happy surprise and his mouth formed a smile. He opened his arms and hurried to the Messiah. "Hail, Master!" said the missing apostle. The sight of him coming out of the crowd of temple guards and soldiers must have surprised the other apostles, but they may have thought that it was Judas who had been arrested.

The treasurer threw both arms around Jesus and lifted his lips up to the master's cheek. The Galilean looked at Judas with compassion. "Judas," he said, "with a kiss you betray the Son of Man?" There was no time for a reply. Some of the guards and soldiers, and indeed some of the priests and Pharisees and Scribes, were standing on the edge of the clearing. Jesus, in feigned innocence, looked directly at those from the great temple and said: "Who is it you are looking for?"

"Jesus of Nazareth," they said as one.

"I am he," he said, touching the tips of the fingers of both hands to his breast. At once those in front dropped back. There was confusion again and it was obvious that the guards from the temple had heard stories of his miracles and they were afraid. The Romans were disgusted with the showing of their temporary allies and now pressed forward to take charge.

"Who is it," said Jesus, slowly and distinctly, "you are looking for?"

The Romans now joined in the shouted reply: "Jesus of Nazareth."

"I told you that I am he," he said after the voices died down. "Therefore, since you are looking for me," he pointed behind him to his apostles, "let these men go unmolested." The raiders began to take courage. They stepped forward and, as they crowded around, not yet daring to touch him, Judas moved away and became lost in the crowd.

"As though to capture a bandit," Jesus said to the temple authorities, "you came out armed with swords and clubs to arrest me." There was a little edge of scorn in the tone. "Day after day I was with you teaching in the temple: yet you did not arrest me." They said nothing. Some looked away. "But then," Jesus said softly, "let the Scriptures be fulfilled."

One of the apostles in the rear passed one of the old swords up to Peter. He unsheathed it and, without a word, stepped in front of Jesus and swung it diagonally upward. He had aimed for the neck of the servant of the high priest, who saw the blow coming and inclined his head away from it. An ear was sheared off and the Chiliarch, expecting a melee, ordered his men to draw their swords.

Jesus was shocked. He looked at Peter and said sternly: "Put the sword back into the sheath; shall I not drink the cup which the Father has presented to me?" Peter did as he was told. The servant now felt the side of his face and screamed. Jesus grabbed him tightly with one hand and touched the side of his face with the other. The man, Malchus, was healed at once, but the healing went unnoticed in any public sense.

The Romans decided that this emotional scene had gone far enough. They came forward and arrested Jesus. The proper manner, taught by the academy of soldiery in Rome, was to take the victim by the right wrist, twist his arm behind him so that his knuckles touched between his shoulder blades and, at the same time, jam the heel down on his right instep. This was the beginning of the pain Jesus would feel this day.

Some of the temple guards, not wishing to be shamed in the presence of the Gentiles, grabbed the other arm and put it behind his back and brought out rope and tied his hands. A long noose was placed about his neck. He was patient with his captors. Now that Jesus was fettered and no one had been struck dead, the Levites began to take courage and issue orders.

The Chiliarch wanted to know whether the prisoner was to be taken to the temple for trial, and conflicting shouts echoed through the grove. The ranking Sadducees and Pharisees consulted and said no, the prisoner was to be taken to the home of the high priest. The men in charge said that it would be preferable not to return by way of the temple gate.

The Romans studied the blasphemer. They could see nothing but a mild, inoffensive man. He stood quietly, and now his head was lowered, so that his beard touched the chest of his garment. Some of the temple guards asked questions of the man—mostly about his alleged divinity— and the head remained bowed. The Gentiles, looking around, were certain that some of the friends of the prisoner were more sinister than he.

Someone prodded Jesus, and the march began. The mob was in front of him and flanking him and behind him. The priests were pleased that the whole matter had been done with such quiet dispatch. Jesus had muttered no incantation, had conjured no balls of blue fire or brimstone to destroy all of them. This, of course, proved that he was no more a Messiah than they. If he were the Messiah, then he had the power to destroy them. If he did not use the power then he did not have it, and if he did not have it then he was just another faker under arrest.

Time had caught up with them, they thought. If he had only remained in Galilee with his preachments of love, he could have been rich someday. But no. He had to storm Jerusalem, and Jerusalem was known to kill real prophets. What chance had a Nazarene magician?

Some of the guards at the rear of the line of march noticed that the apostles of Jesus were following. The guards winked at one another and turned as if to pursue them. All took flight quickly, and disappeared into the darkness so abruptly that the Romans laughed and made jokes about their speed. One guard got close enough to young Mark to clutch his night linen with his fist. Frantically, Mark whirled around and fled down the road, naked.

The march took them from Gethsemane to the Bethany Road. There, they turned left and marched up the big hill to the north of the city and through the Antonia entrance. Jesus, head still down, not answering the jibes, walked barefoot with his hands tied behind his back and the noose jerking lightly at his neck.

When the party got inside the walls, the Chiliarch halted the march and asked the Jews if they needed further assistance. They said no. The prisoner, properly, was a temple charge and they would take him to the high priest. The Romans remained inside the fortress, wondering why they had been needed on the mission, and why so many of them.

The march started again and, fortunately, there were few people abroad in the northwestern part of Jerusalem. These few stopped to stare at the lanterns, the torches, the noisy line of march and the lone prisoner in the middle. But there were no demonstrations for Jesus. In fact, no one, at least thus far, seemed to recognize him.

The priests and the others congratulated themselves on taking the long way back. It had served their purpose. The temple, at this moment, could be teeming with followers of Jesus, and had Jesus been led fettered through the Golden Gate they would have demonstrated and wept, or possibly fought the guards. Then a riot would have started which could end only when Pilate sent soldiers into the Court of the Gentiles.

Now they were safely at the Maccabean Palace, and they moved around the wall of Herod's Palace bearing south by southeast. The road led up onto the little hill called Mount Sion. They were near the palatial homes of Caiaphas and Annas, and now the Scribes and the Pharisees became jocular. The assignment was drawing to a close and they felt free to admit to one another that, for a time there in the little olive garden, each had been secretly worried. Each had heard reports of such wonders that this man had accomplished that there had been a latent and sometimes lively fear in each breast. Who would have expected that he would turn out to be a most ordinary Nazarene? If the elders were ashamed of anything, it was that they had seen fit to take such a large party with them to do the work. One man with a club could have set the companions of Jesus to flight and, as the Galilean did not believe in violence, he could have been bound and led away without a struggle.

The marchers arrived at the big double courtyard before the homes of Annas and Caiphas, and there were happy words back and forth as the servants inside unlocked the gates. Ordinarily, they would have entered by the porter's door, but this was too small for the victorious ones. They surged inside, pushing the victim before them. More lamps were lighted at once, because there was a distinguished company on the premises who wanted to have a good look at this man. Members of the Great Sanhedrin, hurriedly summoned, came running out of the house of Caiphas, holding their white garments off the flagstones as their feet flew.

Some of the women of the household came out and stood in the shadows of the balcony to see the prisoner about whom their men had debated so often. Some of the captors ran off to tell old Annas that the blasphemer was even now standing under guard in front of his house. Caiphas came down the steps slowly. Now, with the end in sight, he had patience. His first interest was not in confronting Jesus, but in getting the reports of his men on how the arrest had been accomplished, what the attitude of the Romans might be, where the disciples of Jesus were, and whether there had been any popular uprising against the will of the Sanhedrin.

The high priest heard the reports. They were all good. The matter had been handled discreetly and the city was not even aware of what had happened. Caiphas was elated. He had struck a good blow for God and for the temple. A sore had festered on the body of Judea and he, Caiphas, had cauterized it. He stroked his silken, square-cut beard, and ordered the so-called Messiah to be taken to Hananyah, which was the Hebrew name of his father-in-law.

This was a diplomatic move. Caiphas could wait. It was proper to permit Annas a first look at the face of the prisoner and to conduct the first examination. Besides, Caiphas knew what his father-in-law would do: he would order the prisoner returned at once to the high priest and the Great Sanhedrin for trial.

So nothing could be lost by this polite move. Caiphas watched the temple guards take Jesus across the courtyard, walking behind him and shoving him roughly forward so that he staggered on the stones. Caiphas was more deeply interested in the fact that the Sadducees and the Pharisees who had been part of the apprehending party were now friendly, and were busy congratulating one another on a good night's work.

This was important to Caiphas because, as the ranking Sadducee, he had been plagued by the breast-beating Pharisees within and without the Sanhedrin. Tonight he felt proud that the dissident forces were united. He, Caiphas, had arranged this by nominating the committee which was to accompany the guards to ensure that everything was done lawfully.

And who but Caiphas had engineered the trap for the Romans? Who went to Pontius Pilate, almost groveling for assistance in an internal matter which was of no concern to the barbarous Gentiles? Caiphas. And now, when sentence of death was passed upon Jesus, how could Pilate admit that the soldiers of Tiberius Caesar had assisted in the arrest while denying affirmation of the sentence? If he refused to confirm the execution he would tacitly be conceding that he had sent a maniple—two companies—to arrest one innocent man. This would make a juicy subject for one of Herod's secret notes to the Emperor.

No, Pilate was trapped and well trapped. However, this was not the immediate matter to occupy Caiphas' attention. At the moment he was most concerned with the need to send out more servants to demand the attendance at once of all members of the Great Sanhedrin at a special convocation; the need to get witnesses from among the Levites in the temple to come to the hearing and to swear that they had heard Jesus, preaching in the Court of the Gentiles, pronounce himself the Son of Man; and the need to arrange for demonstrators at the temple after daylight, so that when Jesus was led to Pilate for confirmation of sentence, all the citizens around him would be unfavorable to his cause.

He was taking care of these items when someone drew his attention to a little man standing in the shadows. It was Judas. Caiphas interrupted his elaborate plans and said: "Pay him. Take him to the temple and pay him the thirty pieces of silver agreed upon."

And it was done. The little man was hurried through the streets down the side of Mount Sion with no friendly words, into the little Tyropoeon Valley and up the viaduct into the temple. There the ranking priests were told the wishes of Caiphas. They told Judas to cup both hands while they counted out the silver. The small coins clinked, one on top of the other into his moist palms. His head nodded with the count of the priest until the number reached thirty.

Then, with deep thanks and proper bows of respect to the priests, he thrust the money into a bag and into his garment. He had sold the man who had promised him life everlasting.

4 A.M.

Annas did not want the prisoner inside the house. He came out on the portico, and ordered Jesus brought to him. The guards pushed and dragged the man, not because they despised him, but because they wanted to show some zeal in front of the old Nasi. When Jesus did not hurry, they kicked him.

The old man sat and studied the young man. No one knows what thoughts crossed his mind, or what questions passed his lips. He sat and he looked and he may have wondered, idly, what motivated a young nobody into posing as the Saviour of the world. This man did not appear to be a lunatic. The reports that had been coming in for over a year tended to show the opposite. Jesus of Nazareth was intelligent; he was well versed in the law although no one knew what rabbinical school he had followed; he was tall and as well muscled as a farmer; he was not given to extravagance or indulgence in the grape; he was not betrothed and no scandal adhered to so much as the hem of his garments.

Then why? Why did he have to be a Messiah? For two years or more, this man had increased the tension in Palestine—first in his native Galilee, then in Jerusalem and even over in Jericho. His basic tenet had been love, which, in the eyes of the old priest, was not dangerous. But the people had begun to fall away from the temple, first in little groups, then in larger ones. Someone had reported—the old man could not remember who— that recently, when Jesus left a town, a good part of the population followed him, leaving homes and work and farms.

Annas looked for a long time. He would not try this man. Let Caiphas do it. The law said that not less than twenty-three members of the Great Sanhedrin could try a capital case, and the old man was certain that, by this time, his son-in-law had awakened and summoned the judges. Still, it was interesting to inquire why a man would want to pose as the Messiah, since he must have known that sooner or later he would be challenged by the temple. In fact, the ratio of the chances of being challenged by the temple was in direct proportion to the success of the so-called Messiah. This one was highly successful. At that, he might have escaped challenge and the charge of blasphemy if he had not kicked over the tables of Annas' money-changers and condemned Annas' animal market.

Annas pulled his striped robe more tightly around his old frame. He asked Jesus why he taught heresy. He also asked who the disciples were, and how many. The Nazarene looked steadily at the man who must soon face the Father and be accountable for his acts.

"I have spoken openly," said Jesus with the soft solicitude all Jews reserved for the aged, "where all the world could listen. I have always taught at synagogue meetings and in the temple, where all the Jews are wont to meet. . . . Why do you question me?" Under the rules of trial procedure, Jesus knew—and so did Annas—that it was against the law to solicit the testimony of any except witnesses and corroborators. Besides, under the law, no prisoner had to undergo preliminary examination.

"Question those who heard what I said. You see," he said patiently, "they *know* what I said." One of the guards walked around in front of Jesus and smashed his face.

"Is this the way you answer the high priest?" the guard said.

Jesus shook his head to clear the effects of the blow and said to the guard: "If I was wrong in speaking this way, then prove me wrong; but if I was right, then why do you strike me?"

Old Annas smiled and shook his head. He got up and ordered Jesus sent to Caiphas.

The night air was now very chilly. There was a wet wind out of the west and the temple guards shouldered their cloaks and built a fire in a brazier. They crouched around it in the courtyard of the high priest and the glow of the coals painted their faces in brief, ruddy flicks.

One of those who crouched with them and kept warm was young John, whom Jesus loved so much. He had followed behind the raiding party with Peter, and the two had seen their master disappear inside the gates. They had argued whether they should follow him. John wanted to go in; Peter favored caution. While Jesus was at the house of Annas, the young apostle knocked on the porter's gate.

A girl had the duties of porter. She opened the door a little way and, holding a lamp in her hand, looked at the face of John. She greeted him and he greeted her, and he was admitted without question because John and his family were favorably known to the high priest. The young man roamed the courtyard, trying to strike up a conversation with the guards, asking gruffly where the prisoner had been taken, and then he crouched by the fire with the others.

When he was certain that he was not suspect, he got up and spoke to the girl porter and said that a friend of his was outside the gate. John said that he would vouch for his friend. The girl admitted Peter. She shaded her lamp and saw a barrel-chested man with wild pale-colored hair and beard; a man with a voice as deep as doom.

"Are you, perhaps, one of the disciples of that man?" she said.

Peter paused. He swallowed and glared at the girl in outrage. "I am not!" he roared.

John led him to the fire and Peter lifted his cloak up to his chin as he stooped to warm his hands. Somewhere, a cock ruffled his feathers. The guards were talking about the raid, and of how the apostles had fled at the first threatening move of the soldiers. John contributed nothing to the conversation. Peter was silent. A man on the far side of the fire stared hard at Peter, and the chief of the apostles pulled the top of his cloak up over the tip of his nose.

The man pointed a finger at Peter. "You," he said, "are one of them."

Peter turned his head from side to side. "No, sir," he shouted through the muffling cloth, "I am not."

Members of the Great Sanhedrin were arriving and they glanced briefly around as they walked across the courtyard. Some were old. Some seemed young. Most seemed irritated from lack of sleep. They walked with dignity to the stairway of the high priest, their hands clutching both sides of their cloaks near the neck as befitted judges, and they went up the stairway and inside.

It was against the law to hold a criminal hearing while the sky was yet dark, and some thought that Caiphas would postpone the trial until morning. Still, whether it was held now or later, no one would cite the law against Caiphas because, in this matter, even the Pharisees were his allies. And if daylight was still an hour away, which of them would uphold the law and stand by the side of Jesus, crying: "Wait!"

No one.

The men around the fire heard a stir and they stood looking toward the house of Annas. Servants were coming down the steps with lanterns and Jesus was between them. Peter, in his fear for the Messiah, permitted the cloak to drop and one of the guards, a relative of the one who had lost an ear in the garden, said: "This man was certainly with him! Why, he is a Galilean!"

Peter cursed loudly and said: "Sir, I do not know what you are talking about."

From somewhere far off, a rooster stretched himself, shook his wings and crowed. The guards passed the little fire on their way to Caiphas. Jesus, in the center, looked full on the face of Peter. The chief disciple stared stolidly at the man in fetters, watched his back as he was led on, and suddenly broke into sobs, covered his face with both hands, and ran from the scene.

Members of the Sanhedrin were still hurrying inside to the private apartments of the high priest after the prisoner had been led in. The latecomers knew the identity of the prisoner and what the charge was because, of late, the Galilean Messiah had been discussed gravely at the meetings of the supreme council and plans had been advanced concerning the best way of trapping him. So that, no matter how late their arrival, the members could take their places in the three-tiered semicircle and listen to the proceedings with comprehension.

The proceedings were secret. There were some whispers later from those who had been privileged to sit on this judgment, but little can be proved as fact. Caiphas wanted a full court, and, before the trial was under way, had the seventy members or a number close to it. The Great Sanhedrin had met at this house before, and the servants were able to have the chairs and tables ready in the proper order, with the two clerks at either end of the crescent of chairs.

The proper way to have opened the session would have been to call the roll of members, starting with the high priest and going through the names of the elders and down through to the most junior member. This would be followed by a recitation of the charge by the Nasi, who would stand to publish it. The charge, simply, was that the prisoner did indeed on divers occasions proclaim himself to be the Messiah, the true Son of God, and in so doing had blasphemed against God and had profaned the temple.

No one asked Jesus how he would plead. He stood throughout, roped and hobbled of foot, with guards standing behind him. The procedure called for the defense to open first, and the high priest, seated, no doubt called upon Jesus three times to defend himself. There was no reply. The steady eyes of the prisoner moved from face to face, from row to row, until he had seen them all. In the group, he saw at least two disciples. Like so many of his highly placed followers, their adherence to his teachings was secret. This was not the hour for them to reveal themselves, just as it was not the hour for Peter and the others. So they sat, maybe with averted eyes, and listened to the procedure. It may be that, when the cry went up for one to defend the man and one to prosecute, a follower of Jesus raised a timid hand and said: "For lack of worthy counsel, I will espouse the cause of this man."

A consultation with the defendant would do the member little good, because the defendant planned no defense. Besides, as Jesus had said, the Son of Man had to die so that the Scriptures would be fulfilled. He and his mission had been rejected by these men; therefore, to impede the tragedy would be pointless.

Jesus could not have been a prepossessing figure. There was dry blood on his cheeks and on his beard. His garments were soiled because he had been pushed and kicked much of the way. His feet were bare and dirty from the march. His lean face was drained of color because so much had happened to him since last he had rested. His eyes were red and heavy-lidded. From a distance of a few yards he looked the part of a man of no substance; a friendless culprit.

The questions came at him from several sides, and he did not bother to answer or even to shake his head. The high priest called loudly for any witnesses in behalf of Jesus to step forward now and to testify. The words rang around the chamber and caromed into silence. No one stood. No one came through the door to say: "This is a good man. This is a man of peace. This is the true Messiah come to save the twelve tribes." No one.

The prosecution opened with the calling of witnesses. These, according to ritual, were heard one at a time. Mostly, they were menials who worked in the temple. They were listened to by the seventy-one and the witnesses struck their breasts and vowed that they had heard this Galilean proclaim himself as one sent by Yahweh himself. They vowed many things and, to maintain the attitude of a proper procedure, the members of the supreme council questioned the witnesses sharply. One after another, the stories of the witnesses collapsed. The elders, the elect, looked at one another. More witnesses were called. These contradicted one another so badly that it was not necessary to question them to prove false witness.

Jesus stood silent. It must have seemed ironic, even to him, to see that the Jews who actively plotted against his life numbered so few, and those Jews who believed that he was the Messiah numbered so many, yet the first group could not seem to prove a case against him while the second lifted not a finger to save him.

The high priest was forced to call witnesses of higher rank, and these testified—with varying degrees of corroboration—that they had heard Jesus say that, if the temple were destroyed, he could raise it again in three days. The difficulty of first-century Palestinian speech can hardly be better exemplified than here, where Jesus was referring to his body as "this temple" and the priests understood him to mean Herod's temple.

Even so, the statement is hardly blasphemy, and not a capital crime. The Pharisees, in their daily interpretations of the law, had been prone to grosser exaggerations. Everyone in the room, except Caiphas, seemed to forget that the particular charge against the prisoner was, in itself, unimportant; the prime concern was to validate a charge which would make him a criminal in the eyes of the Roman Procurator. Of course, even the charge that Jesus claimed to be the Son of God might not do, because the visit of the true Messiah to earth was the last great hope of all Judea; brought up in public it might call forth mockery of a Gentile Governor. But, in the absence of other evidence, this would have to do.

Caiphas had hoped to find Jesus guilty of being a massith and maddiach—one who beguiles and entices individuals to worship idols. The charge would have been ideal, because the Romans were naturally apprehensive about anyone who led the common people into any new way of thinking, whether political or not, because it had been their finding that, sooner or later, such prophets led the people away from Rome.

The charge of being a maddiach was heard from witnesses, but the two required by Mosaic law did not agree either on what was said or how or when it was said, and the charge fell. Caiphas was in a ridiculous position and saw his case against Jesus dying for lack of witnesses who could testify separately to one charge.

Still, he got to his feet and, in full robes and conical hat, pointed sternly at Jesus and said: "Have you nothing to say in your own defense?" The prisoner looked at the man and said nothing. "What about the evidence these men are furnishing against you?" This might have caused some wry expressions among the ranks of the learned judges, but still Jesus kept his peace.

Caiphas was caught. He could not prove the prisoner guilty of a charge, and he could not ask the uncommitted judges to vote for conviction. It is quite possible that the majority of the judges hated Jesus and feared the religious innovations which he espoused, but, by and large these were just men. They wanted to convict Jesus, and they wanted him to suffer death for the peril in which they fancied he had placed the temple, but first of all they wanted two witnesses who, questioned separately, would support the same incriminating evidence.

The high priest was still standing. So long as the prisoner remained silent, the Great Sanhedrin had to acquit. In desperation, and almost pleading, Caiphas shouted: "I adjure you by the living God to tell us outright, are you the Messiah, the Son of God?"

He looked directly at Jesus, and had no hope of an answer. He knew that the prisoner too was well versed in the law, and understood that to say no would be to admit to his multitudes of followers that he had lied to them and was an ordinary man with no ministry; to say yes would be to plead guilty to the charge of blasphemy, because, in the eyes of these men, he was not the Messiah and could not hope ever to convince them that he was. Therefore, as he had remained silent all along, it was expected that he would continue to remain silent to this final question, and thus walk out of the palace of Caiphas free.

But he didn't. At the most dangerous moment of all, Jesus chose to speak, and thus to save face for Caiphas.

"I am," Jesus said to the startled priest, "as you say; but I warn you: hereafter you will see the Son of Man enthroned at the right hand of the Almighty and returning upon the clouds in the sky."

What relief the high priest must have felt! When all else had failed Jesus had condemned himself. He had, in effect, pleaded guilty, though perhaps not *exactly* as Caiphas wished. There was no further need of witless witnesses, even though the law said that the words of a defendant are not to be taken into account. "I am, as you say." That was enough. The entire body of the Great Sanhedrin was witness to the proclamation that Jesus had said that he was sent by God to save Judea.

Further words might vitiate the plea, so Caiphas placed both hands high on the collar of his tunic and pulled down and away, ripping the cloth through the middle. "He has blasphemed!" the high priest shouted. "What further need have we of witnesses?" He desired to close the case as quickly as possible. "Listen, then! You have just heard his blasphemy; what is your verdict?"

A polled vote was not necessary. A crime had been committed in the presence of the judges. They said, in awkward chorus: "He is liable to the penalty of death!"

Jesus stood, his gentle face turning from face to face again, and he saw that now the judicial faces were contorted with anger. He might have said: You have tried me at night and the law forbids it. He might have said: You cannot adjudge guilt in a capital case on the same day on which evidence is heard. He might even have said: Without my words, without my admission that the Father has indeed sent me to you, you would have no case against me.

But he said nothing. And when Caiphas announced that the court stood in recess until after dawn, when it would meet in the temple, the judges came down from their benches and some walked up to Jesus and spat in his face. Others, in the crowd around him, clenched their fists and hit him. He said nothing, though some of the blows caused him to double over.

Caiphas ordered the prisoner to be taken out and guarded well. The servants led him out onto the portico and down the steps into the stone courtyard. They had waited wearily all night and the news of guilt had preceded the prisoner. And they too planned to make sport of the Messiah.

John was in the courtyard. When Peter left to weep his remorse, John remained to find out what the supreme council would do. When word came that Jesus was guilty of blasphemy, and that the judgment had been that he should die, John waited long enough to look once more upon the face of the man who loved him. The young apostle was close to tears as Jesus was led down into the courtyard, because the bound man was bruised and dirty, with spit running down his face, and his legs quivered with weakness and fatigue.

Then John left. He needed wings on his young feet because there was much to do. He had to spread the tragic news among those who believed in Jesus and, sadly, he had also to run to Bethany to tell the news to the Mother of Jesus.

5 A.M.

Some priests came to ask questions of Jesus. He did not answer. He stood tall, looking over their heads as though not seeing them. His hands were bound behind his back and his feet were spread slightly apart. Some of the priests studied him closely now, and in all sincerity they could not see what there was in him that attracted so many of the people. They came to him timidly, and they looked up into his face and asked the same old question: "From where do you derive your power?" They were afraid that at any moment something magical would happen, like flames leaping out of the flagstones, or unheralded claps of thunder. But when nothing happened, they wore expressions of disgust and said "Vah!" and walked away.

The guards moved a brazier full of coals over to the corner where Jesus stood. The sad, bearded face was now bathed in red. The guards were angry because Jesus had not answered any of the questions asked by the priests. It showed lack of respect. So they asked a few questions on their own, and when no answers were forthcoming they slapped him and repeated the questions. They took turns standing before him, and the stinging slaps spun his head to the left and again to the right.

The men began to enjoy the game. They progressed from slaps to heavy punches on the head and chest and stomach. When Jesus doubled up, they hit him in the face and that brought him erect again. They stood close to him and spat in his face and saw their saliva cling to his cheeks.

Someone in the group had a more amusing idea. He got a cloth and blindfolded Jesus. The guards danced around him, cuffing his face and simpering: "Act the prophet, please. Who is it that struck you?" They called him cruel names. And obscene names. He tired before they did.

His knees began to buckle, so they held him up until he was strong enough to stand alone. Then they beat him again. They knew that they were doing nothing reprehensible because this prisoner had already been condemned to death by the Great Sanhedrin, and from experience they knew that a condemned prisoner was legitimate prey for the sadistic pleasures of the guards. So long as he was conscious at the time of stoning or strangling or crucifixion no one would be reprimanded.

This particular man, they found, was weak. Either he had not been properly fed in recent days or he had not been getting rest, because he lasted only about a half-hour. He sagged and fell forward on his knees, and as they lifted him, they saw that his eyes were rolling upward. The face was gouged along the cheek lines and across the forehead, and in the ruddy glow from the fire, the blood made his face look raw and battered; it had matted his beard. The guards had trouble holding him erect.

Word came out that the high priest expected to take the prisoner to the temple shortly after dawn. So the guards got some water and used the blindfold to wipe the face of Jesus. If he was going to the temple, they did not want him to excite the pity of the morning worshipers. The first pale flush of pink was over the courtyard when Jesus was able to stand by himself. The stomach blows bothered him, because he shuffled around the fire, bent over and hobbling, and he could not seem to stand up straight.

A Levite with temple duties stood on the highest pinnacle of the temple. He faced east. His deep brown eyes reflected the first pale greens and reds from the horizon. Below, one of the chief priests, surrounded by others, stood looking aloft. The Levite said nothing. He kept watching the rim of the horizon beyond the Dead Sea and over the tabled Mountains of Moab.

His eyes did not move from the east. Had he chosen to be a little derelict in his duties, he might have gazed below and drunk in the heady view of the snowy temple and the city behind him, and the Cedron below. He could have seen, in a fraction of a glance, that the twenty-four gates of the temple area were spread with people, all of whom were waiting for his word. Had he wavered just the slightest bit, he could have seen the movement of thousands of families on the slopes of Olivet, directly ahead. But he had a solemn duty to perform, and even if his eyes dried in his head, he would not turn away. He would not dream of looking behind him, where blue smoke already curled from many homes and hung, like a veil under an invisible ceiling, flat over Jerusalem. Nor would he look toward the west, where the pilgrims in caravans were approaching the city from Joppa. Those from the north were coming across the last of the hills, and this road and the one from Joppa met outside a western gate at a place called Golgotha, or Calvary, and the two roads formed a pale white cross as they passed each other.

The sky came alight, dimming the pale greens and the rose, and these colors changed to yellows and bands of unbelievable pink. The colors became diffuse and spread over the dome of the sky until, at last, the dedicated Levite saw the sun's first touch of light on a mountain.

He cupped his hands and called down: "The morning sun shineth already!" Far below, the ranking priest called back the ritual question: "Is the sky lit up as far as Hebron?" This was a city seventeen miles away. The Levite shaded his eyes and studied the hills to the south, and looking beyond Bethlehem he saw the reflected brightness of the walls of Hebron.

Again he cupped his hands around his mouth and called down: "Yes!" At that moment, the daylight hours began for Jerusalem. The time was 5:44 A.M. The priest below turned and clapped his hands. In a court, several priests brought long silver trumpets to their lips and blew three mighty blasts in concert, so that the echoes of the sound caromed swiftly around inside the walls of the city.

Jerusalem began to awaken. Inside the temple, the fifty priests who were assigned to temple duty on this day moved about silently, their bare feet slapping softly against the marble. With many others, they had assembled before dawn in the Hall of Hewn Polished Stone; these were the fortunate, chosen by lot. All duties were assigned by lot, starting with the one most desired: the daily solemn offering of incense.

The man who drew that assignment could never again draw for it. There were middle-aged priests in the group who had never been lucky enough to draw it. Some of the fifty priests then disengaged themselves from the others and went to a special room where the sacrificial lamb for this morning had lived for four days. He had been examined carefully for blemishes before he had been found worthy of the sacrifice. Now he was examined again.

Outside, the guards opened all the gates of the temple and the people poured in like a dammed-up flood, spreading to all the courts of the temple and cascading up and down the stairs. The men assembled in one court; the women in another. This was the time for morning prayer. They stood, and each man began by murmuring his sins to Yahweh. Then two sections of Scripture were read, there was a sermon followed by the recitation of the Ten Commandments, and they closed with the singing of psalms. In all the known parts of the world the same service would follow the first glimpse of the morning sun.

The sacrificial lamb was given water from a golden bowl. At a signal, priests came into the altar room with the sacred utensils. The lamb was led up to the altar, and there his right forefoot was tied to his right hindfoot.

Then the left side was tied. He bleated with fright when his head was forced through an iron ring in the floor. He faced west.

At that moment, two priests solemnly vested entered the holy place and one placed incense in the burners and lit it. The other trimmed the candlestick of seven branches. At the altar, a priest straddled the lamb, lifted its head and laid the blade of a knife against the little animal's throat. He remained this way for a moment. Then he stroked upward hard. The lamb struggled in silence. Another priest caught the blood in a golden bowl and sprinkled it on the altar stone.

In the Hall of Hewn Polished Stone another servant of God, followed by two assistants, took a hammer and struck a solid blow on a huge gong. As the sound reverberated, the priests and the pilgrims met and "fell down before the Lord," and blue clouds of sweet-smelling smoke rose from the holy place and hung in the morning air.

This day began with an old sacrifice. It would end with a new one.

At the home of Caiphas, members of the Sanhedrin waited for the propitious hour to meet. They and their servants walked in and out of the courtyard; some, in their great robes and conical hats, paused to look at the condemned man, others did not. It was a busy house, with messengers running in and out and notable persons standing on the porch, but withal it was a happy house.

The elders had trapped a religious faker, and not only that, they had managed to bait him into admitting his own blasphemy. In front of all, he had had the brazen effrontery to refer to himself as the Messiah! This had led a few of the milder members of the Sanhedrin to think that Jesus might be insane, but if this point were admitted they would not be permitted, under law, to put him to death, so they were silenced by the majority.

Jesus had already been found "guilty." Now they had only to sentence him by daylight and the job was done. Any member who had the slightest qualms about the possibility of Jesus' being the Messiah had only to walk over to the corner of the courtyard and look at him. He was not Godlike. He was manlike, and currently, a poor specimen of man. His face was gashed and raw and swollen so that purple welts marked his cheekbones, and both eyes were puffed. His hands shook in the fetters and he was bent over like a person of twice his years.

The Messiah? Not a chance. He was a sinner who had been caught after doing enormous damage to the minds and the faith of the people. The elders knew that if his followers could see him now, they might revolt and riot in the temple, and anyone who wore the trappings of the high priesthood would be likely to be stoned by the infuriated mob.

The Great Sanhedrin had had an informal meeting and an informal trial; now, when Caiphas was ready, the body of sages would meet in the temple and pass a resolution condemning this poor man to death. This would be *formal,* and the certification of it would be carried to the Procurator for endorsement.

No one in the group—except the one or two members who were secret disciples of Jesus—felt any pity for him. Pity was an emotion used with economy in that era. One felt pity for a hurt child, and sometimes for a good woman at the point of death. But true pity had been scrubbed from the minds of some people by the severity of the religious observances of the time and by the callousness of the plagues—from locusts to leprosy— which hit them indiscriminately. Life was an unimportant commodity to the community at large; the termination of it was important only to the man who was about to forfeit it.

Jesus showed signs of weakening. The guards walked him to a column of stone, bound his arms around behind it, and tightened the ropes so that it would be difficult for him to fall down without increasing his pain.

The light of day was strong now and the sun rose over the top of Olivet. Its direct rays were falling inside the city. Everywhere merchants and their clerks were on the narrow roads of Jerusalem, keys jangling, prepared to open the shops. To many this was not only the first day of the Passover, but this evening at six would be the beginning of the Sabbath for all, and many merchants had already closed their shops.

The Gentiles from Greece and Egypt were also abroad at that early hour. Some were tourists, but mostly they were businessmen and they understood and respected the religious laws of the Jews.[24] They would finish their transactions by noon and some would be in an outbound caravan by 3 P.M. Small detachments of the Roman garrison were also on foot in the city, but the people were accustomed to the sight of the alien oppressor parading his might in small squads. The people were accustomed to the sight of them, but their pride would never become accustomed to the pressure of the Roman sandal on their throats.

The ultrareligious Pharisees averted their faces when they saw the soldiers. Women drew their veils tighter at sight of them, and sometimes, when the soldiers saw young Jewish women, they made suggestive noises. It is a tribute to the virtue of the women of the land that there were few scandals.

In the morning light a servant came down off the porch and told the guards to take the prisoner to the temple, there to await the pleasure of the high priest. The bonds were loosed and Jesus was led out of the courtyard. Outside, a small knot of people watched from the opposite side of the tree-lined road. Among them were a few disciples who wanted to be close to the Messiah, but not close enough to risk arrest.

They watched in sorrow, and when the eyes of Jesus lifted and looked into the eyes on the far side of the street, a few turned away, weeping beyond control. The Galilean was taken northeast, through the Mount

Sion area and down into the Tyropoeon Valley and then to the viaduct which led to the temple proper. In the streets many saw him, but few could have recognized the swollen purplish face as that of the Messiah they had followed, Jesus of Nazareth.

Among those who stood waiting outside the home of Caiphas was Judas. He had been paid for his work, but he wanted to know what had happened to his lord and master. He waited, and when Jesus came out Judas looked and was sickened by what he saw. He was shocked and a wave of contrition engulfed him. He did not believe that Jesus was the Messiah but he knew of his own experience that this was the gentlest man one could find in the world.

The party passed him, and Judas watched the guards push Jesus and kick him when he stumbled. His sorrow grew into horror and he told himself, over and over, that he had not meant this to happen! Perhaps Jesus deserved punishment: perhaps banishment to Galilee or further. But not this.

Judas grew frantic. He had to find out what would happen. He hurried after the small group, throwing his cloak over the lower part of his face and keeping a distance between himself and his great friend.

BACKGROUND

The Roman World

At this time the Roman Empire was over seven hundred years of age and still growing—though already it included a great part of the world Jesus had come to save. And certainly it touched his life, his immediate human awareness, in a sense that the other great areas of the earth could not. It hugged the rim of the Mediterranean Sea and it included many peoples of many colors. The banners of Rome snapped in breezes along the Rhine, the Danube, the Atlas Mountains of North Africa; in Portugal, Syria, Belgium, Egypt and over much of the civilized world between.

Tiberius was the Emperor. He was seventy; a lean, acidulous man who suffered from acne. His greatest happiness came from study. His deepest unhappiness had come from his mother, Livia. She nagged him all the way up the political ladder and, when he finally stepped on the top rung, he never looked at Livia again.

He was a strong man, dedicated to the Empire, but he was unfortunate in two respects. He was prone to become caught in the trivia of administration, and he found it impossible to show emotion. Some of his colleagues in the Roman Senate called Tiberius "The Mask." Years before, as a young officer, he had learned to repress any clues to his inner feelings and, in age, he found it impossible to show either joy or sorrow. He took comfort in astrology and he neglected the gods of Rome.

Once he had fallen in love. The woman was Vipsania, who became his wife. In her presence Tiberius was animated and gay, and to her he showed his depth of feeling as a child exhibits secret trinkets to a friend. But his mother and Caesar Augustus intrigued to have him divorce Vipsania for Julia, and Tiberius had done it. Julia cuckolded him.

The reign of Tiberius was, according to law, a constitutional one. Under analysis it wasn't, and yet, in the early part of his reign, he was overly deferential to the Senate and referred even the smallest matters of state to this august body. He made a point of sitting in the Senate and speaking as a member, often in the minority. Decrees were passed against his wishes and Tiberius had no comment. Some of the wits ridiculed him and his family, and when Caesar was asked about it, he said that the Empire should enjoy free speech and thought.

Tacitus opposed him, but admitted that the nominations for office sent to the Senate by the Emperor were "made with judgment." What Tiberius wanted was a Rome of the old days, a Rome in which consuls and procurators and other magistrates enjoyed the full prerogatives of their rank; he wanted peace along the frontiers and no new taxes and no suppression of subject peoples; he admonished anyone who disagreed with him to take the matter to the proper court.

At the age of fifty-six, he had assumed the throne with little knowledge of economics. Now, at seventy, he knew a great deal about the subject.

It is a matter of record that, when his reign began, there were 100,000,000 sesterces in the treasury. When he died, he left 2,700,000,000 sesterces.

The rigid observance of law and the rights of others lasted through the first nine years of the reign of Tiberius. During that time, he said often that he derived his power from the Senate and the people, and that he was only the chief magistrate of the nation. If, later, Tiberius became an autocrat, little by little, the law may have been at fault, because under it Caesar was absolute ruler of the provinces but a democratic appointee at home. This dual aspect of his reign proved an impossible situation in the long run; in time, the autocratic side of the position manifested itself in Rome. Caesar became absolute ruler at home as well as abroad. More and more power passed into fewer and fewer hands; the appointment of magistrates in Rome became a favor for friends; somewhere around the seventh to ninth year of the reign of Tiberius, he posted a huge garrison of soldiers outside the walls of Rome, responsible solely to him. They were an acute threat to all who opposed Tiberius, and a latent threat to him.

As a monarch, Tiberius was in many ways a just though merciless man. His rule in the provinces was more efficient than at home, and the legate or procurator whom Tiberius caught oppressing subject peoples was subject to the unpleasant consequences of his anger! He kept these officials in an almost constant state of dread; as we have seen, Tiberius was chronically suspicious and he used informers. Having appointed Pontius Pilate to the small post of Procurator of Palestine on the endorsement of Pilate's wife and of Sejanus, a confidant and spy, he would still remove Pilate from office and banish him on the slightest pretext, although he had once said that he liked to keep procurators in office for long periods of time on the theory that, once they had fattened on their stealings from the people, they would leave the people alone.

The city of Rome, as a hub around which revolved the wheel of empire, was a marvel of culture and laxness, of business efficiency and gutter politics, of enormous strength and cheap chicanery. Even in the field of jurisprudence, the Romans managed to blend a mixture of progressive thinking with the ridiculous. All law seemed to be divided against itself, beginning with the written law, which was in two parts: *Ius Civile*, the law of the citizens, and *Ius Gentium*, the law of the nations.

Legalities aside, the habits and customs of the people of Rome were, in themselves, of interest when compared with the hyperreligious fears of a city such as Jerusalem. The moral lives of Roman girls were carefully guarded, whereas those of their brothers were leniently supervised. It was not considered shameful for a young man of good family to go to a lupanaria and rent the services of a woman. All such places were licensed and controlled: two of the main rules were that the brothel had to be outside the walls of the city and that it could open for business only after dark. All prostitutes were registered by the authorities and had to wear togas instead of the stola.

At this time, the woman-for-a-fee was losing steadily to the educated amateur who could sing, dance, recite poetry and engage in topical conversation. Both types solicited business in every section of the city, and could even be found flirting in the temple of the goddess Isis. At one point, Ovid found them under the city porticoes, in the theater, at the Circus Maximus—"as numerous as stars in the sky."

Male prostitutes were also available and could, for a fee, be summoned. Homosexuality was condemned by a law which winked at it. (In Jerusalem, the punishment was stoning.) "I am stricken with the heavy dart of love," sang Horace, "for Lyciscus, who claims in tenderness to outdo any woman." The home and marriage fought these rivals and in fear parents employed marriage brokers to find husbands for their daughters at the earliest respectable age. After the age of nineteen, unmarried women were considered to be old maids.

As in Palestine, marriage was a game played by the older generation. A boy and a girl who were betrothed seldom saw each other. There not only was no courtship; there was no word in the language for it. Jaded Seneca said that the Roman tested everything before purchase except a bride. A young man of gifted pen never wrote poetry to the girl of his dreams. He addressed it to married women whom he admired, or to one whom he had no intention of marrying. Flirtations and affairs by married women were common. The younger Seneca wrote that a married woman who was content with but two lovers was virtuous. The callous Ovid said that "Pure women are only those who have not been asked. A man who is angry at his wife's amours is a rustic." Juvenal wrote of a woman—not considered to be extraordinary—who married eight times in five years. The women too were cynical, and some of them said that it was equitable to surrender one's dowry to one's husband and one's body to one's lover.

The attire of the women of Jerusalem was strictly prescribed. But the ladies of Rome were just learning the uses of delicate fabrics as undergarments. Attractive scarves dressed the shoulders carelessly. Filmy veils hid nothing of the face of a woman except a mediocre complexion (cosmetics were in use then too—to say nothing of wigs, hairdresses and manicures). In the chill of winter the women covered themselves with attractive fur coats. Silks and linens were used by both men and women, but dyes were expensive. It was fashionable to embroider rich materials with gold thread or silver, and dresses, carpets, curtains, coverlets and head veils were thus decorated.

The richer homes of Rome were, by any standard, elaborate. Floors were made of grained marble or mosaic; the fluted columns which decorated large rooms were made of polychrome marble or pure onyx, sometimes of alabaster. Walls were hand-painted as murals of battle or land-scapes. Ceilings were covered with gold leaf or made entirely of plate glass. Wood tables stood on purest ivory legs. Divans were decorated with ivory, silver or gold. Large beds were made of bronze and were fitted with canopied mosquito netting. Candelabra were fashioned of bronze or glass; statues and paintings were everywhere; vases of considerable size filled room corners and were made of Corinthian bronze or murrhine glass.

Of course, much of this could be seen only in the better homes, but Rome had plenty of such. Slaves had to be purchased to guard the wealth of such manors, and some houses had four hundred of them. The one thing which the master of such a showplace could not buy was privacy; he ate while two slaves stood in attendance at his elbows; he undressed with a slave at each sandal; even in the privacy of his bath, the silent, elo-quent eyes of his slaves were upon him.

Small businessmen were in their shops and at their benches in factories at sunrise. Lunch was at noon, followed by a short sleep. The men then returned to business, and worked until sunset. For recreation, the little man attended the public baths. Practically all Romans were more particular about personal cleanliness than they were about the worship of their gods. They bathed frequently, and often in public, and they were the first race to carry sudaria (handkerchiefs), for wiping perspiration. They were devoted to toothpastes and tooth powders and consulted their physicians about the care of their teeth.

The diet of the poor was made up mainly of wheat and barley, cheeses, vegetables, fruits and nuts. The rich ate meats of all kinds; the favorite was pork roast. Vendors in the streets pushed wagons and hawked hot botuli (sausages). The rich had jaded tastes which needed freshening. For the pleasure of guests, a big fish was often brought in alive by slaves and dropped into hot water, so that the diners could watch the change in colors as the fish died. They also prized the wings of ostriches, the livers of geese, the pointed tongues of flamingoes. It was Apicus who devised pâté de foie gras by fattening the livers of female pigs on a diet of fresh figs.

The streets of Rome were the best paved in the world, and on them crowds of men walked to their work in the early hours. All men looked rather alike, inasmuch as practically all male citizens of Rome wore short hair and loose-fitting dresses and sandals. The men bunched in groups, usually by professions, and walked to their offices gesticulating in business conversations or shouting greetings to friends. These were the men who, through the agency of a Senate and an Emperor, ruled most of the known world. Caesar Augustus, who had preceded Tiberius, wanted all the men of Rome to show their "apartness" by wearing the toga, and when his chariot rolled through the streets and he saw few togas, he became angry. By law, he denied the use of the toga to any but citizens of Rome, and he would leave a social gathering if he noted that the male guests were not wearing them.

Many Roman fashions and customs were transferred to the provinces. In Jerusalem, what angered and embarrassed the Jews most was the Roman theater built close to the temple and the amphitheater on the plain. Like true provincial works, both had been copied from the originals in the capital of the world, and each tried to be grander than the original.

Women were permitted to act in the theater, but only on condition that they were classified as prostitutes. Much of the material used was either Greek and tragic, or Roman and obscene. On some occasions, the audience was permitted to call upon actors to remove all clothing. No Jewish women were among the performers, and none were in the audience except some of King Herod's friends, who were Jews by blood, but Roman by disposition.

The amphitheater on the plain was not used often because the staging of brutal sport was expensive. Sometimes, it was said, five years passed without a spectacle being seen there and, in these dull periods, the soldiers used the grounds for drills, for simulated battles, and for the torture of slaves and prisoners of war.

When the games were staged by Herod, they were modeled on those staged by Caesar, which is to say that all the better-known Romans and Herodians were present to watch war captives, armed with spears, fight condemned prisoners gathered from all over the province, armed with short broadswords. In all cases, the combatants were told that if they fought bravely and beautifully they might be granted freedom.

High in the terraced wall, in a private box called the suggestum, sat the Procurator and his kingly host and their court guests. The rest of the amphitheater, from the top wall down to the sandbarked floor, was occupied by lower echelons of Roman sycophants. Admission was free. Instead of the customary Roman statuary, there were fountains here and there throwing scented water into the air in mist.

Spectators could buy food and drink from vendors, who hawked their wares between the rows of seats. Opposite the suggestum, an orchestra of musicians played on stringed instruments, trying to match the mood of the music to the mood of what was happening on the tanbark floor. Still, the games were not so clever or so cruel as those in Rome, where the preliminary events often included trained apes riding on dogs, small animals driving chariots, barefoot boys dancing on the backs of bulls, and elephants who had been taught to trace Latin letters in the sand. In Rome, one morning's festivities included four hundred tigers fighting to the death with bulls and elephants; on the day that the Colosseum was dedicated, five thousand animals died. Animals unwilling to fight were put to death by iron darts and hot irons.

One of the most popular events, and one of the simplest to stage, was a fight to the death between a man and a bull. This seemed to arouse the lust of the crowd more than any other event, and they roared with approval when a gladiator was impaled on a horn, or when a bull staggered, his black hide glistening as a long knife was plunged repeatedly into his body.

Condemned prisoners, who were always reminded before the day's events that they were doomed anyway, were dressed in the skins of animals and sent out on the floor. Then hunger-crazed wild beasts were loosed on the other side of the arena. It was thrilling to the crowd to watch the man in the skin crouch against the wall boards and hope not to be seen, while the emaciated lions and tigers loped around the floor, looking up toward the crowd and sniffing, all the time unconsciously drawing closer to the man, who was unarmed. After such an event, physicians used the cadavers of these men to learn more about internal anatomy.

It is not known whether, in the Jerusalem games, they staged such spectacles as were common in Rome, in which a sentenced prisoner was ordered to play the part of Medea's rival, garbed in a striking costume which, at a certain point, would burst into flame and burn him to death. Part of the thrill of watching this lay in the fact that the actor knew what was going to happen, and the crowd always lent an attentive ear to his words to discern whether or not there was a quaver of fear in his voice.

In Rome, the people thought that they were being lenient in permitting condemned men or surly slaves to fight for their lives. Their feeling was: "They are to die anyway. We give them a chance." Almost always, the winners killed the losers in the gladiatorial contests. A man who fought with outstanding bravery, and who won, might gain the approval of the crowd and immediate freedom; a man who fought and won without distinction, or was wounded, was given medical attention and, on recovery, was assigned to fight again. A prisoner of war who survived all contests for three years was released into slavery. If he satisfied his master for two years, he won complete freedom.

The suicide rate was high. Some threw themselves headfirst off high places; some inserted their heads between the spokes of moving chariot wheels; some plunged broadswords into their bellies. Wounded gladiators who feigned death were touched with white-hot irons first. If they twitched, they were hit repeatedly on the head with wooden mallets.

Practically all Jews averted their faces when they passed the Roman theater and amphitheater.

One of the historic advantages of the Roman Empire—and the Republic as well—was that the system united Europe. The Romans ruled, and they pooled the raw stuffs of man's needs. Their fleets and their caravans carried the best of each nation's produce. Another advantage was that the Roman legions kept peace throughout the Empire. This included, besides Rome and Italy, thirty provinces. There was always the threat of rebellion, of course, and the most serious of these usually came from Gallia, Hispania, Mauretania and Thracia.

Palestine was seldom a source of worry to the Legate in Syria. It was small and weak and without a native army. Moreover, it was flanked by Egypt and Syria. At the time of the trouble between Jesus and the high priests, Palestine—or parts of it—had been a protectorate and a province of Rome for ninety-three years.

No matter how benevolent Rome was to Palestine, the Jews were unhappy because they cherished freedom above all else. Their greatest annual festival was the celebration of the passing of their people out of the bondage of Egypt. Even if the Romans had treated the Jews as equals, the people of Palestine would not have been happy in the partnership. In a world in which confraternity was becoming increasingly important, the little sandy garden on the eastern shore of the Mediterranean wanted to stand alone.

Still, the responsible Jews readily admitted that they had learned much from the Romans in the field of engineering—how to build better roads, drainage ditches, aqueducts, sewage-disposal plants. They had even learned some social graces. On the other hand, the Hebrews detested the sight of the Roman patrols—four soldiers and a centurion—on their roads and, even more than that, bridled at the many small taxes imposed on them. There were taxes on deed transfers, hidden taxes on food bought in stores, taxes on slaves (the Jews owned few), taxes on profits, duties on exports, duties on imports, a general sales tax of one percent, death taxes and emergency tax to defray the cost of putting down rebellion in any of the other provinces.

Most galling of all was the fact that the Romans did not collect the taxes themselves. In all towns and villages, they leased the right to collect taxes to Jews. This traffic was administered by the Procurator, who knew that, say, 50,000 shekels should come from the town of Cana each year in all types of taxes. He would lease the right to collect this tax to a local citizen, and back the man's authority with soldiers. For this service, Rome might be willing to let the publican keep 10 percent as his fee. Of course, if the tax collector was voracious he might collect more than 50,000 shekels, in which case he would earn more than 5,000 as his share. The Romans kept close watch on these matters, and seldom permitted the collectors to gouge the people beyond small amounts of graft. They also watched the collectors to prevent double-dealings. For example, if a merchant owed an annual tax of 500 shekels, he might bargain with the collector to take 250 shekels officially, and give the collector 150 more secretly. The publican then made up the deficit by overtaxing the poor and the ignorant. Rome flogged such men.

In the eternal city, all taxes came under the eye of an appointee of the Emperor called the Censor. He had to know how many subjects of Caesar there were in each of the thirty provinces, how much gross business was done by each province, and how much should come to the treasury in Rome from each province.

Every emperor issued his own coins with his image on the face of them, and recalled the coins of his predecessor. There was the aureus and the half-aureus and the silver denarius. One aureus was the equivalent of 25 denarii. It also equaled 100 sesterces or 400 asses. Each emperor proclaimed that his currency was legal tender throughout the world, but that local currency had value only in the province of its origin.

In and around Rome people traveled by chariots, drawn by good horses; by sedan chairs, carried by slaves; by wagons, singly or in caravans; and on the backs of donkeys. Travel by sea was slow and often dangerous. The Mediterranean Sea was closed to all but emergency traffic between November 10 and March 10, because in that interval it was considered stormy and unreliable. The swiftest time for a courier between Rome and Jerusalem was forty-six days.

The owners of merchant ships always announced in February that Roman Jews could book passage at once for the Passover pilgrimage to Jerusalem. When these were heavily booked by the eight thousand Jews who lived in Rome, the merchants extorted bribes from the passengers. This practice became so flagrant that Caesar Augustus took official notice of it and issued an imperial rescript guaranteeing to all Jews the right to go "home" for the holy days at a nominal fee.

Twenty-one years before the birth of Jesus, the Emperor Augustus split all Roman provinces into two classes. Those which were considered to be secure—Italy, for example—were called senatorial provinces and were administered by the Roman Senate. This body appointed proconsuls to manage them. They served one year and were seldom reappointed. The second type of province was usually on the frontiers of the Empire and was administered by the Emperor through his appointment of procurators or legates. The Senate proconsuls were usually Romans of Senate rank; the Procurators were often businessmen who were owed a political favor. These served until they displeased the Emperor.

Palestine was a frontier province.

As a unit, the Roman army lasted longer than any other military institution in the history of man. It was born as a crude instrument of defense; it lived as a gleaming spear ready for flight. It began with citizen soldiers; it ended with long-term professionals. It started with the protection of the City of Rome; its history was climaxed with the conquest of the world.

It was a malleable instrument of policy. It was changing—ever changing—from decade to decade. When its infantry was defeated by barbarian horsemen, the Roman legion acquired horses. When the spear was "outgunned" by the *machina* slingshot, Rome trained cohorts to use the new weapons. It copied and it invented. In time of peace the army remained slightly stronger than the needs of empire. In time of war it recruited all males between the ages of seventeen and sixty who could walk—and all of those under the age of forty-seven had to fight in the field.

In long-term strategy, the Roman army was superb. It required almost three hundred years to conquer Europe and civilize Asia and Africa, and it began by conquering Italy first. It failed only once in its long march—against Hannibal—but even he could not, in victory, rip the Roman army loose from its entrenchments.

In this era, the main unit of the army was called a legion. It consisted of 4,500 men: 3,000 heavy infantry, 1,200 light infantry and 300 horsemen. The real strength of the army lay in its heavy infantry. Each man had a large metal shield, a metal helmet, a leather cuirass which protected the soldier from neck to navel, and weapons. Half carried short Spanish thrusting and cutting swords; the other half carried throwing spears.

The legions were broken into maniples of 120 men each, and each maniple, like a chess piece, was advanced in battle to fight and retire. Spaces were left between maniples so that those in front could retreat while alternate maniples advanced through the gaps. The field in A.D. 30 were for the odd-numbered maniples to charge the enemy on the field of battle, sending forth first a shower of spears, then to follow with close fighting using short swords. On signal, these maniples returned to line while, on the same signal, the alternate maniples were moving up to battle. In command of each legion was a tribune, or a *legatus legionis,* deputy to the general. The maniples were in charge of centurions, who were usually officers of long service or young noblemen beginning military careers.

In support were "allies"—armies impressed into service from the subject peoples. These were organized and trained by Roman officers and were broken into small units, called cohorts, which numbered about five hundred men each. Rome used them to support the flanks of its legions.

Many of them came from the conquered Italian provinces, although Numidian horsemen were used in battle, and so were Balearic slingers, Cretan archers and others.

In battle, the Roman legions were in the center, the "allies" on the outsides, and Roman cavalry on the wings. The tribunes and consuls attacked with their center, holding the "allies" in reserve. In Spain, at the battle of Ilipa, Scipio Africanus surprised his adversary by reversing the order, putting the "allies" in the center, with Roman legions on the flanks, and cavalry out on the wings. Then he ordered his flanks to the attack, holding pat with his center. He won.

The average *professional* Roman legionary enlisted in the army for a term of twenty years. The pay was meager and the service was disciplined. When he retired, he was given a bounty, a small quantity of money, or farm land in a province. Those who served in the armies of "allies" were kept in uniform for a longer term, received less pay, and on retirement were given Roman citizenship for themselves, their wives and their children.

In Palestine, the Twelfth Legion was divided into two brigades. The first, composed of Roman soldiers, served at Caesarea. The second, mostly Syrians, was quartered along the Arabian frontier and garrisoned at Fortress Antonia. With them were special cohorts of camel corps, archers, engineers, besiegers, medical service, base hospitals, veterinary hospitals, and the questionarii, or military police.

Although the Jews did not eat meat except on holidays, the Syrian troops stationed in Jerusalem received two pounds of meat and grain per man per day. The shepherds in the hills around Jerusalem and Bethlehem sold a great deal of their lamb and mutton to the Romans.

The Syrians, officered by Romans, were seldom sent elsewhere to battle. They remained on duty in Palestine, and the aloofness of the Jews toward soldiers far from home and lonely bred ill will. The people often spat when they saw squads of men marching along the roads, each man with a metal helmet, a coral-colored cape pinched at the neck, a short-sleeved tunic which covered him to the thighs and hard leather sandals fastened with ropes across the instep. The soldiers were not permitted to reply to hostile actions by citizens. Even in off-duty hours they found no amusement in Jerusalem, and spent the time rolling dice on the big Lithostrotos.

After two or three years of service in Palestine, the Syrians were taken to Antioch-on-the-Chrysorrhea for a rest tour. It had been built to the east of the Jordan River for Greeks and Romans and Syrians. Swine were kept there for those who liked pork, and all manner of whiskey was distilled. Along the main street were small shops where rugs and weaving could be purchased. There was a hippodrome for plays, and two amphitheaters for Roman games. At the theater, the humor was coarse and to the taste of common soldiers.

A greater contrast could not be imagined than the lax, indulgent, highly civilized life of Rome, and the strict life of Palestine where every last detail of daily living was regulated by the law of a stern religion. Yet these two worlds must have figured with equal importance in the mind of Jesus as he spoke parables to teach the people, and these two worlds joined to pronounce the most important death sentence in the history of man.

NARRATIVE

❖❖❖

April 7, A.D. 30

6 A.M.

Judas, following the maimed man he had betrayed, trailed alone behind the group to the Xystus, which bridged the upper city to the temple area, and then on to the Huldah Gates. He mingled with the worshipers and got inside without attracting attention. He was now in a panic. If only he could have grabbed Jesus by the arm, and fled . . . ! If he could go back to Caiphas and talk . . . ! The terrible feeling that had replaced the tickle in his stomach was not due to his faith in Jesus, not even to his friendship for Jesus, because a traitor has no capacity for friendship. What troubled Judas was the recollection of the sweetness and goodness of this man, even to those who hurt him most. Now—too late—Judas could not bear to see Jesus hurt.

There was a stone room in the southwestern corner of the temple, adjoining the place where the largest court flared out toward the Pool of Siloe. Here the Great Sanhedrin met. The walls inside were of grained black and white marble and there were the three rows of semicircular chairs which faced three similar rows against the opposite wall.

Jesus was led inside and held, standing between the facing rows. Two hundred feet away his Father was being worshiped unceasingly. One hundred feet away many of the Jews who believed in him walked on the royal porch in the morning sunshine, and some asked others whether Jesus the Christ would come to the temple on this bright day to teach and to heal. Here, where he stood, he was a dangerous creature who must be exterminated quickly and quietly to make the land safe for his Father.

It was enough to bring a wry smile to the puffy face. His leg muscles twitched with fatigue; his tongue touched the dry bloody lips and he hoped for water. To ask for it would be foolish, for this would give the guards one additional cruelty with which to play. So he remained quiet and asked his Father for additional strength.

When he saw the elders come in, slowly and solemnly, glancing fleetingly at him, and then edge into their seats, Jesus straightened up and looked at the wall above and behind them. The alternates came in and sat on the opposite side, and when all had been seated Caiphas made his entrance and at once began to review the evidence. He wasted no time on the prisoner, and neither solicited information from him nor taunted him. Caiphas had his mind on the larger goal: the death of Jesus. So he addressed himself to such of the seventy as were present, who listened to the summing up. They stroked their beards, wagged their heads in assent at various points, then pursed their lips and squinted at the ceiling as though in pontifical thought.

The high priest reminded them that it was already the judgment of this court that the man before them deserved death on a charge of blasphemy, and that the recitation of evidence and the admission of guilt on the part of the prisoner were no longer of any account. They must vote now, individually and formally, to certify the sentence. Ordinarily, he said with some unction, it would be fitting to deliberate for another day as prescribed in the law, but one could not deliberate on the Sabbath, which would be upon them in a matter of hours. He reminded them that the prisoner was a chronic desecrator of the Sabbath, having been witnessed healing the sick, curing alleged blind persons, and raising confederates from a stupor giving the appearance of death, all on the Sabbath. And, if the law says that he who lives by the sword shall die by the sword, what finer sense of justice than to kill the blasphemer just before the setting sun ushered in a particularly holy Sabbath?

"He has spoken giddupha [blasphemy]!" Caiphas shouted.

The clerks then began to call the roll, starting with the youngest members. Each in turn stood and said: "He is guilty! Death!" When the roll was completed without a dissenting vote, the clerk wrote the prisoner's name, the charge, the finding of guilt, and the sentence. This, along with the prisoner, would have to be taken to the Roman Procurator for confirmation of sentence.

Two seats in the Great Sanhedrin were empty: that of Nicodemus and that of Joseph of Arimathia, friends of the accused. The total number of men who held the life of Jesus in their hands, excluding Caiphas, who as Nasi had no vote, was no greater than sixty-eight, two for each year of his life.

The high priest left his post and walked toward the rear of the room. There he removed the golden band of his office from his miter. On it in Hebrew were the characters: "Holiness unto Yahweh," and it was an ancient legend that, when the final day of atonement came, God would read these words on the golden band and, pleased, would forgive all blasphemers.

The bonds of the prisoner had been loosed throughout the brief hearing and he stood chafing his wrists and holding his stomach. In the back of the Boule (council), Caiphas sat in whispered consultation with some of the Scribes. The next move was to take Jesus to Pontius Pilate, and in all the long, hard road of the apprehension, trial and conviction of this criminal, there was nothing that Caiphas feared more. A man of restraint could bear with Pilate's ironies, his sarcasms, his spurious puzzlement regarding Hebrew law, his disclaimers, his faintly veiled scorn of all Jews. But if he denied that the crime was of sufficient gravity to warrant death, then all the pleas of logic and justice would avail them nothing. Jesus would be freed and he would be a greater voice among the people than ever before. One might as well close the temple.

A Scribe sitting with Caiphas said that he had been present a few days ago when Jesus had examined a Roman coin and had said that it was just to render to Caesar the things that were Caesar's. A small group of conferees suggested that there was the germ of an idea in this, and they discussed it at length. What the Galilean actually had said could not but please Pilate, because the little speech favored just taxation and coin in kind. But if the statement could be perverted a little—to a point, say, where they might tell the Procurator that this man had counseled the populace *against* Caesar—that would be inciting to rebellion under Roman law, and Pilate, no matter what his knowledge of the truth, would not dare to free the man Jesus. If word got back to the Legate in Syria, or to Tiberius in Rome, that Pilate had dared to set free one who had taught the downfall of Caesar, then Pilate's own freedom would be in jeopardy.

The high priest promised to give this matter some thought. Only two years ago Caiphas had had to combat Pilate in a test of strength precipitated by the Procurator. Pilate had been told that the Roman soldiers could not carry votive shields, which bore the image of Caesar, into Jerusalem. The Jews, he was informed, would riot. So Pilate had hundreds of the shields set up on the wall of Fortress Antonia, which faced the temple grounds. The people rioted. Caiphas and Annas conferred and protested directly to Tiberius. The Emperor sent orders to Pilate to remove the shields at once and to secure them in the temple of Augustus at Caesarea.

Caiphas arranged for the people to stand in the Court of Gentiles, near Antonia, as the shields came down. They jeered. Pilate had been humbled. He had been beaten by the Hebrews. The protagonists remembered this. Nor had they forgotten the time Pilate expropriated temple moneys for his viaduct.

The high priest felt that Pilate would make the case of Jesus another test of strength. Not that Pilate cared for the prisoner, who was just another inconsequential subject. The life or *death* of Jesus was without meaning to the Procurator. The worry of Caiphas was that, in spite of the fact that he had inveigled the Roman into participating in the arrest of Jesus, Pilate would do anything he could to embarrass Caiphas and his father-in-law, no matter what the legalities might be.

And yet, in matters that concerned the internal affairs of Palestine, the scornful Gentile was not supposed to interfere. Pilate had been confirming the death sentences of Jews without a murmur. The three wooden beams stuck in the ground at Golgotha-Calvary had been used for several crucifixions in recent days. The Romans, of course, also put them to good use for their own criminals, and for such Jews as were found guilty of crimes against the state. Only yesterday, the Great Sanhedrin had condemned two criminals, and both Jews were now lying in the Antonia dungeon awaiting crucifixion. Pontius Pilate had not hesitated to confirm sentence of death.

Maybe he would not hesitate this morning. It was possible that Caiphas and his little coterie of Sadducees were needlessly worried. They were clever men, and they knew that their best chance of success lay in minimizing Jesus as a religious factor. They had to make him appear a small, cheap religious fraud from Galilee. If Pilate guessed that this man had a huge following then all was lost, because the Procurator would begin at once to play one set of Jews off against another. If he could split Palestine he would soon have the people at one another's throats, and this, from the standpoint of an oppressor, would be ideal.

But it worried Caiphas to think that any schism in this matter might prove to be the people versus the temple. In such a fight, more and more people would turn to espouse the faker because he could perform works of wonder and the priests could not. In time, the holy temple would be like the pyramids of Egypt—a huge tomb.

One of the elders suggested that it would help if they brought along a crowd to shout against Jesus in the presence of Pilate. The little knot of men marveled at the simplicity of this weapon. Whom would they get? They would requisition the services of the temple guards and the "police" force. Those who earned their living at the temple should work for its preservation. It did not matter what they believed, or even whether or not they were influenced by that wild story of Lazarus being raised from the dead—they would do as they were told.

So it was decided to take along a large number of temple employees, and to have them shepherded by several priests. On the march through town to the Antonia these people would press closely around the prisoner so that his disciples in Jerusalem could not get close to him, or even properly see who the prisoner was. Then, at Antonia, the employees would take their cues from the priests, who would lead the shouting from the double arches of the fortress.

Caiphas felt better. He ordered the prisoner to be made ready for a journey as soon as the priests and employees could be drawn from the temple.

Jesus waited, standing.

Outside the room the priests on the Royal Porch issued orders. Guards and messengers listened to their words and then ran off through the throng of worshipers, who wondered at this unseemly conduct in the house of the Lord. It was a bright, crisp morning now, and already there were about thirty thousand people on the temple grounds. The number would be greater toward midday when the late caravans from the diaspora arrived. People jammed all the gates and the stairways leading up and down to the various courts; sometimes fathers, caught in the squeezing tide, had to lift their growing sons and carry them until they could be safely set down again. Others, who had come from far off and had not seen the temple before, turned their eyes on its beauties and the eyes dimmed with tears. In the places of prayer some prayed loudly in semirhythmic chant; some lay prone on the floor and pressed their hot faces to the cold marble with arms outstretched; some knelt and murmured to themselves; some merely stared, too overcome to remember to pray.

Judas, standing on the edge of the portico, saw the excitement. He was afraid to ask what the supreme council had decided. He was afraid not to. The messengers ran off, and in minutes they were back. The priests whispered among themselves and rudely brushed aside the questions of passing pilgrims. Judas stood against the railing, the side of his molasses-colored face catching the morning sun, and several times he started off to ask outright what had happened inside, but each time he sensed that he would be putting himself in danger. They might accuse him of trying to deliver Jesus to freedom, and only Caiphas and a few others knew that, but for Judas, the high senate would not have Jesus in custody right now.

The betrayer grew older as he stood there. The sun mercilessly sought the ever-deepening hollows in his cheeks, the leathery pouches under his eyes. He had to ask. He had to know. He wished that he had remained at home in Kerioth, where life was uncomplicated. He wished that he had not volunteered to strike a blow for Yahweh, for his brain had been beset by worry ever since and there would be no end to it.

He would have to make the priests understand somehow that they were mistaken. Jesus had committed no crime. He had done no wrong. He was as innocent of evil as the lamb they had sacrificed at dawn. If he could make this known to Caiphas, Judas was sure that everything would be all right, because Caiphas was a just man, a lawgiver. He became increasingly nervous. The skin of his body felt uncomfortable. People began to notice the wildness in his eyes, and his hands tugging at his chest and thighs and the back of his neck. Some paused to look at him and smile. He stared back at them. Then he looked at his hands and saw that they were soiled. Fiercely, he thrust them inside his garment. They touched the old leather apron where he kept money.

Judas stared sullenly at the faces around him. Some of them resembled Jesus in features or bearing. He feared that he was losing his mind. The little man pressed his fingers against his temples and ran through the crowd.

He almost collided with a messenger, and paused, breathlessly, to ask what the supreme council had decided. The messenger said he had no time for questions. Judas begged. He said he must know what had happened to the prophet from Galilee.

"Oh, that one," said the messenger. "He will be lifted on a tree this morning."

7 A.M.

Judas clutched at the messenger's garments. He asked to see the high priest at once. The messenger slashed at him with his hand. The high priest, he shouted, was too busy to spend time with people of unsound mind. The furtive eyes of Judas saw a knot of people gathering around him and the messenger. He was certain that they were all trying to stop him from explaining how this trifling matter had got out of control.

He swallowed and determined to try to speak softly. What he wanted to say amounted to breast-beating remorse, but the voice was so subdued and quavering that no one could understand the words, and people began to laugh. The messenger laughed too, and then he broke through the little cordon to deliver the messages of the priest. Judas, still whispering hoarsely, begged him to please stop and listen. When the messenger continued at a trot, Judas threatened to return the thirty pieces of silver. Then the high priest, in justice, would have to return the prisoner. This, he mumbled to himself, was simply a matter of justice or lack of justice.

The people in front of his eyes diffused into vague forms and melted against the whiteness of the marble columns. He was alone again. He clutched at his neck and he too began to run through the crowds of people. He ran northward on the porch, toward the Court of the Priests. He swerved around people with remarkable agility and he ducked and skidded and jarred people and kept on without apology.

When Judas reached the Court of the Priests, he turned into the inner room of the offerings. Several priests were in a group, holding a discussion. They knew Judas, because these were the men who had paid him. When they saw him, their tongues froze into stiff silence and he approached bowing and groveling and rubbing his hands together and smiling. He had come to ask a favor and he did not want to alienate them, so he pretended not to notice the aloofness.

He wet his lips and was determined that he would not shout. He cleared his throat and said, with forced sweetness: "It was wrong for me to betray innocent blood."

The priests looked at one another and then back to the traitor. They could not be further out of sympathy with this man. The high priest had negotiated for the deliverance of a dangerous fool, and had paid for it. The matter was closed. The priests did not even know what had happened to Jesus, and they cared less. They had been ordered to pay to the apostle thirty pieces of silver out of the temple treasury and they had done this; there had been witnesses to the transaction. What did he want now?

"What does that matter to us?" said the ranking one among them. "That is your worry."

Judas' mouth opened to emit sound, then it closed. The shock of their words was beyond bearing. Didn't they understand? The whole bargain was a mistake. He tried again to speak to them, but they were in animated conversation, and penitents were waiting outside the east door to come in and make sin offerings. Judas wanted to weep, but the tears of remorse were denied.

He stood, wild-eyed, mouth open, staring at the priests. His thoughts, imprisoned in the confused brain of the traitor, kept racing around in circles. It was then that he realized, firmly and irrevocably, that what they had meant was that the entire matter was out of their hands. They proposed to do nothing to save Jesus, and if Judas had, as he protested, betrayed innocent blood, then it was his crime, not theirs.

Judas stood indecisively a moment. Then he made a resolve. He could expiate the murder by returning the money. If he accepted nothing for treachery, then it was no longer treachery. That must be so. The law said that no bargain was complete until each of the contending parties had full possession of the merchandise. Well, Caiphas had Jesus. But Judas would nullify the agreement by returning the money.

He reached into his garment and untied the long leather strings around his money apron, and pulled it out. The priests paused in speech to watch him. Nervously, Judas counted out thirty silver coins. Then, not being certain whether he was not perhaps returning thirty-one, he counted them again. He had thirty; he held them in his right hand, and with an oath cast them to the floor.

The music of the money tinkled through the big room and the coins danced and spun and rolled in ever-lazier circles until they all came to rest on the floor. Then Judas turned, apron in hand, leather strings flying behind him, and fled.

One of the younger Levites went about picking up the coins, though he had qualms that in touching them he might be unclean. The other priests had similar feelings. To a man, they agreed that this was now blood money and could not be returned to the treasury. The corban had never been tainted by money which was not given, with fullness of heart, by one who did it for love of Yahweh. They were still debating when the Levite brought them the coins, glinting in his hands.

No one wanted to touch them. One of the older priests, watching this display of purity, observed that there was nothing in the law to prevent the use of any money—even blood money—to help the poor. Another said that every year the temple was plagued by the deaths of unknown pilgrims, who had to be buried at temple expense. The priests nodded, and the older one reminded them that on the opposite side of the Valley of Hinnom a potter had offered to sell his plot for the burial of unknowns.

They bought it. It became the first Potter's Field and it was known as Haceldama, the Field of Blood.[25]

Judas ran from the temple like a man who dares not stop. He clutched his cloak in his fist and hitched up his garments; in the other hand he swung the money apron. He ran wildly, almost purposelessly, and he bumped into people. Finally he got across the Xystus piers to the southwest, and then ran down the west side of the Tyropoeon Valley.

His lungs burned and cried for air, but he did not stop. He went through the wealthy residential section of the city, little legs flying, eyes bugged like those of one who does not see, and to families out for a holy day morning stroll he was a comical figure. Some called to him as he passed, but Judas heard nothing.

When he reached the broad white Roman steps, he hurried across them, skipping so that he would not fall, and then ran through the tall cypresses pointing green apostrophes at the sky. Instead of breath, little cries came from between his teeth. He ran as far as the inside of the wall, and then, like an animal looking for an exit, he turned right and ran to the west. When he came to the gate leading to Bethlehem, a sea of people was coming in, and Judas swam the tide with his legs churning and his arms flailing.

Outside the wall, he ran along the little path which hung over the Valley of Hinnom. The little field he had helped to buy lay directly across from him, but Judas did not know; nor would he have wanted to know. Now he was slowed to a walk, because the path clung to the wall and hung over the edge of nothing. Far below were the jagged chunks of rock left over from the building of the wall.

Judas walked carefully along until he came to a lonely fig tree. It grew out from the path and hung its spring leaves over the valley. The apostle placed his foot against the tree trunk and pushed violently. The tree barely shook. He breathed hard; painfully hard. He cast about, looking for something, and could not find it. Then he looked at the money belt in his hand and crept up the small trunk until he found a strong branch. Judas leaned out and tried to rock the branch. It moved slightly.

He leaned out, straddling the branch, and tied the thick leather thong to it. Then he took the other string, on the far side of the apron, and tied it securely around his neck. He made several knots behind his ear and then slowly, carefully, he crept off the branch. The little man clung to the wood with both hands for a moment. His eyes looked directly up into the sun, and he whimpered like a child who is afraid that something is going to hurt.

Then he released one hand, and the other. He dropped a few feet and, in the morning sun, swung back and forth like a lazy pendulum. The branch creaked as he swung. After a few seconds, he reached up to the leather thong and tried to grasp it and lift himself up. His mouth opened and contorted, but no sound came. The legs convulsed and drew themselves up, almost to his chest.

He made one more attempt to pull himself up, then his hands fell back and settled by his side and he swung back and forth in a wide arc. There was a loud snap of sound, and the big branch cracked. It snapped off at the trunk and followed Judas and his money apron, like a marionette on a stick, down, down into the Valley of Hinnom. There the body of Judas landed and moved no more.

He was the first of the twelve to die, and he died before the Messiah he sold.

The priests came out of the meeting room first. Then came the guards with Jesus in their midst, then the Levites and the temple hirelings, who made a sizable crowd. They had changed their clothes so that no one could identify them as men who worked in the temple.

They could have led Jesus straight north through the temple to Antonia on the other side, but their method was secrecy, and so they took him out through the west side of the temple to the main road near the Palace of the Hasmoneans. There they turned north, so large a crowd that the prisoner had to be led in the middle of the road. At all times, he had many people ahead of him and on both sides and behind him. No one casually walking these roads on that morning could tell whether a prisoner was being led somewhere, or whether a group of temple priests and Levites were on their way to some solemn ceremony.

The high priest was already at the gates to Fortress Antonia. He could not enter without defiling himself, so he stood under the twin arches over the east-west road and sent a Gentile messenger in with news that the Great Sanhedrin, in its wisdom, had found guilty of blasphemy one Jesus of Nazareth, who deceived the people by pretending to be King of the Jews. This man Jesus had been arrested, tried under law, and condemned to death. If it pleased the Procurator of his imperial majesty, Tiberius, the supreme council asked that he, Pontius Pilate, endorse the sentence and see that sentence was executed this day before the hour of the oncoming Sabbath.

The Romans, like the Jews, were early risers, and especially so the Roman provincial officials, who worked from 6 A.M. until noon. They spent the rest of the day reclining in conversation, or touring, or inspecting. The petition from Caiphas was taken across the Lithostrotos court, up the cascading stone steps leading to the fortress apartments, and into the presence of the Procurator. It was read without comment and the messenger was told to ask the high priest to wait.

This was a rude opening move, and Caiphas had expected it. He stood under the arches in a party of elders and watched the despised Gentile sentries pace their posts. Someday, with the help of God, the Holy City would be rid of all of these. He knew the history and the strength of this mighty fortress as well as he knew the history and strength of his Sadducean family, and that was very well indeed. The four towers of the fortress were so built that even if the fortress, with all of its garrison space and subterranean chambers, was taken by the Jews, the bowmen of the Roman army could still deal a peculiarily devastating type of death from these four towers. And worse, they commanded the whole north side of the temple immediately below them. Another factor, as Caiphas knew, was that a relief column could come down and march into the fortress at night without coming under the walls of the city. In time of tumult, the high priest had seen the Roman soldiers pouring out of their subterranean exits onto the temple grounds. Caiphas knew that the Twelfth Legion, numbering many thousands of men, had been split between garrison duty on the eastern frontier of Palestine and Caesarea. Still, Pilate always managed to keep a sufficient number of men garrisoned in Antonia so that, should the high priest ever become ambitious to reduce the fortress, he could reflect on the pillage of the Holy City within the first twenty-four hours of struggle, and this was sufficient to moderate a man's thoughts.

Caiphas sighed. He watched the comings and goings of the Romans. One of the elders, standing outside the arches, said that Jesus was coming up the street. At almost the same moment, Pilate came out on the balcony with a staff of officers behind him.

8 A.M.

The priests ordered the crowd to part to permit Jesus and his guards to come forward. He was brought to a point inside the arches of Antonia, slightly forward of the high priests. Across the big broad court, Syrian soldiers in Roman uniforms lounged. They looked up toward the balcony where the Procurator stood, flanked by his aides. Had he given them the slightest sign, the Syrians would have massacred the Jews standing under the arch. They looked up hopefully, but Pilate only gestured toward the crowd and whispered to his assistants.

A servant brought out a regal chair and the Procurator walked down the right-hand stairway—the one closest to the temple—and, five steps up from the Lithostrotos, sat on the chair which was placed on a stone landing. Jesus saw this through swollen, purple eyes. He stood with but one binding on him; his wrists were held behind his back with a short rope. He stood alone, in front of the mob, and Pontius Pilate looked at Jesus for the first time, as Jesus, for the first time, looked at Caesar's Governor.

What each one saw was hardly monumental. The Messiah looked at the Roman and saw a short, patrician-looking man of about fifty years of age. He appeared to be nervous. His eyes darted from side to side, swinging quickly to anything or anyone that moved. His hair was graying and he wore an expensive toga and gilded sandals. The Governor's personal guard of two soldiers replaced the aides, who bowed and left, going back up into the fortress. The guards stood in short tunics, legs apart, leaning on spears which they held before them. The Procurator stared at Jesus and saw a rather tall Jew with puffed lips and discolored cheeks. There were flecks on his garment and it was soiled. Behind Jesus he saw Caiphas and some of the other ranking priests, deferential but uneasy in the presence of Gentiles. And behind them, the people jammed the arches, some even hanging from the wall-bracket lamps.

The Procurator held his right hand aloft. In a few seconds, the babbling of the crowd subsided. A centurion named Abenadar marched forward from the rear of the court, followed by four legionaries, and took his post by the side of the prisoner. The temple guards dropped back. From this time onward, the disposition of the case of Jesus versus temple law was in the hands of Rome.

"What charge," asked Pilate loudly, "do you bring against that man?" He pointed to Jesus.

The high priests appeared to be shocked at the question. Caiphas had been there the night before to discuss the case with the Governor, to explain to him the seriousness of the matter in its relation to Hebrew law. Besides, all the ranking priests knew that the Tribune who had led the raiding detachment had surely returned and told Pilate everything about the case. Why, then, this pretense of no knowledge of Jesus?

The priests exchanged uneasy glances. This could mean that the cruel oppressor was ready to have Jesus tried before him—and, in that case, might dismiss the charges against him for lack of evidence. Outside, Pilate's question was passed to the crowds, which roared so much that Caiphas had to wait for silence before he answered.

"If this man," said the high priest, pointing to the back of Jesus, "were not a criminal, we should not have handed him over to you." These words constituted a legal sarcasm. It did not answer the Governor's question, which concerned the nature of the charge. Now, in the name of the temple, Caiphas had assumed the pietistic manner of the priest who would never turn a man over to the authorities unless he were a criminal.

Sarcasm can be a dangerous effrontery when used against a man who, on whim alone, can thwart the person who utters it. Pilate masked his surprise at the reply of Caiphas. The Procurator understood this case thoroughly. He even understood the desperation which prompted the sentence of death by a Sanhedrin, and he knew the size of the threat to the masters of the temple presented by the gentle gospel of Jesus. Still, all this knowledge was unofficial, and as Caesar's deputy it was correct to open a hearing by asking the manner of the charge.

"Then take him in charge yourselves," shouted Pilate, standing and preparing to retire, "and try him by your law!"

He knew of course that the Great Sanhedrin had already tried this blasphemer and had condemned him to death, but the coldly angry Procurator was determined to have the final thrust in this semantic sword play. To bring the high priest to his knees, symbolically, all Pilate had to do was to pretend innocence of the entire matter and walk off the scene.

Several of the priests cupped their hands and shouted together: "We have no power to put anyone to death." They did not say that they had no power to condemn a prisoner to death; only that they could not carry out their own sentence. Blasphemy was an internal crime, and Palestine had the power to try such offenders. Pilate and Caiphas knew this equally well.

Pilate did not answer. He turned his back on the priests and started to walk up the steps. The accusers were dismayed. It looked as though the hearing was closed. The crowd of temple employees was stunned! One of the ranking priests shouted: "We caught this man inciting our nation to revolt. He opposes the paying of taxes to Caesar, and passes himself off as the Messiah—a king.''

The Procurator paused and looked around, halfway up the steps to his quarters. He held his long toga off the stones and thought about the words which had just been uttered. He knew that unless these words were denied by Caiphas at once the charge against Jesus had been altered.

Blasphemy was one thing. Any mentally unbalanced person might think that he was God. And any deceiver who was not unbalanced could make the same pretense for profit. But when a responsible group of citizens used the words *revolt* and *taxes* and *Caesar,* they were charging the prisoner with a high crime against Tiberius and the Empire.

Pilate studied the little knot of elegant priests and was forced to show a brief smile of admiration. They had rid themselves of Jesus as a local problem and had thrown him to Pilate as a menace to the Empire. The Procurator could hardly put himself in the position of defending Jesus. That was not his function. He was the highest judge and the top administrator of the country. However, there was still a little room for maneuver. Not much. A little.

In Pilate's private apartment, high in the southwest tower, Claudia Procula was awakened by the noise of the crowd. The wife of the Governor remained in her big bronze bed, staring through the white netting overhead. The roars from outside sounded surflike. Claudia called her female slave and asked what time it was and what had excited the crowd.

The maid said that it was the third hour of the morning watch (8 A.M.) and that the Procurator was out in the courtyard, listening to a case brought by the Jews against a man named Jesus. Claudia Procula sat up in bed. She remembered that Caiphas had come last night with an urgent matter to present to her husband. And when the clever priest had left, Pilate had explained the case of Jesus to her before she retired.

This woman was a true Roman. She believed in many gods, and she tried hard not to anger any of them. And she had heard from some of her husband's aides about this man Jesus, and of the miracles he had performed among the Jews. Now she was worried because she did not want the fate of this man to rest in Pilate's hands.

It was possible, she knew, that Jesus might be a god come to earth to test the faith and goodness of these fretful people. If that were so, he might be displeased with any Roman who disposed of the case with malice. Claudia Procula, dark hair in disarray, asked for parchment and quill. The servant brought them and the mistress said that she had had a dream about the man Jesus and that her husband must do nothing to hurt him. She wrote: ''Have nothing to do with that just man,'' and sent it out to Pilate.

The message reached him just before he turned away from the crowd at the gate. He read it and frowned and crumpled it in his hand. The eyes of Jesus burned on him. Pontius Pilate, his bearing regal, left the scene and walked off the balcony into his suite of offices.

There, as he sat on his couch, he could drop the judicial indifference. He was worried. All along he had been certain that when the time came for Caiphas and Annas to make their move against Jesus, he, as Procurator, could frustrate them easily by pretending to find no guilt in the provincial Messiah, and would free him. This, if done publicly, would set Jew against Jew and would diminish the authority of the wily old man who ran the internal affairs of the province through his son-in-law.

What should he do now? There was a whole new question, since the elders had now placed Pilate in the position of espousing a radical who was leading the people against Caesar. He sat and thought about it, pounding his fist against the upholstered arm of the couch. Then he noticed the crumpled note from his wife. He unfolded it and read it again and cast it from him. Her fearful superstitions never failed to irritate him. The Procurator, unlike his spouse, believed in nothing. He was a man of the world. In his youth, he had tried to advance his fortune by worshiping all the gods, even old Caesar Augustus, but it had availed him nothing, as his good sense had told him all along. He had realized then that all gods were nonexistent, that these supernatural beings had been invented by man to allay the fears of the peasants and at the same time dispose believers against personal wrongdoing. In his wisdom Pilate had ceased to beg the gods for success, and instead had married Claudia Procula and had attained success almost at once.

Pilate dispatched a servant to go out into the courtyard and tell the centurion Abenadar to bring Jesus to him. At the same time, he sent an aide to his wife's quarters to tell her not to worry, that he did not intend to confirm the sentence of death.

Jesus was brought in and stood in the center of the room. The Romans and Syrians studied him closely for the first time. They wanted to see the greatness that had frightened the high priests. But there was nothing to see except a pathetic figure of a man, shorn of dignity. Pilate looked at his men. They shrugged.

The Procurator walked over to Jesus and stood close to him.

"Are you the king of the Jews?" he said.

The swollen lips began to move. "Do you ask this question from personal observation," Jesus said, "or have others spoken to you about me?" The words do not convey the intended shadings of meaning. *Did you, as a Roman governor, observe me acting as king of the Jews or have others told you about my spiritual kingship?*

Pilate misunderstood the interrogative reply and he stood before the Messiah and said: "Am I a Jew?" This brought chuckles from the Gentiles in the room. "Your own nation and the high priests have handed you over to me. What have you done?" The tone now was soft and sympathetic. Pontius Pilate looked up at Jesus hopefully. All he needed was a denial. He knew that Jesus had not pretended to be the temporal king of the Jews and had not aspired to it. He also knew the story about the coin with Caesar's image, because he had spies everywhere. He knew that self-preservation is of enormous importance to all human beings, and now he was giving Jesus the chance to preserve his life.

"My kingdom," Jesus said slowly, almost as though he were selecting the words with special care, "is not a worldly one." He offered sensible proof of this. "If mine were a worldly kingdom my subjects would exert themselves to prevent my being surrendered to the Jews. As it is, my kingdom is not of an earthly character."

Pilate was vexed with the stupidity of the pious faker. "Then you are a king after all!" he said. He glanced at his staff helplessly. There was no accounting for the obstinacy of Jewish religious fervor.

"You are right," Jesus said, further confounding the Governor. "I am a king. For this purpose I was born, and for this purpose I came into the world—to give testimony to the truth. Only he who is open to the truth gives ear to my voice."

Pontius Pilate drew himself up to his full height. His lips curled with scorn as he snapped: "What is truth?"

He motioned for the soldiers to take Jesus outside. The soldiers and the prisoner led the way, followed by Pilate and his officers. The crowds at the gate watched tensely as the Procurator came all the way down the steps and across the Lithostrotos to a point near the high priests. A servant carried the curule chair to him and placed it behind him. This was the cobalt blue chair on which the Procurator sat when he was about to render judgment.

The people watched, almost breathlessly, as Pilate sat. The Messiah stood at his right side and some of the soldiers stood between the chair and the crowd with swords drawn. The Governor wasted no time.

"I can detect no guilt in this man," he said. There was a moment or two of stunned silence, and then a riotous babble of voices arose. The soldiers turned and faced the crowd. The high priests struck their foreheads repeatedy and turned to the people in mute appeal. The roar became louder. Some of the off-duty soldiers ran into the garrison room and got their cuirasses and swords and ran into the garrison.

Pilate sat. He smiled a small smile as he looked at the frenzied faces. Caiphas and the others of the Sanhedrin knew that Pilate was turning the man loose not on the legalities but to confound them. Jesus looked up at the hundreds of faces under the arches and all the eyes he saw blazed with hatred of him. He was alone. The soldiers began to make threatening gestures. The crowd quieted.

The priests approached Pilate and, bowing formally, said: "He stirs up the nation"—they pointed to the people—"by his teaching throughout the whole Jewish country. He began in Galilee and ended here."

The Procurator, who had been listening with annoyance, suddenly grabbed the arms of the curule chair and sat up. Galilee? He had forgotten that the prisoner came originally from the up-country. Pontius Pilate began to look pleased.

He asked if the prisoner was a Galilean. Certainly, the priests said. Everybody who knew this mocker of God was aware that he came from a little town called Nazareth. Indeed, his name was Jesus of Nazareth, son of Joseph the carpenter.

"Well then," said Pilate, "this is not properly a case for me. It should be under the jurisdiction of Herod, Tetrarch of Galilee. Take him then to Herod."

9 A.M.

The priests could hardly believe their ears. Pilate had been aware of this troublemaker and his origins, and if it were a matter of jurisdiction, could have told Caiphas last night that the prisoner properly belonged to Herod, who was in Jerusalem for the Passover. This amounted to dangerous meddling in the internal affairs of Palestine. The mock Messiah was a Jew, charged with a religious crime in Jerusalem, to which was added a crime against the Empire. How then could he be brought before Herod, whose jurisdiction was confined to Galilee?

Besides—and this was what worried Caiphas—the Sabbath was approaching inexorably and Pilate knew that time was now of the essence. If Jesus was not put to death soon, the holy day which could not be defiled by an execution would be upon them.[26] Pilate was temporizing with the people. He was delaying purposely, so that nothing could be done on this day. If the execution were to be postponed until after the Sabbath, it would have to be delayed until after the eight-day Passover season, and by that time the proponents of Jesus would rally by the thousands against the authorities of the temple and this would lead to bloodshed and perhaps a schism in the country.

Pilate stood. He would not entertain an argument about the matter. He had first acquitted Jesus, then reconsidered and ordered him to be sent to a man Pilate had offended a long time ago. The Procurator nodded to the soldiers to take the man Jesus in charge and to bring him to King Herod. The sweet unction of belated pleasure twisted the face of Pilate into a smile as he walked back across the court and up the steps to his quarters.

He had, he thought, done a bright thing. There had been no communication between him and Herod since the time that Pilate's soldiers had mistakenly killed Herod's subjects on the temple grounds. The Roman was now making a gesture of friendship, or respect. Herod could not interpret it in any other way. Pilate was bowing deferentially to the Jewish Tetrarch, and Herod would be forced by custom to reciprocate in some way. Thus the breach between the two would be healed over the worthless body of a Galilean. Further, the gesture forced Herod to become part of the trial of Jesus, and now no matter what happened the King could hardly write any lying, poisonous letter to Tiberius about Pilate, when it would be so easy to prove that the case had been turned over to the Herod for full disposition.

In one brilliant stroke Pilate had removed himself from a highly sensitive case, had embroiled Herod in it, had at the same time made a gesture of high regard to Herod, and had placed Annas and Caiphas in a dangerous, almost untenable position. The Procurator returned to his office well pleased.

At the gate of Antonia the priests argued among themselves about what should have been said to Pilate, and what had been said. Outside the gates people who were not in the employ of the temple had been attracted by the tumult, and among them were surely some followers of Jesus. The high priests were worried because, a few hours ago, this had been a small, secret case. Now it was threatening to become a public cause, and they could not afford to permit the people to debate the merits of it. When Jesus was dead the priests would not mind a discussion, because after the fact the case would expire in a day or two of its own inconsequence. Besides, if Jesus were put to death, this would silence his disciples. How could one argue that Jesus was God if he had been put to death by man?

There was nothing to do but proceed to Herod. Caiphas dispatched a courier to run ahead and acquaint the Tetrarch with the circumstances, and to tell him that the prisoner and priests would be there with all speed. The Romans, under Centurion Abenadar, formed a box around Jesus, and the big party, closely pressed in the streets by the ever-swelling mob, went through the gates and moved west down the sloping hill. At the bottom of the Tyropoeon Valley they touched the edge of the big shopping district, and the thousands in the shops paused to look. Some called questions: "Who is it?" "What did he do?" "Why are the high priests in the party?" "Is it a visiting king?" The questions were not answered because word had been given to the soldiers not to attract more people and not to mention the name of the prisoner.

When they reached the inner side of the west wall the party turned left toward the palace of Herod. They passed the gate at the top of the hill which led to Golgotha-Calvary, the Roman ground for crucifixion. The people had long ago tired of collecting outside the gates to watch the drama of death, because in crucifixions the condemned often took a long time to die. In Syria the Legate Varus had once crucified two thousand Jews on one day for preaching rebellion, and it was more than two days before the last of them hung his chin on his chest.

Herod and his court had come down from Galilee three days before to sacrifice at the temple. According to his custom when he was in residence in Jerusalem, he was using the Hasmonean Palace, which was close to the Xystus Gate of the Temple.

When he heard the news from the courier he was elated and at once he resolved to heal the breach between himself and Pilate.[27] He thought it was unusually diplomatic of the Procurator to send the Galilean to the King of the Galileans. Then too, he welcomed the chance to meet the man who had once referred to him as "that fox!"

Herod went to his quarters and waited for the party to appear. Word was left with the gatekeeper to escort the high priests and the prisoner to the royal presence at once.

Herod used the waiting time to discuss what he knew of the case with his royal advisers. He knew a great deal, and he announced at once that, unless someone could advance a good reason why he should sit in judgment on this case, he planned merely to see Jesus and then send him back to Pilate for final disposition. Herod's argument was succinct and sensible: Jesus had many followers in his home province of Galilee. Why alienate these people? Let the onus of his death rest on the high priests here in Jerusalem and on Pilate.

No one in the royal retinue argued against the reasoning of the King. The case against Jesus and the evidence came from Jerusalem. Let the culprit be brought to the presence of the King—as a token of respect from the Romans—and then let him be sent back to Pilate.

The appellation "fox" was apt. Herod was crafty, a schemer. He was not cruel, as Pilate could be cruel, or mercenary, as Annas could be mercenary. He may have been mentally disordered. His father had killed his mother, and then had called her name loudly through the palace corridors for weeks. His ancestors had showed extremes of ambition and extremes of jealousy, coupled with chronic fears of persecution. All the Herods changed political allegiance as a weathercock changes direction in a variable breeze. They were shifty allies.

Herod was a medium-tall man with a paunch and a square-cut beard. He wore the trappings of his office—crown, royal cape, scepter—at all possible times. And, as his father's haunting specter was the wife he had killed, so too Antipas had one which he could not blot out of his mind. This was John the Baptist, whom the King had had beheaded because Herodias' daughter, Salome, had asked it as a favor for a dance. The King had been reluctant to do it—more than reluctant—but he had promised Salome anything within his power, and she wanted the head of the Baptist. When it was presented to her, Herod Antipas found that he could never shut the scene from his mind.

Now he was about to confront the man who, in Herod's eyes, resembled John the Baptist. He could atone partially for what he had done to the Baptist by sparing the life of this one. In any case, he was as eager to see Jesus as a child would be to watch a fire-eater.

The big party of marchers arrived at the gates of the palace of Herod, and the servants told the high priests to keep the crowds outside. Only the priests, Jesus, and the Roman guards were admitted. The Messiah saw the palace close to for the first time. It had beauty that would rob a peasant of his breath. Some said that it looked like a big white eagle with its wings out, about to land.

It was built in two wings of snowy marble without grain or trace of discoloration. Inside the porter's gate the terrain had been built up so that one had the impression of climbing a hill toward the palace. As the visitor walked up the steep incline, the wings of the palace appeared to be between him and the cobalt sky. Between the wings was a great hall. The dining room alone held one hundred dining couches. In front of the wings and around the grounds tall colonnades sparkled in the morning sun with the many colors of the world's richest marble.

Jesus could not be impressed. The things he knew about Antipas had engraved themselves firmly on his mind. The King was the murderer of the Nazarene's cousin John. The King was a coward who could remain loyal to no one. The King was an adulterer who had stolen his own brother's wife. The King would do nothing in this case except ask for a show of power.

The group went into the palace and Herod treated the prisoner as a guest. He offered chairs to all, but Jesus stood. The high priests were nervously excited and they did not want to sit. They considered all this a waste of time. They could not prove charges of blasphemy in Galilee, and they hoped solely to get the vindictive support of Herod so that they could hurry back to Pilate and announce that Jesus was also a blasphemer in the country of Herod.

The King sat. He was cordial; he admitted that he had heard much about Jesus. Jesus said nothing. He looked at the King, then he looked at a spot against the wall and his eyes remained fixed and his mouth remained closed.

Herod did not like this, but he hoped to soften Jesus with further words about the powers of a Messiah. If Jesus of Nazareth had indeed been sent by God, he, Herod, would be happy to witness a few simple demonstrations of this power. Would Jesus mind performing? There was no answer. A small feat of magic, perhaps? A little miracle? Could he make water pour from the walls or thunder roll through the sky?

Silence. It might help the case for Jesus, the Tetrarch said, if Jesus were more cooperative. The priests started to talk, and they filled the gap of silence with recitations of all the crimes Jesus had committed. Herod frowned. He waved his hands for silence. What cared he about charges and the legalities? He had called his friends and his retinue into the room with a promise that they would see things from the Galilean that they had never seen before. Now Jesus not only refused to perform for the King, but also had the ill grace not to reply to him who had the power to command.

Herod tried once more. Time was going by. Jesus stood looking at the wall, the lines of fatigue under his eyes deepening. Herod's words were sweet and friendly. Jesus did not answer. Herod waited. He asked Jesus if he could hear his Tetrarch. Silence.

The King was vexed. The behavior of Jesus was an affront to royal dignity. The priests were encouraged by this, and started anew a recitation about curing on the Sabbath, claims to be the Son of Man, Messianic pretensions. Herod, irritated, shouted them into silence. He had promised a show of magic to his friends, and the magician had disappointed him and humiliated him.

Herod stood. He reviled Jesus. From the dregs of memory, he brought up epithets recalled only in unreasoning anger. He mocked Jesus and taunted him. He called him a king of nothing and a monarch of no one. The Tetrarch walked around the prisoner, making personal remarks about his shabby appearance, his lacerated face, his dirty garments, the now-unwashed feet, the swollen eyes. A king indeed! Pray, king of what?

Antipas had an idea. He called one of his assistants and whispered to him. Then he winked at the priests, and everyone waited in silence. In a few minutes, the aide returned with a beautiful cloak. It was a garish red garment such as might be worn by the king of a nomadic tribe. It was more theatrical than kingly. Herod took it in .his hands and shook the dust from it. Then, with a friendly smile, he swung it over the shoulders of Jesus and tied the red ropes at the collar.

It was comic. Even the high priests were forced to smile. Jesus made the most sorrowful and ridiculous king any of them had seen.

King Herod Antipas ordered the prisoner returned to Pilate. And Jesus staggered with weakness as he left. He had been standing for many hours.

The young apostle John had done a good thing. The best way of circulating the tragic news, he thought, would be to go to a few key places and to ask them to spread the news. He called first at the home of Mark's father; then he met Peter and one or two of the other apostles and told them that the Messiah had been condemned to death and, so far as he knew, the Romans had Jesus at the praetorium. Then he ran out to Bethany to tell Lazarus and Martha and Mary, but most of all to break the news gently to the Mother of Jesus.

This was a special assignment which John had given to himself. He realized that Mary had heard from her son's lips what would happen to him, but John knew that even the warnings of the Messiah himself would not stay the grief in the heart of the Mother. At Bethany he sat panting, and in halting phrases told them all in detail of the next to the last scene in the life of Jesus. He told everything that had happened at the Passover supper, and even recited the prayers that Jesus had uttered in the gethsemane. He told of the raid, the arrest, the verdict.

His audience wept quietly, but there was no loud lamentation. They listened, the tears came, they asked questions, they bowed to the will of the Father. Mary especially was determined that she would not cause anguish to her divine son by a display of emotion. When the story was finished and none could think of more questions to ask of John, Mary said that she would accompany John back to Jerusalem.

The young man demurred. He did not want to expose the gentle woman, whom he had learned to love and respect almost as much as Jesus, to the harsh cruelties which might be imposed on her son. He asked her to stay with Mary and Martha and he promised that he would be back before the Sabbath erub was set out to relate everything.

Mary shook her head. No. She would go. If, as Jesus had prophesied, he would die in the Holy City, then she wanted to be with him. John looked to Lazarus for help. Lazarus looked away. Argument, however polite and logical, would do no good. Mary had been with her son when he drew his first breath; she would be with him when he drew his last.

10 A.M.

The sun was high and a warm breeze from the south swept the sky clean of clouds. There was a freshness, a buoyancy in the city and some of the late caravans from Joppa and Galilee came in through the gates with singing pilgrims. Jerusalem felt the surge of the festive mood; a time when the heart is light because it is held in the hand of God.

A few shopkeepers stood in front of their doors shouting to the passersby to hurry up, that all places of business would soon close because of the Sabbath. Young children hurried through the streets with handfuls of wildflowers picked from the hills to the west and rushed to be first to bring them to the temple. Old men with long curling hair and thin snowy beards walked the porticoes of the temple in pairs, exchanging pieces of information about families and crops and minor neighborhood heresies and the bewildering idiocies of the younger generation.

On the far side of Olivet the shepherds whistled; the sheep, heads down to the early spring grass, followed. Up from the south, families coming all the way from Alexandria paused on the road out of Bethlehem when they caught the first glimpse of Jerusalem. To them, the sight of the spires of the temple reflecting the gold tossed by the sun was almost too much. This was where the heart belonged. This was home.

In this atmosphere, Jesus was led back to the Fortress Antonia. It was obvious to the guards that this man was fatigued. His steps were slower. The face was weary with pain. The mouth was open a little to make breathing easier. The eyes moved from side to side.

The high priests were in a dilemma, and their only consolation was that the Procurator was in a deeper one. He had refused to dispose of this case, and had sent it to the King of the Galileans. Now the case was coming back to his doorstep and he would be forced to judge, one way or another. The dilemma of the priests was that, having started this action against the prisoner, they must see it through successfully. The way was too narrow for turning back. A matter which had started, to their way of thinking, as plain blasphemy, had grown and grown until, at this hour, it was big enough to endanger the nation.

Had Pilate, who had lent aid to the arrest the night before, listened to the charge and adhered to the Roman custom of permitting local authorities to try and judge local offenses, he would have endorsed their findings without argument and would have told the priests to have the prisoner stoned according to their law, or he would have had Jesus crucified according to his. But no—because he was vexed with Annas and Caiphas, the Governor preferred to pretend ignorance.

On the way back, the ranking Sadducees agreed that Pilate would not be persuaded to confirm sentence by any eloquence on their part, but he could, and probably would, be persuaded by a violent public opinion. If Pilate thought that, by making the case bigger than it really was, he was embarrassing the high priests, they in turn could make it outlandishly bigger by instructing their crowd to scream for the blood of Jesus. This, in turn, would throw the dilemma back once more into Pilate's hands, because he would hardly dare to defy public opinion in an internal affair which was in reality a small one. So the word was passed from mouth to mouth to wait for signals from the high priests and to demand the death of the prisoner as loudly as possible.

The party arrived under the double arch and word was sent in that Herod had interviewed the prisoner and had found in him no crime against Galilee. In a few minutes, Pilate came out with his men and again sat in the curule chair on the Lithostrotos. He smiled faintly as the parties to the action assumed their places because he thought he had won a victory. He had acquitted Jesus once; Herod had come to the same conclusion. The graying little man was ready to squeeze a small triumph from his enemies.

As he sat waiting, some soldiers to the left stood on the huge flagstones and played knucklebones. This was done with two dice, which were cast out from under the sandal. The stones had been chiseled long ago with the symbols of the game: a bird, a triangle, a rooster and a monarch with crown. The game was called Kings, and the men gambled on each cast of the dice. Each player had a marker on his symbol, and the goal was to move the marker across the faces of the symbols, until the winner reached the mock king who, according to the rules, was not a real king in any sense but rather an object of amusement.

The crowd was hushed and Pilate was about to speak when he noticed the prisoner. He realized at once that Herod had made a spurious king of Jesus, and had mocked him by returning him with a red robe. The Procurator interpreted this as meaning that, to Herod, Jesus was comical. A clown among kings.

"You brought this man before my tribunal," Pontius Pilate said loudly, "on the ground that he incited the nation to revolt. Now see the result: in your presence I personally conducted this hearing, but detected no guilt in him regarding the charges you preferred against him." The people listened, but they were already muttering. "Nor did Herod either!" the Procurator shouted, and then, subsiding said: "For he referred his case back to us. This, then, is the verdict: he has done nothing to deserve the penalty of death." The crowd, on signal, began to cry for vengeance. "Accordingly," shrilled Pilate, "I will discipline him, and then set him free."

He stood, having pronounced a second verdict. But the bedlam of venom from the crowd was so shattering that, for an instant, Pontius Pilate lost his poise and turned to look at the people. For the moment, his eyes showed that he was not the Governor; he was a frightened man. Out of the roar of sound, Pilate heard snatches of words, parts of phrases, and became aware that some were asking a Passover pardon for a prisoner named Bar-Abbas.

It was the custom to pardon a prisoner annually at the inception of the Feast of the Passover. Pilate had forgotten about it. The people who were asking for freedom for Bar-Abbas were not the same people who had come with the high priests. These were political friends of the man now in the dungeon below Antonia, a rebel who had incited a riot and, in the melee which followed, killed a man. He was scheduled to die that day, along with two thieves.

Pilate decided to use the Passover pardon to close the case against Jesus. He would give the people their choice of having Bar-Abbas or Jesus returned to them, and, pitting the known murderer against a man of obvious gentleness, Pilate was certain that they would choose to free Jesus, who had been called the Christ.

The Governor was naïve. Through the morning, he had made mistakes. First, he had acquitted the prisoner from the curule chair, which made the acquittal official, and then he had permitted himself, influenced by the tumult of the high priests and the people, to send Jesus to a Jewish King to be judged according to Jewish law. This, in effect had canceled the first verdict, or at least had thrown it into doubt. Now, having learned that Jesus was acquitted by King Herod as a buffoon unworthy of attention, Pontius Pilate was prepared to acquit a second time, but, to appease the Sanhedrinists, Jesus would be "disciplined"—scourged. The crowd was asking for the release of Bar-Abbas and the Governor, still temporizing, proposed to give them a choice of the murderer or the teacher.

The Roman turned back to the people. He held both hands high for quiet, and then he said: "Which do you want me to release as your choice, Bar-Abbas or Jesus, called the Messiah?" A truly fatal question poorly phrased. The crowd was composed of two elements: those who worked in the temple and who formed a claque against Jesus, and those who had arrived within the hour to try to effect the release of their political compatriot, Bar-Abbas. Besides, he had described Jesus as the "Messiah" or King, and this was bound to further alienate those who worked at the temple.

"Bar-Abbas!" they shouted, almost in a chorus. The high priests did not have to prompt the people this time.

Pilate was shocked. "Then what am I to do with Jesus, called the Messiah?" he said plaintively.

"Have him crucified!" they roared.

"Why, what wrong has he done?" Pilate said.

The people, not having been told what crime was involved, shouted: "Have him crucified!"

Caiphas and his friends could not help looking pleased. Once more, they had beaten this obstinate Gentile and beaten him thoroughly. Pilate correctly judged the temper of the people to be getting out of hand. He did not want to have a riot at the gates to the fortress and he surely did not want to be known as the instigator. So he marshaled what dignity was left to him, and, turning from the gates, ordered the centurion to release Bar-Abbas at once, and to proceed with the scourging of Jesus.

Throughout all this the Galilean had stood in his funny cloak before the Governor, with his back to the crowd. A soldier took him by the arm and led him diagonally across the Lithostrotos and into a small enclosed courtyard. On the walls hung some of the gear the soldiers used. In the middle of the court were three small thick stone pillars, each about three feet tall. Each one had embedded in it two big iron rings. They took Jesus to the nearest of the posts and removed all of his clothing and bent his body forward. They pulled both wrists down the far side of the post and tied them to the ring. The entire cohort of soldiers on garrison duty was summoned and the men—about four hundred—stood around the perimeter of the court to watch.

Roman scourging was called the "halfway death" because it was supposed to stop this side of death. It was not administered in addition to another punishment. The two "thieves" who would die on this day were not scourged. And the Jewish law—Mithah Arikhta—forbade any manner of prolonged death for condemned criminals, and exempted any who were to die from the shame of being scourged.

The Jews called their scourging the "intermediate death," although it was far less severe than the Roman. The custom in Palestine was to administer to the prisoner "forty stripes save one." It was done by a paid executioner, who, armed with a long supple rod, beat the prisoner thirteen times on each shoulder and thirteen times on the loins. The prisoner seldom died but, although in time the scars might fade, the shame and humiliation seldom did.

The scourging of Rome was deadlier. It was administered by a trained man, called a lictor—there were none in Palestine—and he used a short circular piece of wood, to which were attached several strips of leather. At the end of each strip, he sewed a chunk of bone or a small piece of iron chain. This instrument was called a flagellum. There was no set number of stripes to be administered, and the law said nothing about the parts of the body to be assailed.

Jesus was standing, bent over the short column and tied to it securely. The Tribune then addressed the cohort and explained that the crime of this particular prisoner was that he had pretended to be the King of the Jews. This caused raucous laughter. The callous Syrian soldiers knew that the King of the Jews was no one but Tiberius, their own King. Anyone presumptuous enough to try to usurp the place of Caesar was a fool indeed. It was the custom, at times like this, to permit the soldiers to enjoy some play with the prisoner, provided that the play did not kill the culprit. Several, who had amusing ideas, asked the Tribune for permission to return to barracks, and it was granted.

The fresh coolness of the morning breeze came down on the back of Jesus, and the muscles of his legs trembled involuntarily. The soldier who performed flagellations for the Jerusalem garrison approached and, out of curiosity, bent down to see the face of the victim. He then moved to a position about six feet behind Jesus, and spread his legs. The flagellum was brought all the way back and whistled forward and made a dull drum sound as the strips of leather smashed against the back of the rib cage. The bits of bone and chain curled around the right side of the body and raised small subcutaneous hemorrhages on the chest.

A moan escaped the lips of Jesus and he almost collapsed. The knees bent, then, by effort, they straightened. The soldiers murmured approval because they had seen others who passed into unconsciousness before the punishment was fairly under way. The flagellum came back again, aimed slightly lower, and it crashed against skin and flesh. The lips of Jesus seemed to be moving in prayer. The flagellum now moved in slow heavy rhythm.

The men who watched made self-conscious witticisms about the fragility of the Jews, and of how unkinglike this one looked. The Tribune was also watching, but he had a special motive. It was his responsibility to stop the "discipline" when he thought that the guilty one might not be revived. He stopped the executioner and went over to examine Jesus.

The Tribune did not touch him. He bent close, to see how much life was left. He could not judge by the tortured and bruised skin of the face, so he contented himself with watching the respiration of the rib cage. It was swift and shallow and he ordered the executioner to stop.

The scourging had not taken more than about three minutes. It was over, and the Tribune sent two men for cloths and cold water. The executioner, with no more feelings of compassion than the priest had for the lamb with its head through the ring, untied the wrist ropes and Jesus at once fell off the pillar and rolled onto his back on the stones. He was unconscious.

The washing of the body was hardly an act of mercy because it returned the prisoner to gasping consciousness.

The Tribune ordered a soldier to help the Messiah to stand. He could not remain standing without two hands under his arms. Jesus was held in this position until he felt a slight return of strength. Then he was permitted to sit on the stone column. Little by little, his entire body began to throb with pain. It began as a pulsing thing, dull and enervating and it worked up until the entire body screamed with agony.

No one felt pity for him. To the soldiers' way of thinking, any man who permitted himself to get into this position was either stupid or knavish and, considering the manner in which they had been treated by the local populace, they would not have felt commiseration even if they had understood the emotion. Just as the high priests sincerely felt that they were striking a blow for God in plotting against Jesus, so too these soldiers were certain that, in beating him half to death, they were performing a routine duty.

The few soldiers who had asked permission to leave were now waiting. They looked at Jesus and they were grinning. They had with them an old scarlet sagum—a wool cloak—a heavy reed, and a hat made of thorns. The Tribune rubbed his chin and smiled as he understood the joke. Jesus had pretended to be a king, and the soldiers would costume him like a king; a comic king. It would be in the nature of Herod's joke, but exaggerated. As they prepared, the victim sat, thin and bearded and subject to shivering, which started in spasms and shook his whole being and rattled his teeth, and stopped. He looked up into the sun and his face was a suffering mask.

The shivering started again and a soldier dropped the scarlet cloak over the naked back and they dragged Jesus to his feet to drape the garment correctly. The soldier who had made the hat of thorns had gouged his fingers in doing the job. The hat was a clever piece of work because, instead of braiding a mere crown, he had fashioned it in the shape of a pileus, a Roman hat shaped in oval form, usually made of felt, which fitted like a skull cap. The dead thorns[28] were always stacked in piles around the courtyard and were used for starting fires.

The plaited hat of thorns was placed lightly on the head of Jesus and the soldiers stepped back a little to see that it was on straight. The heavy reed scepter was placed in the hand of the Messiah. The soldiers knelt before him on one knee and bowed their heads and shouted: "Long live the King of the Jews!" They paid mock homage to Jesus and walked up close and spat in his face and slapped him. He said nothing, but watched them at their game.

One soldier felt that there was too much homage, and not enough punishment. He snatched the heavy reed out of the hand of Jesus and struck him with it. The priests outside wondered when the soldiers would finish with their amusement because the sun, inexorably, was drawing higher. And to some at least this was becoming sickening.

The soldiers were finished. They helped Jesus to his feet and placed a winding cloth around his loins and dressed him. This, they wanted him to understand, was a concession to the inordinate modesty of the Jews and was further proof of the leniency of the Romans in the small niceties. Jesus did not answer, and had not said a word in a long time. It is possible—in fact, probable—that, as a human being subject to the stresses and strains of a human being, he was now in a state of shock.

11 A.M.

The crowd around the Antonia arches had thinned. Even for the temple hirelings the day was too glorious, too beautiful to be spent in utter meanness. The waiting was tiresome, and there were duties to be performed at the temple. The followers of Bar-Abbas left in triumph with the murderer. The high priests stood in front of the arches, their tall hats and garments lending dignity to their persons, their hands composed and twined in front of their bodices.

They conversed in whispers and they were certain that, when Pilate had completed the flagellation of the prisoner, he would submit to them that this was punishment enough. He would try to free Jesus on the premise that he was now a broken and pathetic figure. Caiphas was nettled by this type of reasoning. It was beyond him why the Procurator could not understand that, as long as Jesus was alive, he was a dangerous threat to both civil and religious authority.

The people under the arches were still sufficient in number to set up a roar, and they had been primed to call for the blood of Jesus no matter what Pilate said. They were whispering about this when Pilate, preceded by Abenadar and a squad of soldiers, came down the steps for the third time. At once the deep growl of many men talking in low voices was hushed.

Once more, the Governor sat in his chair. This time he seemed to be impatient. He glanced angrily at the crowd and, raising his right hand high, he said: "Now look! I am bringing him out to you, and you must understand that I find no guilt in him!"

The priests' followers muttered. Caiphas studied his adversary and knew that he had him close to defeat. A little more pressure, a little more of the dissenting uproar, and Pilate would quit the field. He looked across the Lithostrotos to the left and saw a centurion and some soldiers leading Jesus out. The prisoner could not be seen, because two of the soldiers in front blocked the view. But the slowness of the procession indicated that the prisoner was not in good condition.

The group drew up close to the arches beside the Procurator. Then the soldiers pulled away, and Jesus was left standing, with but two soldiers flanking him and holding him erect.

The crowd looked, and sucked in its breath. This man was a shocking sight. The hair, under the thorns, was damp and discolored. The face was so marked that individual features were almost indistinguishable. The top of the garment under the cloak was stained. The body teetered slowly backward. The soldiers leaned closer to keep him erect, eyes straight ahead.

Pilate looked on the prisoner. He looked at the crowd, and saw the natural pity of common people for suffering. Their eyes also showed horror and some turned away. The Roman wanted to capitalize on the pity and the revulsion. He stood up and walked over to Jesus. Then he seized his hand and held it aloft.

"Behold the man!" he shouted to the crowd.

The high priests and the crowd chanted: "To the cross! To the cross!" Shocked, Pilate dropped the prisoner's hand. He could not believe that, even under the tutelage of Caiphas, the crowd could be so callous in the face of what was left of this human being.

He felt nervous, but he could not understand why he was so apprehensive. Did they not realize that, at the snap of his fingers, he could have freed this man at any stage of the hearing? Then why did they press for crucifixion when it was so obvious that the magistrate did not want to countenance capital punishment in this case? Did they not realize that he could order the immediate arrest of them all? He saw now—too late—that he should not have argued with either the priests or the people. It would have been much better if he had exercised the *ius gladii*, the power of the Procurator, and ordered Jesus to be freed for lack of evidence.

Pilate glared at the people and made two or three false starts to say something. Finally he said bitterly: "Then take him in charge yourselves and crucify him! I find no guilt in him!" Caiphas knew, and so did Pilate and everyone present, that the Jews had no power to crucify.

"We have a law," one of the elders said, "and according to the law he must die, for he has declared himself to be the Son of God!"

The Governor was at his wit's end. He had assumed all along that Jesus had presented himself as some sort of Hebrew prophet, but the assumption of divinity was something he had not heard before. He worried about it now, once more remembering that Procula had begged him please not to do anything about this man—that she had suffered a great deal in a dream about him. Pilate believed in none of it—from divinity to dream— but he was strangely troubled. He turned away on his gilded sandals and walked back into the praetorium, ordering Abenadar to bring the prisoner to him.

Inside, it was Pilate who appeared to be harried. Originally, he had planned to set Jesus free as a means of thwarting Caiphas and Annas. Now a cold fright laid hold of him and he could not understand what frightened him. He studied the wounded man standing before him and said gently: "What is your origin?"

He did not say, "Where were you born?" or "What is the place of your nativity?" "What is your origin?" is a much deeper question. . . . Jesus seemed to gather a little strength. Not much. But now he could stand alone. He studied the Roman briefly, then lowered his head and did not answer.

Pilate looked at his retinue in abject frustration. In three hours of one golden morning, he had moved himself from a position of command to one of entreaty. He was trying to save a man who had no interest in being saved.

"Do you not know," Pilate said through set teeth, "that I have power to set you free and power to crucify you?"

The dry, broken lips moved. The voice was hoarse. "You have no power whatever to harm me," said Jesus, "unless it is granted to you from above. . . . He who surrendered me to you is guilty of a graver offense." These were most important words. They seemed to mean that, unless God the Father wished Jesus to die, no one, including Pilate, had the power to harm the Messiah.

The Governor had Jesus brought out again before the remaining crowd. Then he came out and once more seated himself on the chair. The high priests and others called out to him: "If you release this man, you are not a friend of Caesar! Anyone who declares himself a king renounces allegiance to Caesar!"

This was a naked threat to Pilate, who understood the suspicious nature of Tiberius, and knew that he would lend ear to any charges brought by the Jews, more especially if they were "responsible" persons like Caiphas.

He raised his hand and the noise died slowly. "Look," he said in sarcasm, "there is your king!" The people shouted: "Away with him! Away with him! Crucify him!"

The Procurator pretended to be shocked. "Am I to crucify your king?"

This angered the high priests and the people and, in a jumble of sound, Pilate made out the words "We have no king but Caesar!"

Ironically, this group of Palestinians had now turned the political table askew so that they appeared to be more loyal to the cause of Tiberius Caesar than Caesar's hand-appointed Governor. At that point, Pontius Pilate gave up the fight. He had a basin with water brought to him and he stood, dipped both hands into it, and looking directly at Caiphas said: "I am innocent of the blood of this just man. The responsibility is yours!"

This was not an original gesture. It had been used many times, and in the juridical sense it merely meant that the judge refused to argue further, and would permit the contender to have his way. Members of the crowd called out: "His blood be upon us and upon our children!"

Caiphas had wrested a great victory from the Roman and now he said nothing that might make Pilate reconsider his gesture. Jesus was to die.

The Centurion Abenadar ordered the royal cloak taken from Jesus. Pilate walked to the praetorium slowly. If he looked back, it was to take another glance at the strange prisoner over whom he had fought so hard and so uncleverly. When Claudia Procula asked him about this, Pilate would say, in honesty: "I did not intend to condemn the man. His crime was religious, so I surrendered him to Caiphas."

Almost as an afterthought, the Procurator called Abenadar to him and ordered that a heavy wooden sign be made to nail to the top of the cross, listing the crime of Jesus in three languages: Hebrew, Latin and Aramaic—in that order.

The purpose of capital punishment was always to deter crime, and it was always executed in a public place for all to see. That was why it was necessary for the people to understand the nature of the crime of the victim. The sign, said Pilate, should read: "Jesus of Nazareth, King of the Jews."

That was his name and his crime.

Abenadar asked about clothing, knowing that, in most cases where Jews were involved, Pilate permitted the condemned to wear something. The Procurator ordered the centurion to follow custom. On the cross, he would be allowed to wear a breech clout.

Would the other two prisoners—the thieves—be executed at the same time?

Yes, Pilate said. Form the detail, have the signs drawn up and execute the three prisoners.

Were there any special orders from his excellency?

No special orders. Proceed, and be done with it.

Pilate walked back up the stone steps and into the fortress. The crowd below was quiet. Its work, as the multitudinous mouthpiece of the high priests, was done. So too was Pilate's. And that of Caiphas. The work of Abenadar was about to begin. To his way of thinking this cannot have been the best of duties, but it was much better than patrolling the frontier with a short sword. In this detail, as in war, someone had to die; but the soldier was always certain that it would not be he.

The signs for the three prisoners were hastily painted, and when the high priests saw the one for Jesus, marked "King of the Jews," they became excited and upset and called for an immediate audience with Pontius Pilate.

They were admitted, and as one final favor asked that the sign be changed. They did not want the public to see Jesus proclaimed king of the Jews. He wasn't, and he did not pretend to be. Still, they did not dare say this. They might have pointed out that Jesus had been tried on a charge of blasphemy, and that the sign could rightfully proclaim: "Jesus of Nazareth, blasphemer." But these few were clever, and they knew that if they used this argument, Pontius Pilate might reopen the case again on the grounds that he had misunderstood and had thought that Jesus was a pretender to the throne who had tried to lead the populace away from Caesar.

So they said, as politely as they could, "Do not let your inscription be, 'King of the Jews,'[29] but: 'He said, I am the king of the Jews.'" At this, the Procurator smiled grimly and said: "My inscription stands."

This was the strongest statement made by the Governor and the first on which he proved to be adamant. This man was cruel and ineffectual, the third in a chain of three weak men who brought Jesus to the cross. Judas betrayed him for money; Caiphas brought him to trial in part at least to please his father-in-law; Pilate tried to play a political game with him and found his king in irrevocable check in three moves.

The sign was made as Pilate wanted it made. A laborer at the fortress used thin pine boards, about two feet long by one foot high, and these were coated with a whitish substance, like lead or gypsum. On it he lettered the words in black. It could then be hung around the neck of the condemned by a chain, or, as in this case, carried before him by a soldier. At the execution grounds, the sign would be placed at the top of the cross for all to see.

Abenadar was an efficient soldier. He had drawn this duty before and knew the items he had to requisition—from soldiers to saddles to signs. He ordered a detail sent to fetch the two thieves from the dungeon, and these were placed in single file behind Jesus. He ordered one cavalryman to saddle up and to take a position at the head of the procession. A platoon of legionaries formed a box around the prisoners. The soldiers were armed with spears. Three guards arrayed themselves in front of each of the three condemned men. These carried the signs proclaiming the identity and crime of each.

The centurion ordered the "trees" from the supply room, and three soldiers left ranks to get them. The two prisoners looked longingly at the chatting, joking soldiers who slaked their thirst with wine or water. Nothing was offered to the condemned. One of the thieves asked for a drink and was refused. Abenadar hurried back and forth across the courtyard on his several errands. He talked briefly with the executioner, a soldier who had been trained for this in Rome and who understood the exact ritual. He drew rations for the soldiers who would have to stand guard under the crosses.

When everything was ready, the "trees" were placed on the right shoulder of each of the three criminals. This was the crosspiece only; the upright part of the cross was always left standing at the place of execution and was used many times. The crosspiece was of cypress, about three inches by five inches and about six feet long. It weighed perhaps thirty pounds, and was fashioned roughly with an adze by the executioner. In the bottom of the crosspiece, at the center, was an oblong mortise so that the crosspiece would fit over the upright piece. The sign would be nailed here and the spikes would lock both pieces of the cross together.

Each man shouldered his tree, and this too was done as ritually prescribed. The prisoners' wrists were bound together with rope which permitted a distance of about six inches between hands. As the crossbeam was placed on the right shoulder, the two hands curled over opposite sides of the beam, which jutted about thirty inches in front of the condemned, and about forty-two inches behind him, diagonally to the left. If, in his agony of anticipation, the hands slipped off the beam, the short rope between wrists kept it from sliding to the street in front of the soldier marching behind.[30]

The centurion was worried only about Jesus. The thieves had not been scourged, and were strong. Abenadar noticed that Jesus had trouble holding himself erect, without trying to carry a thirty-pound timber.

When the column was fully formed, the centurion walked the length of it and found it satisfactory. He called a forward march, and the little parade started through the archway. The few high priests moved aside and watched Jesus stagger as he started out under his burden, his eyes doggedly on the back of the soldier immediately in front of him. The work of the priests was finished, but they worried about the effect of the sign on the Amé-Haaretz, the ignorant ones. A few of the elders decided to follow the line of march. If the sign impressed any of the populace, they could jeer and explain that it was a matter of the personal sarcasm of the Procurator.

These learned ones moved slightly ahead of the pathetic group of marchers, and their topic of conversation, as they walked slowly along, was the behavior of Pilate, who had humiliated himself in a manner to make men shake their heads. Then too, his final act of washing the hands—that was a Hebrew symbol, not a Roman one. It had been laid down by Moses in Deuteronomy 21. In its original form, it concerned the action to be taken in the case of a mystery murder. The ancients of the town nearest the scene of the crime had to kill a heifer and wash their hands over the animal, saying: "Our hands did not shed this blood, nor did our eyes see it." The priests, of course, were happy that the people had responded, "His blood be upon us and upon our children," because this was a proper response to a false charge of guilt. When one feels no guilt, full responsibility can be assumed.

The road from the arch to Golgotha[31] was almost exactly one thousand paces—about three thousand feet. The first part of the march was by a narrow road, hardly more than twelve feet wide, up a slight incline, then sharply down into the valley below.

All of this area was crowded with houses and shops. The sun, high now, came down warm on the backs of the marchers. People on rooftops gathered near the edge to watch the mournful march, to see the faces of the condemned and to try to read the signs. The men moved slowly because Jesus could not be urged to go faster than at a staggering gait. Along the sides of the road, pilgrims pressed against the walls and argued loudly for guilt or innocence as the parade moved by. The legionaries moved the crowds back, when necessary with their spears, and the soldier who led on the horse shouted continuously for the people to make way for the soldiers of Rome.

Under ordinary circumstances, Abenadar would have led the prisoners through the main part of the city because the rule was to display the condemned to the populace, so that the people might think well before committing crime. But the Sabbath was coming quickly, and Pilate had been told long ago by the Legate of Syria that, in internal matters, he was to refrain from violating the religious customs of the people. So the march was directed to Golgotha by the shortest way, and Jesus started down the sharp hill to the west, swaying from side to side with his burden, and staggering forward. The Jews who stood watching from the shops and houses were moved to pity and made sympathetic noises and shouted sounds which meant "No! No!" Some, notably the women, covered their faces with their fingers and would not look.

At the bottom of the hill, Abenadar turned his column to the left. This was at the edge of the big market of Jerusalem, and crowds came running when they saw the soldiers and the tips of three "trees" inside the square of spears. Jesus made the turn, following those in front, but he was so faint that Abenadar had to come back several times to urge him to take the next step forward.

Jesus finally got one foot in front of him, but could not seem to bring up the other one. He was not moving, but his body was trying to lurch forward. The big beam began to sway and the people watched as Abenadar ordered him to proceed. The other foot came forward suddenly and the entire body heaved ahead out of control. The Messiah felt that he was falling, but he could not free his bound hands from the beam and, in a moment, he had pitched downward. The front of the big beam hit the ground first, and slid against the right side of his face as it stood almost on end. He landed on his right knee and both elbows, and the crosspiece hung standing for a split second, and then fell away from him.

The centurion wanted everything to be orderly. He was displeased with this and, after a quick glance at the muddy face, and the fresh rivulets of blood starting from the thorns on the right side of Jesus' head, he knew that it was useless, in front of a crowd, to order this man to stand up and again shoulder the beam.

He did the next best thing. With a look of impatience, hands resting on hips, he studied the people in the crowd to find a man strong enough to shoulder the tree for the rest of the journey. He saw a farmer with brown bulging biceps, a man with a big dome of a head and a black beard. Abenadar beckoned to him and ordered him to pick up the crossbeam and carry it.

The farmer cursed the moment he had permitted his curiosity to bring him to the front of the crowd. He was on his way from his farm to the city. His name was Simon of Cyrene. He was not a Jew, but a pagan,[32] and he was a prosperous man who did not want to be a party, however unwilling, to the problems of the Romans or the Jews.

Simon of Cyrene did as he was told. He picked the crossbeam up out of the dust and, with a grimace, threw it over his shoulder and hitched up his garments with his free hand. He was ready. But Jesus lay on his right side, gasping. Abenadar reached down and lifted him by the arm. He told the Messiah, with some show of irritation, that he would not have to carry the tree anymore; that the strong farmer would do this honor for him.

The horseman started forward again, as slowly as possible. The Cyrenean followed behind Jesus and knew that this bleeding Jew was close to the point of total exhaustion because he had trouble moving his feet with only his weight to support. The pathetic parade moved down the street to the south, then turned right.

Ahead was a formidable hill, leading to the Gennath Gate. The walk to the cross was a little more than half finished. The spectators were not so numerous on the hill because this was a residential district. Many who read the signs asked, in forlorn sorrow: "Why did you do these things?" Jesus did not answer. The thieves did not answer.

Under the law, sympathy toward an accused was permitted; sympathy toward one condemned was forbidden. However, there was a society of charitable women of Jerusalem (chaburatir). They presented gifts at circumcisions, betrothals and weddings, and gave money and tears when death visited poor families. As Jesus dragged his feet up the long hill, he was in such acute pain that his breathing could be heard by the citizens who watched, and among them were these charitable women. Their hearts were moved and, when one of them burst into tears, all began to sob. Many could no longer bear to look at him.

The Messiah stopped. His chest heaved with the effort to breathe, and his gaze turned shakily from one woman to the next until he had seen them all and had seen the reality of the tears—the first shed for his death. He pressed his hands together and, for a moment, it seemed as though he would weep with them. Instead, his voice strained, he warned the women of the impending pillage of their city:

"Daughters of Jerusalem," he said slowly and with massive effort, "do not weep for me; weep for yourselves and your children; for, mark my words, a time is coming when people will say 'How blessed the barren are! How blessed the wombs that have never borne children, and the breasts that have never nursed!'

"Then they will actually cry out to the mountains, 'Fall upon us!' and to the hills 'Bury us!'" For the final time, Jesus was a prophet and he had reserved his last warning for the women who were good of heart and who could bear to look upon a strange man reduced almost to the last breath of life.

"Yes," he said, nodding his head slowly, "if this is done to the green wood, what must be the fate of the dry?"[33]

Abenadar came running back and urged the column to continue its march. The women were staring at Jesus through drying eyes. They had heard the words, but they did not understand them. The marchers started up again, and Jesus lifted a foot and brought it forward and set it down. Then, mechanically, he began the effort of lifting the other one and trying to move it ahead.

Beyond the horseman up ahead, Jesus could see the Gennath Gate. The centurion hurried ahead of his column and tacked up a notice on the outside of the gate, which explained who would be executed that day at the pleasure of Tiberius Caesar, and for what crimes. It had been a long difficult road for the Galilean, and it was almost a consolation to know that fifty more steps would bring him to the pinnacle of his promise—the chance to die for everyone.

12 Noon

A tide of people squeezed through Gennath Gate. The horseman sat astride his animal between the giant doors and ordered the people to stand aside. The pilgrims grumbled. Most of them had come from far away—this was at the crossroads of the Joppa-Jerusalem road and the north-south Samaria-Jerusalem road. They did not welcome further delay, because many of them had remained on the road all night to ensure getting to the holy city before the onset of the Sabbath. Besides, they had made this trip in joy; their hearts were hurt when they saw the Romans putting Jews to death.

The people stood aside mumbling; the children babbled questions about the three men carrying timbers. They wanted to know what these men had done to deserve death, and some wanted to know what was death and did it hurt. Even the little ones were moved when, looking between the legs of the soldiers, they saw the blood on Jesus. They held a little tighter to their fathers and asked what that man had done to bleed so much. The fathers read the sign and did not answer the question.

Outside the gate, the little parade continued for thirty yards. The centurion called a halt at Golgotha. This was a rocky hill about fifteen feet high immediately inside the confluence of the two roads. In the little declivity behind the hill was a garden, aflame now with pink and red wildflowers and, one hundred feet northwest, was a sepulcher newly hollowed out by Joseph of Arimathea.

A stranger could not mistake the fact that this was a place of execution, because three upright beams stood naked against the sky. Sometimes there were more, but there were never fewer than three. These were ordinary cypress beams, like those carried by the condemned men, except that, at the top, they had been planed down so that the mortises in the cross-beams would fit across them.

Jesus looked at them wearily. And he looked at the sky beyond them, so beautiful, so bright. He seemed almost relieved. His body was bent forward slightly and his legs were spread, as though this made standing easier. A crowd gathered, and in the front he saw the ceremonial hats of the high priests. The soldiers formed a perimeter line inside the roads, and, when they permitted a small group of people to come through onto Golgotha, Jesus tried to form his face into a smile because, among them he saw his Mother.

If he had not told her, many times, that he was to die at the hands of men, he would not have wanted her to be there. But he had steeled her for this moment by transmuting the natural fears of the Mother, into an understanding that his death would not be defeat, but glory everlasting. She came toward him followed by her sister-in-law Mary (the mother of the younger James), and Salome, wife of Zebedee, and Mary Magdalen, and the beloved apostle John. She tried to speak, but her face contorted and the tears came. Mutely she held out her arms to him.

Jesus wanted to hold her close, but his garments were soiled with blood. The other women, seeing the tears of his Mother began to sob. The Messiah had to admonish them that it was for this that he had come to earth, and that this was the will of his Father. They understood, and they knew of his promise to return to them in three days; but they found it exceedingly difficult to bear the sight of him, a beaten man who was about to have nails driven through his wrists and feet.

The Messiah turned to John for assistance with the women, and was moved to find that the young man whom he loved so much was also wiping his eyes. Jesus was prepared for the suffering he was about to undergo, but the sorrow of those he loved moved him as few other things could. He turned and tried to clear his mouth so that he could talk.

He begged them not to grieve, and his penetrating glance at John warned the apostle to shield his Mother from as much of what lay ahead as possible. John nodded through eyes dimmed. Mary wanted to remain at the side of her only child, but John led her a few feet away with the others. In the remaining minutes of the life of Jesus—about 180—John tried to shield Mary from the heartrending sight of her divine son's death.

The centurion consulted with the executioner, and ordered the crucifixion of Jesus first. One of the thieves was arguing loudly that he was not a robber, but a politician. Some of the soldiers chuckled and one suggested that the robber talk about it to Jesus, who was a king. The other thief seemed frightened. He had no friend or kin in the crowd, and he folded his hands in prayer. The crowd jeered.

Abenadar ordered Simon of Cyrene to set the crossbeam down behind Jesus. The pagan looked at the Galilean with compassion. It was obvious that he wanted to say something sympathetic. He tried, but gave up and walked into the crowd, shaking his head. The centurion ordered the three soldiers who had carried the signs to assist the executioner and to stand guard beneath the crosses. He would share this duty with them.

The Phoenicians were the first to devise crucifixion. They had tried death by spear, by boiling in oil, impalement, stoning, strangulation, drowning, burning—and all had been found to be too quick. They wanted a means of punishing criminals slowly and inexorably, so man devised the cross. It was almost ideal, because in its original form it was as slow as it was painful (men often lived two and more days in the burning sun), and the condemned, at the same time, were placed fairly before the gaze of the people.

A secondary consideration was nudity. This added to the shame of the evildoer and, at the same time, made him helpless before the thousands of insects of the air, while the carrion birds and the small animals held back until the crucified was dead.

The Romans adopted the cross as a means of deterring crime, and they had faith in it. In time, they reduced it to an exact science with a set of rules to be followed. The soldiers of the Empire had much practice in this field. When the revolt of Spartacus was suppressed, six thousand men were crucified in a single day and hung on crosses between Capua and Rome. In the early phases of this form of execution, they had driven spikes through the feet of the victim and tied the hands to the crossbeam; but this, they learned, sapped the strength of criminals so slowly that it was necessary to keep a guard posted at the foot of the cross for several days. Later, they abandoned spikes and ropes and drove nails through wrists and feet and found that, unless the victim was a tower of strength, he would expire within a few hours.

This, they decided, was reasonable because, after that time, the interest of the onlookers began to flag. The crowd went home.

In the early days of the Empire, this punishment was reserved for slaves and revolutionaries. For a long time the words of a magistrate sentencing a man to death were: "Pone crucem servo"—place the cross on the slave. The part which remained permanently in the ground was called *stipes crucis*. The crossbeam, carried by Jesus until he fell, was the *patibulum*.

The upright was six feet tall. This would accommodate most criminals because the knees were arranged in a buckled position. The Romans called the assembled cross the *crux humilis*. They had another cross, rarely used, which was called *crux sublimus*, and this was much taller, but was only used on personages whom the Romans wanted to display—like Regulus or Hamilcar on the sunny field at Carthage, or the condemned Spanish assassin who appealed to Caesar Galba and insisted that he was not a slave; he was a Roman citizen.

The patibulum, in the earliest crucifixions, was a long piece of wood used to bar doors. It was hammered against an upright, and formed a true cross. This was called the *crux immissa,* or *capitata.* Usage, however, refined the cross into one resembling a capital T. It was easier to manufacture, easier to use, and was made by the executioners.

For a time, the Romans used a small pointed saddle—called the *sedile,* or the *sedere cruce.* This was nailed beneath the pelvis of the criminal and, as his fatigue increased, he tended to try to rest on the point of it. It was used on occasion in the time of Seneca, but it did not merit the extra time its use entailed, and it was abandoned.

The crowd was quiet. Abenadar had assigned four soldiers to each of the thieves, and they awaited a signal. The entire party now stood on the black rock, which bulged above the crossroads like a man's hat. Golgotha was crowded. The people pressed in upon the soldiers and, with the muttering of the curious, the shouted orders of the soldiers to stand back, the sobbing of women spectators, there was considerable noise. Then through the cordon of guards came some of the charitable women of Jerusalem, bringing a jar and chalices.

They brought wine, slightly drugged, to all men who were to be crucified. It was an act of mercy which the Romans permitted. Abenadar waited patiently until they had finished. The women approached one of the thieves—the one who had remained silent throughout the march. They poured the wine from the jar into the chalice. Ordinarily it contained a grain or two of incense, and this, it was said, had the property of drugging the senses.

It didn't, but the belief, when shared by the culprit, was of some help. The silent thief drank the potion and stared at the women, who wept. He seemed stunned: his life was about to be forfeited and yet his eyes remained dry; they, who would continue to live, sobbed for someone they had never known.

The women moved across the rock to Jesus and poured the drink into a fresh chalice. He looked at the wine and at the women and shook his head. He would not drink it. He had to feel the fullness of pain.

The women moved on to the other robber, some looking back at the strange man who had spurned their wine, and who, only a half hour ago, had said such strange things to them. The third man took the drink, gulped it down, and began a loud speech on the injustice of crucifying political opponents. The witnesses had called him a thief, and this was not so. He was truly an opponent of the political powers of Jerusalem, and if he had stolen, it was a matter of policy not personal gain.

He was still talking as the women moved off the rock of Golgotha.

Abenadar gave the signal. Four soldiers moved in closely around the prisoners and began to strip them of their clothes. A murmurous sound came up from the people below. The crucifixion had begun.

When the prisoners were naked, a cloth was wound around their loins and between the thighs with the loose end tucked in at the back. Their clothes and sandals were set in a loose pile before each of the three.

The time was a few minutes after noon. The sun was high and warm. Below the big bald rock, the leaves of the olive trees and the wildflowers shimmered in a soft breeze. Coveys of little swifts darted across the rock and down into the garden below, there to peck for food and to keep a wary eye on man. At the first murmur from the crowd, they took flight.

The executioner laid the crossbeam behind Jesus and brought him to the ground quickly by grasping his arm and pulling him backward. As soon as Jesus fell, the beam was fitted under the back of his neck and, on each side, soldiers quickly knelt on the inside of the elbows. Jesus gave no resistance and said nothing, but he groaned as he fell on the back of his head and the thorns pressed against his torn scalp.

Once begun, the matter was done quickly and efficiently. The executioner wore an apron with pockets. He placed two five-inch nails between his teeth and, hammer in hand, knelt beside the right arm. The soldier whose knee rested on the inside of the elbow held the forearm flat to the board. With his right hand, the executioner probed the wrist of Jesus to find the little hollow spot.[34] When he found it, he took one of the square-cut iron nails from his teeth and held it against the spot, directly behind where the so-called lifeline ends. Then he raised the hammer over the nail head and brought it down with force.

At the foot of the hill, John held Mary's head against his bosom—both to comfort her and so that she could not see. Among the spectators many turned away. Some cried. Some prayed aloud. Some walked away toward the Gennath Gate.

The executioner jumped across the body to the other wrist. . . .

As soon as he was satisfied that the condemned man could not, in struggling, pull himself loose and perhaps fall forward off the cross, he brought both of his arms upward rapidly. This was the signal to lift the crossbeam.

Two soldiers grabbed each side of the crossbeam and lifted. As they pulled up, they dragged Jesus by the wrists. With every breath, he groaned. When the soldiers reached the upright, the four of them began to lift the crossbeam higher until the feet of Jesus were off the ground. The body must have writhed with pain.

The four men pushed upward until the mortise hole was over the upright. The two thieves, who had been watching, looked away. The silent one found his voice again and began to pray in murmurs. The other one cried, and appealed to the four guards around him that this was all a mistake as far as he was concerned. One high priest looked at another and said that this was a very poor example of a Messiah; in his time, he had seen better.

When the crossbeam was set firmly, the executioner reached up and set the board which listed the name of prisoner and the crime. Then he knelt before the cross. Two soldiers hurried to help, and each one took hold of a leg at the calf. The ritual was to nail the right foot over the left, and this was probably the most difficult part of the work. If the feet were pulled downward, and nailed close to the foot of the cross, the prisoner always died quickly. Over the years, the Romans learned to push the feet upward on the cross, so that the condemned man could lean on the nails and stretch himself upward.

Jesus was crucified. He faced the Holy City for the last time.

The workman moved to the others, and went through the same ritual with each one.

To the watching crowd in front, death appeared to come slowly astride the shoulders of fatigue. The four wounds, in themselves, were not fatal. But the constant pain forced the dying men to move in agony.

The spectators observed Jesus closely because the high priests had passed the word that this was a mock Messiah, and that part of his crime was saying that if the great temple were destroyed he could raise it in three days. To the strangers, Jesus looked like any other pain-racked criminal they had ever seen. To the casual viewer there was nothing different about him, or unusual.

Like the others, his head at times was lowered, with chin touching chest. Again, moved by sudden spasms, his head tossed from one shoulder to the other and his eyes looked directly up into the sun as his lips moved. When his body sagged, in fatigue, its weight hung on the nails in his wrists and his knees bent far forward.

His arms were now in a V position, and Jesus became conscious of two unendurable circumstances: the first was that the pain in his wrists was beyond bearing, and that muscle cramps knotted his forearms and upper arms and the pads of his shoulders; the second was that his pectoral muscles at the sides of his chest were momentarily paralyzed. This induced in him an involuntary panic; for he found that while he could draw air into his lungs, he was powerless to exhale.

At once, Jesus raised himself on his bleeding feet. As the weight of his body came down on the insteps, the single nail pressed hard against the top of the wound. Slowly, steadily, Jesus was forced to raise himself higher until, for the moment, his head hid the sign which told of his crime. When his shoulders were on a level with his hands, breathing was rapid and easier. Like the other two, he fought the pain in his feet in order to breathe rapidly for a few moments. Then, unable to bear the pain below, which cramped legs and thighs and wrung moans from the strongest, he let his torso sag lower and lower, and his knees projected a little at a time until, with a deep sigh, he felt himself to be hanging by the wrists. And this process must have been repeated again and again.

The elders could not refrain from pouring some scorn onto the pain. Cupping his hands, one yelled at Jesus: "You are the one that can pull down the sanctuary and lift it up in three days!" This savage sarcasm was appropriate because every time the body of Jesus sagged, it looked as though he could hardly lift himself up again.

Another shouted: "Help yourself if you are the Son of God, and come down from the cross!"

There was no reply from the cross. Caiphas sneered as he said loudly: "He helped others! He cannot help himself!" Others in the small select group of priests joined in the cry: "He is the king of Judea; let him this instant come down from the cross, and we will believe in him!" (Lord, give us a sign!) "He trusts in God; let God deliver him if he cares for him. Did he not say, 'I am the Son of God'?"

One of the soldiers, who had been playing knucklebones, joined in the taunting. He walked around to a position in front of the cross, and, placing his hands on his hips, looked up into the agonized face of Jesus and said: "If you are the king of the Jews, then save yourself."

A woman told her husband that it was becoming difficult to see. He looked into the sky, and others looked. There were no clouds. But the heavens had deepened from a pale azure to a deeper hue. The sky continued to darken. It was not a sudden thing; the color of the sky continued to deepen to a robin's-egg blue and then on to a darker blue.

The people forgot for a moment the three men on crosses, and many in the crowd pointed to the sky. Some said that a storm was coming. The crowd began to break up, and many hurried toward the gates, the women flinging shawls over their heads and running with their children to get to shelter before the storm broke.

There was no sound of thunder. There were no lightning flashes. There were no clouds. The sky darkened until the sun could be stared at with the human eye. The blue deepened until the darkness of dusk descended over all.

The people were afraid, and many asked what this was. And some, calmer than others, said that it must be a gigantic dust storm which had flung millions of tons of sand between the land and the sun. But others said that even the oldest living Jew had not seen a sandstorm of more than minor proportions over Jerusalem.[35]

The darkness lasted for the rest of the day.

1 P.M.

Traffic on the two main roads was lighter now. One or two caravans came plodding down from the north, pausing to ask questions and to gesticulate at the three men on trees. None left the city except pagan merchants going west to make connections with a ship at Joppa. A Persian astride a camel rocked through the gate, outward bound, despite the stronger weather, glancing disdainfully at the wretches on the stony hill.

Death was a cheap transient in Palestine. It came, it went. It visited many; it remained in no home for long. Many families, seeing a dead beggar on a road, would scarcely pause. Children were prone to so many kinds of sickness and fever that the mother who could boast that she had four growing youngsters with none lost to death was rare and lucky. The median age was somewhere between twenty-five and thirty.

There was little interest in the fate of Jesus after the first hour. Only a few high priests remained; the others had hurried back to the temple. Most of the curious had left because they were afraid of the midday darkness. The birds were hushed. The little olive trees and the wildflowers held a steady pose in the still air.

The only sounds were the deep moans of pain wrenched from the throats of the dying. Each had come a long way in pain; each had a long way to go. Once in a while, the few observers pointed to one or another of the three and said: "This one is dead. He does not move."

It is likely that one or the other of the condemned fainted from time to time. But never for long, because the moment the sweetness of unconsciousness embraced him he could not breathe. If death did not overcome him quickly, the return to consciousness was more acutely painful than that which had originally caused the spectators and the wall of Jerusalem to dance before his eyes and to revolve amid ringing sounds and darkness.

Behind the crosses, the soldiers rolled knucklebones on the slope of rock and argued loudly. Under the law, the effects of all condemned persons were confiscated by the state. The spoils of drawing this particular duty were that the four soldiers assigned to each prisoner were permitted to divide his clothes among them.

One of the four behind the cross of Jesus was Abenadar. He could have asserted his rank and braved the grumble of his men in taking the clothing. But he decreed that all should have their midday rations first. After that, they drank cheap wine, toasted Jesus and, raising their cups, asked him to toast them in return. They inquired about his state of health how he was feeling and so forth.

They drank considerable wine and played knucklebones and insulted one another at play. Abenadar walked around the cross and picked up the garments of Jesus. To one, he tossed the worn sandals. To another he gave the bloody cloak. To a third he threw the broad white band which was worn as a hat. For himself, he kept the girdle. Then he nodded to the other soldiers to portion out the clothing of the thieves. They jumped to their feet and scrambled for the pathetic spoils.

There had been one article of clothing left over after the garments of Jesus were divided. This was a tunic—an undergarment made like a long petticoat. It was stained with the Saviour's blood, but Abenadar was interested because it appeared to be a garment without a seam. He stood on the rock with his fingers inside the neck band, turning it around trying to find a seam. There wasn't any.

The centurion was just. He wanted the garment. When it was washed, it would be worth more than the other items, but he decreed that he and his friends should have a little more wine and then roll the cubed bones for the tunic. The soldiers passed it around, feeling and looking for a seam, but found none.

When they began to gamble for the tunic, Jesus looked up to heaven and said loudly: "Father, forgive them, for they know not what they do!" It was so unexpected that the soldiers stopped the game briefly—for even in their half-drunken state the extraordinary words must have brought a moment of wonder; Mary, who had been weeping, stopped suddenly and broke away from young John to look up at her Son.

What Jesus had uttered was a prayer asking for forgiveness for the soldiers who callously crucified him and who divided his garments. But when he uttered the word "them," it embraced more than the soldiers. The ejaculation asked pardon for the high priests, the Pharisees, Sadducees, the people, the world. It included the man with the disordered mind who had destroyed two people in one day—Judas Iscariot.

Love. This is what he meant by love.

The watchers noted that the three men were failing. Some of the soldiers looked at the sky and wondered what had delayed the storm which was so long in coming. Others, fairly full of wine, pulled their helmets off and dozed on the big rock.

Each minute required sixty slow steps to cross the faces of the condemned. With each second, the pain mounted. But death was not ready. The arms, the limbs, the torso screamed with pain; the nerves were pulled across a bridge like that on a violin, and the nerve ends were screwed tighter and tighter and tighter.

The political robber to the left of Jesus[36] glared at him. It was as though he had a secret grievance against the stranger who was dying with him. He kept glowering across his right shoulder, and at last exploded in anger.

"Are you not the Messiah?" he roared. "Save yourself then, and us!"

Jesus looked toward the man whom pain had conquered. He said nothing. The silent one raised himself high on his bloody feet and looked across Jesus to reprove his friend. "Do not you even fear God, though you have been condemned to the same punishment?" The political robber had sunk to the bottom of his cross, and could no longer hear. "Besides," the silent one said, "We suffer justly and are getting what we have deserved for our crimes. But this man has done no wrong." There was no reply. The robber was groaning in anguish. The silent one took an extra long breath before he started to sink, and he said in humble desperation: "Jesus, remember me when you return in your glory."

The Messiah raised himself, breathed painfully and said: "Today you shall be with me in Paradise."

The Messiah—who was dying as man and with the physical limitations of man—found himself in a multiplicity of pain. Slowly, steadily, he was being asphyxiated as though two hands were on his throat.

The loss of blood had not been fatal. No arteries in wrists or feet had been severed, though there was considerable loss from thorns and wounds. The cause of death, in Roman crucifixions, was never loss of blood. It was almost always asphyxiation.

The thieves were weaker too; the whole scheme of crucifixion was progressive weakness under increasing pain. But their weakness did not keep pace with that of Jesus because he had been beaten and had been given no food or water since eleven the night before—almost fourteen hours. The mouths and throats of all condemned men cried for water and, as the victim went deeper into shock, he lost more fluids and his skin became increasingly moist to the touch. Jesus was closer to death than were the robbers.

2 P.M.

Jesus began his final hour on the cross.

The traffic through the Gennath Gate was down to a trickle. The beggars whistled, and their kin came and carried them off. The soldiers dozed on the dark rock. The cluster of people around Golgotha was composed of hardly more than the few who loved Jesus and the few who despised him. The sky remained under a dark veil, and some said that it must be an eclipse of the sun, although the more learned knew that this could not be, because the sun was now in the western side of the sky and the moon would rise in the east after sundown.

Even in gloom, the city inside the gates was in a holiday spirit; the crowding of religious people at the temple, far from being an irritation, was a source of brotherly joy to all. In the outer courts, thousands and thousands of men assembled, awaiting the call to the mid-afternoon sacrifice.

Few knew about the fate of Jesus. The exact whereabouts of the apostles other than Judas and John at this time is not known. In any case they were ashamed—and quiet in the agony of their shame. The priests said nothing, because they did not want the execution of Jesus to become known to his many followers. On the temple porch that afternoon, scores of men asked: "But where is this great Jesus, who teaches in the name of the Lord?" "Where is the Galilean who raises from the dead and makes the blind to see?" "We have heard much of this Jesus. Where can he be found?" No one knew. No one would tell.

The few who had seen him on the cross, and had recognized him by the sign behind his head, would not discuss the matter because it dampened one's holy joy to know that a fellowman was up on a Roman tree; besides, a man would be ashamed to admit that the one he had thought might be the promised Messiah was dying like a slave outside the west wall of the holy city. Sadly, if the thousands who believed in

Jesus could have seen his wretched condition now, they might have been angered at the plot of Judas and Caiphas to kill him; but, on reflection, they would have had to admit that what they saw at Golgotha did not coincide with their image of a Messiah.

Better than anyone, Jesus knew the imminence of death. He could have willed himself to die at any time, but he wanted to show his love for mankind by suffering *in extremis,* and he had not reached this point. In severe and unremitting pain, it required a strong will to keep from dying.

Jesus looked at the little party of loved ones standing only twenty-five feet away. Young John's arm was around the Mother of Jesus in protection. On the other side of Mary was the "sister" of the Blessed Mother. There too was Mary Magdalen, whom Jesus had once delivered of seven devils, and she stood beside the faithful Salome.

The Messiah nodded from his cross to John. The apostle saw the sign through tear-dimmed eyes, and did not know whether to go forward alone, or to bring the Mother of the Messiah with him. After a whispered conversation with the women, he decided to step forward with Mary.

The soldiers saw them approach and two got to their feet with spears, but the centurion ordered them not to seek trouble. They sat on the warm rock and watched. Mary and John walked up on the rock slowly until they stood almost in front of Jesus. They stood only a foot below his eyes, and what they saw caused Mary to sob and lower her head.

Jesus did not want to excite their pity. He had a message for both of them. His foster father had been dead for a long time, and now that he, the only child, was dying, there would be no one to watch over Mary and to take care of her in her declining years. Their many kin would not see Mary in want, but Jesus did not wish his Mother to be shunted from relative to relative, no matter how kindly disposed they might be.

He drew himself up on the cross, so that he could speak. He clenched his teeth against the pain until his knees were straight again and he could breathe. Then, in an economy of words, he said: "Mother, behold your son." And Mary looked at John. Jesus looked steadily at John, and said: "Son, behold your mother." John the apostle fastened his arm around Mary a little tighter. He looked up into the eyes of his Messiah and nodded. He understood.

They turned and walked back to the others. This was a tragic moment for the Son of Man. He watched the back of his Mother, her head covered with the cornered veil which hung down to the waist. As she retreated from him, with the arm of John where he wished his could be, the eyes of Jesus misted and the pain of dying faded, for a moment, in the face of a greater ache.

It wasn't much of a farewell. He could have said much more. He could have unlocked his reluctant man's heart, which does not usually speak eloquently of filial devotion, and he could have told her how much he really loved her, how much her teachings had meant to him, how deeply he understood all her sufferings through the years of his work, and how he was torn by the heaviness of her heart in this terrible moment. But he didn't.

All too well, Jesus knew that words like these, far from decreasing her grief, would add to it and bring all her sorrow to poignant life. It was better to say it all in a few important words. But underneath her grief she must have had a deep sense of her son's ultimate victory.

The minutes moved on. The high priests were worried. The water clocks were nearing the ninth hour and it was not seemly that Jesus and the robbers should continue to struggle. The priests did not want to appear to be callous about the matter of time, but, in a little more than three hours the Sabbath would be upon all. So, after some discussion, they sent a messenger hurrying back into the city to ask Pontius Pilate to order the centurion to dispatch these three, so that they might be interred before sundown.

The Galilean was close to death. For a time, he hung down, and the vision of his loved ones and the wall of the city and the high priests dimmed before his eyes. The dusk deepened and Jesus felt the chill shock of the imminence of death. He struggled valiantly for another breath and pulled himself up on his wrists to stop his vision of the world from fading. When he reached the top, he panted and looked again at the world of men.

"Eli, Eli!" he cried. "Lema sabachthani?" ("My God, my God! Why hast thou forsaken me?") The voice was so loud that some of the spectators thought that he had called Elias, the prophet.

"This man is calling for Elias," one said in wonderment. Another said: "Let us see whether Elias is coming to help him." But Jesus had not called the prophet. He had called his Father. And, in his agony, which had not reached the point where the human nervous system will refuse to accept more and short-circuits itself into unconsciousness, Jesus prayed these words of the psalm.

Full consciousness returned, and he looked around him. The world before him was clear. He saw the anguish of his friends. He saw the triumph of the priests, who reasoned that he could not be the Son of God if, in his pain, he was calling for help from one who was only a prophet.

"I thirst!" Jesus said. The words made a mockery of hollow sound on the little hill. Who could help him? He was there to die, not to drink. The muscles of his upper arms danced in spasms as he tried hard to hold himself high on his cross. Behind him, a soldier had heard the words. He stirred and stood and looked up at the dark sky.

He picked up his spear and stabbed it into a sponge,[37] then dipped it into a jar of posca. This was the ordinary drink of the legionaries, and was made of sour wine, water, and beaten eggs.

The dripping sponge on the spear was lifted up to the lips of the Messiah. He uttered a loud cry but he did not drink. The vinegar mixture glistened on his cracked lips and rolled down off his beard. The soldier shrugged. He flicked the sponge from the spear and sat down behind the cross.

3 P.M.

Now, at the end, Jesus again pulled himself up to the top of his cross. Again he spoke. "Father," he cried, "into your hands I commit my spirit!" One of the soldiers came around to the front of the cross to take another look. Then he went back and lay down on the rock.

From Jesus' lungs came a final cry: "It is finished!" The body sagged on the cross. Jesus willed himself to die.

A sound went through the air as though a herd of animals had stampeded underground. A fresh breeze expelled its brief breath on the wildflowers.

The earth trembled and a small crack fissured the earth from the west toward the east and split the big rock of execution and went across the road and through the gate of Jerusalem and across the town and through the temple, and it split the big inner veil of the temple from the top to the bottom and went on east and rocked the big wall and split the tombs in the cemetery outside the walls and shook the Cedron and went on to the Dead Sea, leaving fissures in the earth, the rocks and across the mountains.[38]

The centurion and some of the soldiers jumped to their feet in alarm. They came to the front of the cross and looked at him and at the darkened sky and the crack across the big rock. The centurion bowed his head. "Assuredly," he said to the others, "this man was the Son of God." He was troubled, and he turned to look at the friends of Jesus—perhaps to ask a question—but he saw that they had moved the Mother of the Messiah back toward the crossroads near the gate.

All of them seemed to be weeping. The centurion noticed a man— one who was attired as a wealthy person—walking rapidly toward the city gate. Abenadar did not know the man but he had seen him in the last hour standing apart from the others, watching the face of Jesus with obvious compassion. This was Joseph of Arimathea. The centurion also saw that two of Pilate's guards were now conversing with the high priests. He wondered about this and returned to his post.

The guards came across the rock and told the centurion that the high priests had been to see Pilate. They had told him that, if the crucified were still on the trees at sundown, all of Golgotha would be defiled, and no Jew could set foot on it henceforth. Pilate had been in a mood to be done with this matter of Jesus. He had called two guards and had told them to accompany the priests back to Golgotha and there to apply the crurifragium at once.

Abenadar nodded toward the three crosses and ordered the guards to do their duty. One of the guards was armed with a spear. The other carried a board, about one inch by three inches and about four feet long. The two men conferred and decided to begin at the left, with the silent one. He saw them coming and he knew that the crurifragium meant the breaking of both legs to hasten death. . . .

When the robber sank to the bottom of his cross, and showed no sign of trying to pull himself up again, the two men moved on to Jesus.

The man with the spear said that this one was dead. He waved the other away, then stepped back a pace. He held his lance midway down the shaft, and drew it back, aiming for the right side of the Messiah's chest.

He would make certain that this one was not feigning death. The spear flipped forward and drove inward between the fifth and sixth ribs. It went through the pleura and the thin part of the lung and stopped in the pericardium. The dead do not bleed, ordinarily, but the right auricle of the human heart holds liquid blood after death, and the outer sac holds a serum called hydropericardium. When the soldier withdrew the spear, blood and water were seen to emerge and drip down the side of the body.

The pair moved on to the political robber, who had exhausted himself with protests, and could only stare in mute horror as the man with the board took a stance beside him. . . .

The two guards of Pilate stood before the crosses and their glances moved back and forth across the condemned, to watch for signs of life. The silent one, the Messiah, and the political robber hung quietly toward the bottom of their crosses. The guards secured the permission of the centurion to return to Fortress Antonia. Abenadar said that he too would leave with his platoon as soon as he collected all his gear.

It required a degree of courage, indeed gallantry, to do what Joseph of Arimathea did that afternoon. He hurried to Antonia and requested an audience of Pontius Pilate. It was granted, and Joseph asked for permission to bury Jesus of Nazareth at once.

Pilate was startled. He did not believe that Jesus was yet dead. Joseph insisted that he had seen him die with his own eyes. To settle the matter, the Roman ordered a horseman to Golgotha at once to get a report from Abenadar.[39] Joseph waited. This was an embarrassing interview for him because, in asking for the body for burial, he was making known to the Procurator that he, a member of the Great Sanhedrin, the head of the well-known Sadducean family, was a secret disciple of Jesus.

Why else would he ask for the body? Why would he demean himself by coming to Antonia, when at this moment he should be in the temple across the courtyard holding a baby lamb as thousands of men were now doing, while they waited the three separate calls to sacrifice? He must have known that it would please the pagan Procurator to know that, even in the Sanhedrin, there were secret followers of the Galilean.

He waited. Word came back that the man Jesus had died first, just prior to the work of the guard with the plank. Pilate shrugged. He bowed pleasantly and gave permission for Joseph to take the body down, in conformity with Jewish custom, and to bury the body before the onset of the Sabbath.

The Hebrew senator thanked him and hurried back through the double arch and out into the streets of Jerusalem. There, by accident, he met Nicodemus, the Pharisee who had once sought Jesus in the dead of night, and Joseph said that he had just built a sepulcher in the garden at Golgotha and was about to inter the body of Jesus there. Nicodemus did not hesitate. He said that he too had been strangely moved by the words and deeds of this man, and he wanted to assist in the funeral arrangements to see that Jesus was buried as an honorable man.

It is an almost melodramatic irony that, when Jesus died, his burial was arranged—not by Peter, or John, or the others who, only last night, had beat their breasts at dinner and argued about who loved him the most—but by a Sadducee, a Pharisee, and a pagan. The Roman custom was to permit the bodies to remain on the cross until the carrion birds, the dogs and other small animals and insects had had sufficient time to reduce the body to bones. It was Caesar Augustus who broke the custom and gave the Jews permission to take down those who could be certified as dead, and bury them before the Sabbath.

Joseph knew—and so did Nicodemus—that, when they reached Golgotha a few of the priests would still be there, and would be scandalized to learn that two of the most respected men in the land would publicly lay the blasphemer to rest. Thus, though they had hidden their devotion to the Messiah throughout his life, now, in death, they were bringing down on themselves the condemnation of their own kind for the rest of their lives. The elite of Jerusalem could never forgive these men for assisting a scoundrel who had been crucified.

It was Nicodemus who sent a servant to his home for one hundred pounds of spices, a mixture of myrrh and aloes—which was necessary for the final anointment of the body. Joseph purchased wide bands of fine linen to be used as funeral shrouds. He also secured other unguents and a small downy feather.

When they arrived at Golgotha, Joseph and Nicodemus approached the friends of Jesus and told John that the Romans had given the body to the Arimathean for burial. John searched their faces, and saw love and pity. They discussed the need for haste so that the Sabbath would not be profaned, and Joseph pointed to the proximity of the sepulcher which was newly hewn from rock.

John said that he would help to take the body down. The two men of compassion said no, that John should remain at the side of the Mother; they would do this thing, now that the Romans had left. The few high priests who were watching came closer to listen and were shocked to the point of momentary muteness when they saw two of the great Jewish leaders of the temple with the kin of the blasphemer. And, when they understood that Jesus would be buried in Joseph's own crypt, they muttered against their leaders and hurried into Jerusalem to confer with Annas.

John insisted that he should perform the final loving-kindness for his Messiah; Mary could be left with the women. He was ashamed that the other apostles were not present. As the master had warned, they had scattered like sheep when the shepherd was attacked. It grieved John to think that his beloved Jesus might still be in the hands of strangers in these final hours. He said that he would be of service to them; insisted on it. Who better to lay loving hands on the body than the one to whom he had entrusted his Mother?

The little party of women remained near the gate. There was no one else.

The three Marys expressed a desire to send someone into the city to buy rare spices and perfumes. It was the custom for women to do this. The men wanted to agree, but this was going to be a hasty burial and there was no time. They pointed out that Nicodemus had brought spices, but the women were not impressed. They had offered nothing but tears. They too wanted to be a part of the last loving-kindness. John suggested that they could return tomorrow or Sunday with perfumes. He saw the sorrowful disappointment in their faces. Then Joseph of Arimathea said that the women should supervise the impregnation of the spices in the linen winding cloths. Their heads lifted a little. Joseph was a middle-aged man. He understood women better than the young apostle.

The men moved on to the cross. . . .

It was not a simple feat, but they managed to rock the patibulum loose. Once Jesus was free of the patibulum, the three men lifted him and moved him to a flat rock for bathing.

They saw the women approaching. From a distance they could see that Mary of Alpheus and Mary Magdalen were trying to dissuade the Virgin Mother, who was pressing forward and weeping. John left the body and hurried to the side of the Mother. Softly pleading, he reminded her that Jesus had said that his death was not a defeat, but a glorious victory; that he had come here to perform this act of sacrifice and it would hurt him to know that she mourned. As he argued gently, John too began to weep.

She would not be persuaded to turn away. Mary came to the side of her son's body. He lay on the rock as though he were still on the cross. Joseph of Arimathia knelt behind the head of Jesus and, with a wet cloth, wiped the face softly, soothingly. With his thumb, he closed the eyes tight. When the neck and shoulders had been washed, he took a dry strip of linen and tied it tightly around the head, closing the mouth.

Mary sat on the rock with her son, and the men glanced at her often as they proceeded with the urgent work. They wished—in commiseration— that she would go away; the work was heartrending enough without having to listen to her sobs. Hastily, the three men washed the body as best they could. Two had to hold the body on its side while a third washed the back, from the bloody head down to the heels. Mary shared the rock with her son, the two other women standing before her, patting her hands, trying to infuse courage.

Nicodemus unrolled some linen sheeting and placed it on the rock beside the body. The three men lifted Jesus, and set the corpse on the linen. Parts of the body were anointed with perfumed spices. When this was completed, the men knew that the arms would have to be brought down and the legs laid flat. They did not want to proceed in the presence of the Mother.

Joseph solved the dilemma. He suggested that the men take the body into the vestibule of his tomb to complete the obsequies. The women did not object. The three men lifted the body on the linen and carried it slowly and tenderly 120 feet north-northwest to the middle of the low garden. In the vestibule of the sepulcher, the body was laid on a slab of stone. John brought the rolls of linen back to the Marys and asked them to impregnate it with the aromatic spices. They were grateful to be asked, and in performing this service for the redeemer they eased their grief in work.

The tomb was not an ornate one. Judged by the standards of those who could afford sepulchers, it was ordinary. It was set in the side of a twelve-foot hill facing the Gate of Gennath and, from front to back, measured fifteen feet. From floor to ceiling, it was seven feet, and from wall to wall about five. The Arimathean had built it for himself, with an idea of further enlarging it if any of his children, or their children, wanted to share it with him.

There was an atrium, or open forecourt, in front. The entrance was less than five feet high and was closed by a millstone sixty inches in diameter and nine inches thick. The weight of this stone was beyond the strength of one person to move. It sat in a curved groove and, when two or more men tried to rock it away from the entrance, an extra man had to crouch below with a heavy stone to use as a chock. Whether it was rolled to the left or the right of the entrance, the groove turned upward. The tendency of the stone was always to roll back into place before the aperture.

Behind the stone was a vestibule, about six feet deep and, like the whole, it was hewn from limestone. The ceilings and the walls were roughly finished. A thin ledge of rock separated the vestibule from the main sepulcher. The doorway between was about forty inches high and loved ones always had to bend deeply to enter.

On the right side of the vestibule was a flat slab of stone for the use of visitors who might want to sit. It was on this stone, in cramped quarters, that the three men hurriedly prepared Jesus for final entombment. They lit tapers and stuck them in the walls. Nicodemus was well versed in these matters and, when the body of Jesus had been laid flat, it was he who placed the downy feather under the nose of the deceased for a specified length of time, which was about fifteen minutes. If, in that time, the feather had not moved, the soul had left the body.

The feather did not move.

Around the temple, thousands of lamps were already being lighted in anticipation of what to some would be a doubly great Sabbath which was only two hours away. The final sacrifice of the day was almost finished and men carrying baby lambs seemed almost to be cascading down the rich marble steps. In an inner room, Annas sat in informal discussion with the high priests who had seen the man Jesus die.

Annas was old and wise and he listened to the ranking priests as they told, in tones of horror, about the apostolic actions of Joseph and Nicodemus. The old man could hardly have been less moved. The heresies of a few members of the Great Sanhedrin were matters that he had witnessed again and again over a span of years. In his time, Annas had seen new schools of rabbinical teaching become fashionable, fade, and die. And he had seen the crowds rush to each new religious philosopher, bowing before him as though he had been sent by God himself.

This was of no moment. Nicodemus and Joseph would soon come back to the temple contrite, or they would be challenged in a formal session of the Great Sanhedrin and charged with espousing heretical doctrine. They would acknowledge it and leave, or deny it and keep their places among their honored fellows.

What worried Annas was that the faker Jesus had said, in his teachings, that he would rise again in three days. Now that he was dead, there was one more chore to do. The high priests would have to go to Pontius Pilate in the morning and ask for guards to be posted over the tomb of Joseph of Arimathea so that the scheming disciples of this man could not come and steal the body and claim later that he had risen from the dead.

So when his son-in-law and the others had concluded their horrifying story of dishonor, Annas wet his aged lips and advised them to be more concerned with the promise of Jesus to resurrect himself from the dead. The high priests had not thought of this, and at once they began to babble. Annas shushed them all, and told them to delegate a committee to go to the Gentile at Antonia and, if possible, to have him post a Roman guard over the tomb for several days.

The importance of this was twofold: first, it would have the same effect as having the Romans participate in the original raid on the gethsemane—once they became a part of it, the Romans would have to protect their interests by not permitting anyone to steal the body; second, the word of the Romans would have more weight with the people of Jerusalem at this time. If the priests said that Jesus did not rise from the grave, the thousands of followers of the Galilean would say that the priests were lying to cover the darkness of their deed in having him crucified; if the Romans said it, the people would believe, understanding that the Gentiles had no interest in the matter one way or the other.[40]

Caiphas praised his father-in-law as a man of great wisdom.

4 P.M.

The feather was removed. John went out to the women and gathered up the strips of linen, into which they had rubbed the spices. These were two: a resin extracted from agave, and soccotrine aloes, which has a scent of balsam, midway between myrrh and saffron. The men hurried noiselessly.

One anointed the body with balm oil, rubbing it in with the ball of the thumb; another tore the big bolt of cloth into strips; a third wound the strips around the legs and the arms.

A large white linen cloth was fitted down over the body and the three men cut it a few inches beyond the tips of the toes. Narrow strips—or bandages—were now cut from the remainder. The big shroud was tied with these bandages, at the neck, at the waist, and around both ankles. The upper part of the shroud covered the head, but the bandage around the neck enabled anyone at any time to flick the head covering off to identify the body. In the first week or two after burial, the cloth was turned down from the head to expose it. The bandage around the waist was to keep the hands from slipping from the body. The third one was to prevent the ankles from separating.

When this was done, the three men carried the body of Jesus inside, stooping low to get through the stone opening. They laid him on a shelf of rock on the right side. The body faced Jerusalem, and the rock was chipped so that the head rest was slightly higher than the remainder of the shelf.

Swiftly, they arranged the body so that it appeared to be in proper repose. The white shroud was off the face. The odor of the spices was heavy in the sepulcher, and John hurried out to bring in the three Marys. On the way back, he told them that this was a hasty work, that Jesus was not properly anointed, but, again, that Mary Magdalen and Mary of Alpheus could, on the morrow or on Sunday come with spices and perfumes and pay homage to the Lord.

The interior was dark, except for the fitful shadows and yellow light thrown by the dying tapers. The main part of the sepulcher was so small that the men had to leave in order to allow the women to enter. The Virgin Mother bent low and was the first to go in. Her shadow, with long veil, was thrown darkly across the body as she looked down upon her divine son and found that she could weep no more. Behind her stood the other Marys, their memories telling them that this was what he wanted; their hearts telling them that this was a tragic moment for man.

They remained a few minutes and, as they stooped to leave, they whispered among themselves that they would be back to do honor to the Messiah. The Magdalen wanted to leave at once to purchase perfumes in the city, but Nicodemus told her that the Sabbath was too close. Besides, the morrow would not be too late.

John went back in and extinguished the little tapers, one by one. The body of Jesus faded from his vision little by little. At last it blended with the velvet of darkness inside. He stepped outside, and tried to thank Joseph of Arimathea and Nicodemus formally, but they would not listen. They assured him that there were things he did not know.

The three men laid hold of the rolling stone and moved it farther away from the opening, so that the rock holding it back could be removed. Then slowly, reluctantly, they permitted it to slide back down the curved groove until it rocked into place before the tomb.

Nicodemus took the empty spice boxes and the linen strips which were left. He gazed long upon the face of the Mother of Jesus. Then, with no farewell, he turned and went away. Joseph bowed to the women, and followed him. Young John looked helplessly at the big millstone, then told Mary, the Mother of Jesus, that it was time they started for "home." Mary nodded slightly and managed a small smile for her new son. He took her arm, and they left, walking through the garden of wildflowers and up onto the rock shelf where the three uprights stood, and across the roads and through the gate into the Holy City.

Mary of Alpheus said that she did not want to leave. She sat before the golet—the great rolling stone—and leaned her back against its beige roughness. Mary Magdalen sat down beside her. Both leaned against the stone.

It had been a long day. A very long day. There was much to remember, and some would remember it this way and some would remember it that way. Much of it had been done in secret, in spite of the public execution, and it would be weeks before the news reached the small towns of Galilee and the settlements east of Jericho.

The grief among the followers of Jesus would be poignant, a volatile fuel which, in its own fierce flame, burns itself out quickly. They did not understand. (For a moment in time at least, they could not understand.) To their way of thinking, this was now a tragic defeat. It was not.

It was victory beyond their most exalted imaginings. He had come here to die. And he had died. He had come to preach a new covenant with his Father, and he had preached it. He had come to tell man that the way to everlasting life was love—each for the other, each for him, and his love for all—and he had proved this by laying down his life in a torrent of torment—for them.

He did not die particularly for the Jews, or for the Gentiles. He died for man. All mankind. He came to Palestine to lay the foundations of his new covenant because he and his Father were dissatisfied with the old. The Father had never made a covenant with the Romans, or the Greeks or the Egyptians. He had made it, through Moses, with the Jews. And the leaders of Judea had, over the centuries, perverted that covenant until worship became a matter of externals in which all inner love was missing. If a new covenant was to replace the old, it would be negotiated with the same people.

That is why he had to die in Palestine; that is why, of all the cities in Palestine, he had to die in the Holy City—the city of his Father. The high priests rejected him and plotted against him and killed him. The people didn't. The people were looking for the Messiah, waiting eagerly. And, although Jesus did not fit their conception of a resplendent Messiah clothed in clouds of glory, they were willing to listen. They did listen. And many of them gave up their worldly possessions to follow him. The people were of good heart.

Inside the sepulcher now, Jesus was not dead. If he was, then all men are dead; they creep irrevocably toward darkness. But this is not so. There were too many signs to the contrary. For two and a quarter years, Jesus pointed the way and, had he followed the dictates of his heart, he would have done nothing but cure and cure and cure. In a way, the miracles interfered with his mission, which was to preach the good news and die. His body was to be rended and its functions were to cease. In this immolation, his soul would be glorified and in this too he was pointing the way to man.

The two Marys sat with their backs to the stone. They loved him and, in their love, they missed the enormous triumph; the new promise; the good news.

They did not even notice that the sun was shining.

NOTES

1. I purposely avoid capitalization of the pronouns here even though it is my custom in personal usage. I am writing of Jesus as a man, for the most part, and I feel that such capitalization checks the eye and interferes with the narrative in this present context. It does not imply lack of reverence.

2. It was the year 784 A.U.C. according to the Roman calendar and, in time, would be reckoned as "Thursday," the evening of April 6, A.D. 30.

3. Isaias wrote: "There is no beauty in him nor comeliness, and we have seen him, and there was no sightliness, that we should be desirous of him. Despised and the most abject of men, a man of sorrows and acquainted with infirmity, and his look was as it were hidden and despised. Whereupon we esteemed him not."

4. Great numbers of the Jews would commence Passover observance at this time, Thursday, though some believed the Passover would not start until the morrow.

5. The word *apostle* in this book refers to one of "the twelve." *Disciple* is used to describe one who believed that Jesus was the Messiah.

6. Andrew had been "recruited" very shortly before his brother Peter, for, as a disciple of John the Baptist, he had witnessed Jesus' baptism and had followed him immediately.

7. The Talmud was not to be compiled until two hundred years later.

8. The law as cited here is not complete. My purpose is to *sample* the minutiae of the theocratic rules of the time and place.

9. These were leather-covered square capsules, inside of which were printed four sections of the law: Exodus 3:1–10; 11–16; Deuteronomy 6:4–9; 11:13–21. They were kept close to the head and the heart and great reverence was attached to the wearing of them.

10. *Levite* and *priest* are hereditary titles, though, of course, *high priest* is the title of an office.

11. The rule for candidates, written two centuries after the time of Christ, read this way: "From whence they sent and investigated, and whoever was wise and humble and modest and fearful of sin and well respected by his fellows at first was made a judge in his own city. From

there he was elevated to the Temple Mount. From there to the Hil Court and from there he was raised to the Gazit Court."

12. Actually, this was the "compensation price" for a slave killed by an ox. St. Matthew specifies "thirty pieces of silver," probably meaning thirty Hebrew shekels or the equivalent of 120 denarii. A denarius was the price of a day's labor for a common soldier or worker.

13. Whenever Jesus used the word "Jews" it would seem that he meant the Pharisees, those, in general, who opposed him.

14. Dionysius, a monk who organized the Gregorian calendar, made a mistake in calculation and set the birth six years later than it was.

15. John's parents were old when he was born and, presumably, died when he was young. The Baptist spent twenty years in the desert and did not know his cousin when he saw him at the baptism in the Jordan.

16. *Rabbi,* when used as a title for Jesus in the New Testament, means "master." It does not imply that he was "ordained" as a Jewish religious teacher.

17. Or "Christ," from the Greek *Christos,* meaning "anointed." *Messiah* and *Christ* are practically synonymous.

18. In the Sermon on the Mount, as in some other cases, one is tempted to use a more traditional translation than the Kleist-Lilly *New Testament.* But that excellent work seems to add in clarity what it may lose in either musical quality or the warmth of familiarity.

19. This fulfilled the words of the ancient prophet Zacharias, who said that the King of Zion would come to Israel meek and seated upon an ass.

20. Thus, on this day, April 2, A.D. 30, Jesus predicted the siege and fall of Jerusalem in A.D. 70.

21. A good part of this scene is not well grounded in the Gospel or in any recognized work. The rest of it, particularly the direct quotations and the bargain with the priests, can be found in the Gospels of the synoptists.

22. As man, which Jesus was when he uttered these words, he was subordinate to God the Father. As God the Son, he is equal to and commingled with the Father.

23. The word *Sunday* is used to identify the day in the modern sense—what is now called Palm Sunday.

24. They would certainly not offend those who believed that this year the first day of Passover and the Sabbath would coincide, though

their activity would doubtless already have offended those who believed Friday to be the first day of the Passover.

25. Long before, Jeremias and Zacharias had prophesied: "And they took the thirty pieces of silver, the price of him that was priced, whom they priced of the children of Israel, and they gave them for the potter's field, as the Lord appointed to me."

26. Of course, to many Jews this was already a holy day, the first day of the Passover, but to the Sadducean priest Caiphas it was not.

27. They were steadfast friends after this day.

28. Coming from the Paliurus Aculeatus, which grew around Jerusalem.

29. The sign in Aramaic: "Jeshu han nostri malka dihudaey." In Latin: "Hic est Jesus rex Judaeorum."

30. There were other customs, including tying the beam across the back of the shoulders; but all the evidence indicates that the Romans in Palestine used the system of crucifixion as here described.

31. Its name at the time of the crucifixion was Golgotha—"skull-like." "Calvary" was taken into our language from the Latin translation.

32. He gave his children pagan names: Rufus and Alexander.

33. Jesus was the green wood, the new wood. The sinners were the dry wood. If they would do this to him, what would they do to the jaded and the callous? In forty years, those who were left of these women, and their children, would see the horrors of unspeakable terror at the siege of Jerusalem.

34. The nails were never put in the hands.

35. The darkness, which was like looking through extra-strong sunglasses, seems to have pervaded the world at this hour. Phlegon wrote that in the fourth year of the two hundred and second Olympiad, there was a great darkness over Europe, surpassing anything that had ever been seen. At midday, he said, the stars could be seen. At the same time an earthquake caused much damage in Nicaea. Tertullian said later that he found in the records of Rome a notation of worldwide darkness which the statesmen of the Empire could not explain. Apparently the people of Jerusalem were accustomed to sudden changes in the weather, or there would have been a very wide sense of alarm or wonder at this time.

36. History has given apocryphal names to the two robbers. The one who protested that he was a politician, not a thief, has been called Cestas, which could mean "hardened," "silenced." The other has been called Dysmas, which, in the idiomatic, might be translated as "he who turns

to the setting sun." Other names for them are Dumachas and Titus, Joca and Matha, Nisimus and Zustin.

37. Some authorities say that the soldier used a stalk of hyssop. Père Lagrange, a noted modern scholar who taught in Jerusalem, said that the stalk of hyssop was too slender to support a sponge. He maintained that the original Greek word was not *hyssopo*, but *hysso*—a short javelin.

38. The fissure in the earth must have seemed a "natural" disturbance to the general populace, which had apparently experienced earthquakes before this time. The rending of the temple veil would not have been revealed to the people.

39. The reason Jesus chose to die before the crurifragium was because, regarding the death of the Messiah, the Scriptures had said that "not a bone of the lamb will be broken."

40. A delegation called on Pilate the following morning, but the Procurator refused to be a party to the scheme, and ordered the high priests to set their own guard over the body. They did this and they sealed the tomb too. When Jesus arose from the dead on Sunday morning, the high priests claimed that the body had been stolen while their guards slept.

BIBLIOGRAPHY

The bibliography has been kept short. For instance, I do not separate specific articles of the *Encyclopaedia Britannica* or specific parts of the Talmud. Obviously I did not read every volume of each, though I sampled a great deal of the Talmud and checked every appropriate reference and cross-reference in the *Britannica*.

Barbet, Pierre, M.D. *A Doctor at Calvary*.

Baroni. *Political History of the Jews*.

Bouquet, A. C. *Everyday Life in New Testament Times*.

Burrows, Millar. *The Dead Sea Scrolls*.

Danby, Herbert, D.D., translator. *The Mishnah*.

Dawson, W. J. *The Threshold of Manhood*.

Durant, Will. *Caesar and Christ*.

Edersheim, Alfred. *The Life and Times of Jesus the Messiah* (2 vols.).

Encyclopaedia Britannica, 1956.

Fillion, L. C., S.S. *The Life of Christ* (3 vols.).

The Good News, the New Testament, American Bible Society.

Goodier, Archbishop Alban. *The Passion and Death of Our Lord Jesus Christ*.

Ginzberg, L. *Religion of the Jews in the Time of Jesus*.

Gorman, Ralph, C.P. *Notes on the Passion*.

Greenstone, Julius H. *Jewish Feasts and Fasts*.

Hoade, Eugene, O.F.M. *Guide to the Holy Land*.

Hoenig, Sidney B. *Illustrated Haggadah*.

———. *The Great Sandhedrin*.

Homan, Helen Walker. *By Post to the Apostles*.

Jewish Encyclopedia, vol. II.

Josephus, Flavius. *Works* (4 vols., Woodward, 1825).

Kleist, James A., S.J., and Lilly, Joseph L., C.M., translators. The New Testament.

Kugelman, Richard, C.P. *Political History of the New Testament Era*.

Lagrange, Père M. J. *The Gospel of Jesus Christ.*

Lebreton, Jules, S.J. *The Life and Teaching of Jesus Christ, Our Lord.*

Morgenstern, Julian. *Hebrew Union College Annual,* XVII, XVIII.

Morison, Frank. *Who Moved the Stone?*

Morton, H. V. *In the Steps of the Master.*

McDonnel, Kilian, O.S.B. "Peter, the Apostle," *The Sign,* 1955.

Notre Dame de Sion, *The Lithostrotos.*

———. *The Morning of Good Friday at the Lithostrotos.*

Poelzl, F. X., S.T.D. *The Passion and Glory of Christ.*

Prat, Ferdinand, S.J. *Jesus Christ, His Life, His Teaching and His Work* (2 vols.).

Ricciotti, Giuselle. *The Life of Christ.*

Richmond, Ernest Tatham. *The Site of the Crucifixion and the Resurrection.*

Saint Andrew's Daily Missal.

Sayers, Dorothy. *The Man Born to Be King.*

Schuerer, Emil. *A History of the Jewish People in the Time of Jesus.*

Spencer, F. A., translator. *Gospels of Matthew, Mark, Luke and John.*

Stalker, J. *The Trial and Death of Jesus Christ.*

The Talmud.

Thompson, *The Harmony of the Gospels.*

William, Franz Michel. *The Life of Jesus Christ in the Land of Israel and Among Its People.*

Wingo, Earl L. *A Lawyer Reviews the Illegal Trial of Jesus.*

"The World's Great Religions," *Life* Magazine, 1955.

Zeitlin, Solomon. *Who Crucified Jesus?*